# HOBBES AND
MODERN POLITICAL THOUGHT

# HOBBES AND MODERN POLITICAL THOUGHT

Yves Charles Zarka

*Translated and with an Introduction by James Griffith*

EDINBURGH
University Press

Edinburgh University Press is one of the leading university presses in the UK. We publish academic books and journals in our selected subject areas across the humanities and social sciences, combining cutting-edge scholarship with high editorial and production values to produce academic works of lasting importance. For more information visit our website: www.edinburghuniversitypress.com

© Yves Charles Zarka, 1995 [year of publication of original text]
© editorial matter and organisation James Griffith, 2016, 2018

First published in hardback by Edinburgh University Press 2016

Edinburgh University Press Ltd
The Tun – Holyrood Road
12(2f) Jackson's Entry
Edinburgh EH8 8PJ

Typeset in Sabon and Gill Sans by
Servis Filmsetting Ltd, Stockport, Cheshire

A CIP record for this book is available from the British Library

ISBN 978 1 4744 0121 0 (hardback)
ISBN 978 1 4744 3346 4 (paperback)
ISBN 978 1 4744 0120 3 (webready PDF)
ISBN 978 1 4744 0513 3 (epub)

The right of Yves Charles Zarka to be identified as the author of this work has been asserted in accordance with the Copyright, Designs and Patents Act 1988, and the Copyright and Related Rights Regulations 2003 (SI No. 2498).

# CONTENTS

*Translator's Introduction* vii
*Foreword* xiii

1  Journey: To the Foundations of Modern Politics     1

**Part I    Individual and State**     13

2  Gracián's Hero and Hobbes's Antihero     15
3  The Hobbesian Idea of Political Philosophy     34

**Part II    Language and Power [*Pouvoir*]**     51

4  Theory of Language     53
5  The Semiology of Power [*Pouvoir*]     72

**Part III    Fundamental Concepts of Politics**     105

6  On War     107
7  On Law     123
8  On Property     146
9  On the State     168
10 On the Right to Punish     195

**Part IV    Hobbes According to Two Contemporaries**     217

11 Hobbes and Filmer: *Regnum Patrimoniale* and *Regnum Institutivum*     219

| | | |
|---|---|---|
| 12 | Hobbes and Pascal: Two Models of the Theory of Power [*Pouvoir*] | 234 |
| Conclusion | | 247 |
| *Bibliography* | | 251 |
| *Index* | | 257 |

# TRANSLATOR'S INTRODUCTION

Yves Charles Zarka is indeed one of the most important philosophers in France, though he has been little recognised in the Anglophone world, at least beyond Hobbes scholarship. He is currently the Chair of Political Philosophy as well as director of the Centre de philosophie, d'épistémologie et de politique at the Université Paris Descartes (Sorbonne). He is also the director of several imprints at the Presses universitaires de France, is the editor of the journal *Cités*, and has collaborated with Jürgen Habermas and Axel Honneth. As to his work on Hobbes, he is the director of Vrin's *Œuvres de Hobbes*, in addition to several writings – including this book, *La décision métaphysique de Hobbes* and *L'autre voie de la subjectivité* – as well as a number of edited volumes. Thus, while his work on Hobbes is what he is primarily known for in English, his research extends to political philosophy broadly, both in its history and its current articulations.

Perhaps the fact that I feel the need to state that Zarka's work covers political philosophy in its historical and contemporary registers explains some of the reasons why he is not as well known to English-language readers as he could be. It does not seem to be a great stretch to claim that Hobbes scholarship in the English-speaking world has been influenced by the work of Quentin Skinner, whose fundamental philosophical positions lead him to ask 'why [texts] were written in the form in which we have them'.[1] This question leads to detailed examinations of the surrounding contexts of the material he examines; of other texts of the time that may have influenced by, or been in immediate conversation with, say, *Leviathan*; and so on.[2] This approach is, in its way, laudable, leading to any number of insights as to how and why a certain text came to be written in the way that it did. However, it is not the only approach to historically grounded philosophy, and

I would argue that it is a limiting and limited approach in its way as well.

The limits to Skinner's approach can be seen at the end of the same sentence cited above, where he articulates a problematic approach to the history of political philosophy: 'what can I hope to learn from this text about politics'.[3] Such is not Zarka's approach. For Zarka, what can never be forgotten when reading the history of philosophy, political or otherwise, is that 'thinking philosophically always means thinking from a certain point of view' and that 'thinking philosophically always means interpreting'.[4] That is, both the philosopher being read and the philosopher doing the reading think from a perspective, a perspective that is both an act of interpretation and itself requires interpretation. Thus, reading the history of philosophy is itself a philosophical act, and an act that requires historical precision.

It is for these reasons that Zarka understands his own position in *The Amsterdam Debate* as being 'antihistoricist'.[5] If we take Skinner's historicism seriously as a philosophical position,[6] then it is a philosophical position that 'refutes itself' insofar as it 'denies its interpretative character in order to make out that it is a pure restoration of the content of a text'.[7] In other words, for Zarka, Skinner's approach, if it is itself philosophical, forgets that it thinks from a certain point of view and also fails to understand that it is interpreting in its thinking from that forgotten perspective.

The other author from whom Zarka departs is Leo Strauss. While Strauss is to some degree an ally of Zarka's in the argument against historicism, they are not involved in identical projects. Like Zarka, Strauss argues that historicism is a self-destructive historiographical position, insofar as it takes up the essentially ahistorical position of asserting that all past political philosophical texts can be reduced to their historical circumstances.[8] However, for Strauss, classical and modern political philosophy are distinguished through 'the discovery of history' in the nineteenth century as a scientific discipline, where history can be engaged, like nature, in the discovery of its laws.[9] Because of this discovery, modern political philosophy contains 'the notion of a guaranteed parallelism between intellectual and social progress' as the laws of history unveil a movement towards, for instance, greater freedom and, like the discoveries of the laws of nature, establish progressive floors 'beneath which man can no longer sink'.[10] Insofar as this parallelism and movement fail, the notion of progress reaches a crisis and 'leads to the suggestion that we should return' in the form of a repentance with an eye towards redemption.[11] It is for this reason that political philosophy 'is today in need of a critical study of its history', and that this history 'presupposes that one understand the great thinkers of the past as they understood themselves' in order to redeem our own world with a fuller knowledge of those political ideas that both inform our world and should have been able to sink into inherited knowledge if progress were not in crisis.[12]

For Zarka, if this return is not precisely the mark of historicism insofar as it does not approach the history of political philosophy as a relativistic engagement of a series of equally valid ideas engaged from the distance of an objective observer, its interest in a repentant return to that history fails to take up political philosophical concepts in a philosophical manner. If Skinner fails to attend to both of Zarka's understandings of thinking philosophically, Strauss primarily fails to attend to Zarka's second understanding of thinking philosophically because either he does not think or he refuses to acknowledge that he is engaged in interpretation. Strauss's careful historical analyses, critical though they may be, still presuppose an understanding of the philosophical concepts at hand as the thinkers themselves understood them, and thus at least obliquely adjure responsibility for the interpretation, the philosophical thinking in which they are engaged. It is in fidelity to both his understandings of thinking philosophically that Zarka will explain, in *La décision métaphysique de Hobbes*, that his interest is in 'putting the whole of the work into motion, not in order to repeat it, but in order to rethink it'.[13] Whereas Strauss does not claim to be engaged in the interpretive work of rethinking the concepts of the history of political philosophy, for Zarka such a philosophical or speculative approach to those concepts is indeed the only way to give those concepts the full historical appreciation they deserve.

That Zarka's work offers a methodological alternative to the reading of the history of political philosophy from what is more standard in the English-speaking world means making his work more available to English speakers is important. That his alternative involves a non-reductive, speculative and philosophical approach to the history of philosophy means he offers a philosophical methodology that should be taken seriously in its own right. Finally, that, here, this non-reductive approach shows us some of the crucial concepts that Hobbes contributed to modern political thought means this book is an important contribution to Hobbes scholarship in general.

## TRANSLATION ISSUES

Both *puissance* and *pouvoir* translate to 'power', but *puissance* relates to an individual's power, *pouvoir* to political power. Because, in Chapter 6, Zarka explicitly distinguishes *puissance* and *force*, neither 'strength' nor 'might' suffice as a translation of *puissance*. Therefore, I have opted to place the French term used in brackets every time each of them appears throughout the text in order to avoid any confusion.

However, Zarka's use of *convention, contrat* and *pacte* seem fairly interchangeable. I have translated *pacte* with 'pact', even if a more usual English usage might suggest 'contract'. However, in that 'social convention' is misleading in English, I have translated both *convention* and *contrat* as 'contract', indicating only the latter in brackets. All other appearances of 'contract' may be assumed to translate *convention*.

## ACKNOWLEDGEMENTS

I wish to thank Professor Zarka himself, first, for having the confidence in me to bring this translation to completion, but also for his patience throughout its development and for his extremely helpful suggestions and clarifications when my own ideas fell short. In addition, I should thank Jen Daly at Edinburgh University Press for helping me through the process of getting the translation approved, as well as Rebecca Mackenzie and Michelle Houston at EUP for their editorial and other forms of help in getting the translation to print. An anonymous reader of the manuscript also contributed a number of helpful suggestions.

Several people at DePaul University should also be thanked for their assistance in finding more nuanced words or translation strategies. In particular, I wish to acknowledge Richard A. Lee Jr, who introduced me to Zarka's work and who is always a generous reader. Michael Naas was exceedingly patient with my asking a number of questions as they came up. María del Rosario Acosta López helped in dealing with the material on Baltasar Gracián in Chapter 2. William Meyerowitz, Ian Moore and Ashley Bohrer at DePaul, and Edward Kazarian at Rowan University also helped me with potentially confusing moments and other such concerns.

Chapter 10 benefited from consulting Edward Hughes's translation of the same material in *The Amsterdam Debate*.[14]

Finally, I wish to thank Ali Beheler at Hastings College, who helped the translation acquire much more fluidity than it otherwise would have had.

Any errors or confusions in the final product are, of course, only my own.

James Griffith
Chicago/Bratislava
2015

## Notes

1. Quentin Skinner, 'Debate', in Quentin Skinner and Yves Charles Zarka, *Hobbes: The Amsterdam Debate*, ed. Hans Blom (New York: Georg Olms Verlag, 2001), p. 25. This book, which is unfortunately out of print, is an excellent resource for clarifications as to the respective positions between Skinner's Cambridge school and Zarka's Paris-centred school of Hobbes scholarship.
2. For instance, Quentin Skinner, *The Foundations of Modern Political Thought*, 2 vols. (Cambridge: Cambridge University Press, 1978–9); Skinner, *Reason and Rhetoric in the Philosophy of Hobbes* (Cambridge: Cambridge University Press, 1997); and Skinner, *Liberty before Liberalism* (Cambridge: Cambridge University Press, 1998).
3. Skinner, 'Debate', p. 25.
4. Yves Charles Zarka, 'Debate: Interpreting the Past in the Present', trans. Edward Hughes, in *The Amsterdam Debate*, p. 31.
5. Ibid., p. 33. In Chapter 1 as well as later in this piece, he refers to this position as 'non-historicist'.
6. 'The historical mode is a way of doing philosophy' (Skinner, 'Debate', p. 25).
7. Zarka, 'Interpreting the Past in the Present', p. 33.
8. See Leo Strauss, 'Political Philosophy and History', in *'What is Political Philosophy?' and Other Studies* (Chicago, IL: University of Chicago Press, 1988), pp. 72–3.
9. Leo Strauss, 'Progress or Return?' in *The Rebirth of Classical Political Rationalism: An Introduction to the Thought of Leo Strauss*, selected and intro. Thomas L. Pangel (Chicago, IL: University of Chicago Press, 1989), p. 233. See also Strauss, 'Political Philosophy and History', p. 60, and Strauss, 'Introduction', in *History of Political Philosophy*, ed. Leo Strauss and Joseph Cropsey, 3rd edn (Chicago, IL: University of Chicago Press, 1987), p. 3.

10. Strauss, 'Progress or Return?', pp. 236, 238.
11. Ibid., pp. 227, 245.
12. Leo Strauss, *The Political Philosophy of Hobbes: Its Basis and its Genesis*, trans. Elsa M. Sinclair (Chicago, IL: University of Chicago Press, 1963), p. xv.
13. Yves Charles Zarka, *La décision métaphysique de Hobbes: Conditions de la politique*, 2 edn (Paris: Vrin, 1999), p. 365 (my translation).
14. Yves Charles Zarka, 'Hobbes and the Right to Punish', trans. Edward Hughes, in *The Amsterdam Debate*, pp. 71–87.

# FOREWORD

This work is constituted from studies each of which, in a first version, was to be given as a lecture or in a separate publication in France or abroad. We have, however, reshaped and rethought them in order to integrate them in this volume, which arranges the results of several years of reflection on Hobbes's œuvre. This ordering and the reshuffling that it implies makes it possible to draw out issues which were only implicit in the texts' first versions. Also, it clearly appeared that these are at the same time the fundamental problems and concepts of modern political thought, which were analysed from the different angles under which Hobbes's philosophy is considered. Some studies aiming to confront the English philosopher's positions with those of some of his contemporaries (Gracián, Filmer, Pascal, etc.) will also emphasise the displacements and ruptures which run across modern thought.

*Chapter 1*

# JOURNEY: TO THE FOUNDATIONS OF MODERN POLITICS

HISTORICAL INTEREST AND PHILOSOPHICAL INTEREST

The work that you are going to read relates to the study of the reorienting, transforming and innovative work in political thought undertaken by Hobbes. A certain number of political modernity's nodal problems will follow from this conceptual work. In order to define the stakes of this work, I will first make an effort to point out the general, simultaneously historiographical and philosophical perspective within which it is inscribed, and I will then indicate the places that will bear on the examination of Hobbes's conceptual intervention.

The general perspective of my research concerns, in this work as in my previous works, the moment where political philosophy, particularly in the seventeenth century, conceptually forges ethical, juridical and theological positions which involve the determination of the foundations of modern politics. The direction of this approach is simultaneously historical and philosophical. Historical, because the texts that it is a question of understanding are texts of the past, the study of which must be subject to historically exact criteria; philosophical, because these texts are not simply the vestiges of a bygone era, but are the bearers of interrogations which raise determinations concerning the nature, value and end of the political to the level of concept, and thus involve our comprehension of the political. In this sense, the historical interest that I bring to past political philosophies cannot be dissociated from a philosophical interest. This position supposes two things concerning the status of, on the one hand, the history of philosophy and, on the other, political philosophy's relationship between the past and the present. On the first point, I will say that the properly philosophical stakes of past political philosophies are retrievable and can be reactivated only from a philosophical point of view. On the second point, I will say that, to the extent that they open up the determinations of the political to the thinkable, the texts of past political philosophy are likely to furnish theoretical resources for the renewal of our own reflection.

This double bond of historical interest and philosophical interest is, however, far from being self-evident. We can even say that some of the most outstanding contemporary authors within the domain of political philosophy and that of the history of political philosophy are attached to effecting an entrenched separation of the two interests, and to presenting this separation as the necessary condition of an authentic political philosophy, on the one hand, and of an exact historical comprehension of works of the past, on the other. The convergence of positions on this separation is emphasised since the authors often lead not only by different but absolutely opposed paths. On the one hand, we understand promoting the idea of an authentic political philosophy. To that end, we maintain that politics has for its object a universal essence or truth concerning the best political order and the just political order. So the intervention of history, in particular that of the history of philosophy, displaces at this point the stakes of political philosophy; it exposes the latter to a loss of historicist prestige. On the other hand, we maintain, within a precisely historicist perspective, that there is no more essence than universal truth or permanent question of the political, but that every political text depends on the historically determined intellectual and discursive context within which it appears and where it finds its meaning and its value. So only a historical approach makes it possible to attain an exact comprehension of the works of past political philosophy. This time the promotion of the idea of a historically exact history of political thought supposes putting aside the philosophical stakes, or, more exactly, the extreme particularisation of these stakes in the service of different historico-discursive contexts.

Can we be released from this alternative – to my mind, fruitless – of a political philosophy that affirms its identity as tearing away from history and, in particular, from the history of political philosophy and of a historicism that constructs a history of thought only at the expense of an extenuation of the idea of political philosophy? The whole approach that I am giving here rests on the possibility of a positive response to this question.

## THE IDEA OF A NON-HISTORICIST HISTORY OF POLITICAL PHILOSOPHY

I do not have the ambition in this short introduction to treat all the theoretical implications of this idea, but only to point out certain aspects of it through more detailed examination of the difficulties encountered by authors who remain held within the choice indicated above, principally Leo Strauss[1] and Quentin Skinner.[2]

We cannot overemphasise the importance of these studies dedicated by Leo Strauss to the genealogy of political philosophy's decline in the modern and contemporary world. This decline comes, according to him, from the fundamental modification of the relationship between philosophy and history that introduced and imposed historicism in its different forms. This modification consists in the historical reorientation of philosophical questions, which was progressively deepened from the formation of the idea of a philosophy of history in the eighteenth century up to contemporary researches on the currents of thought and social life and their historical origins, via the Hegelian elevation of the history of philosophy to the rank of philosophical discipline and the 'historical school' of the nineteenth century. Thus, 'historicism is not just one philosophic school among many, but a most powerful agent that affects more or less all present-day thought'.[3] Furthermore, historicism is so powerful that Strauss speaks in historicist terms of 'the spirit of the times'.[4]

In order to show the magnitude of this challenge, Strauss changes the point of view to situate it within the non-historicist perspective for which classical philosophy furnishes the model. From this point of view, which is also where things are given within the truth of their nature, it appears that:

> Political philosophy is not a historical discipline. The philosophic questions of the nature of political things and of the best, or just political order are fundamentally different from historical questions, which always concern individuals ... In particular, political philosophy is fundamentally different from the history of political philosophy itself. The question of the nature of political things and the answer to it cannot possibly be mistaken for the question of how this or that philosopher or all philosophers have approached, discussed or answered the philosophic question mentioned.[5]

This does not imply that political philosophy should be absolutely indifferent to history in general and to its own history in particular, but these have only the subordinate role of preliminaries or exterior auxiliaries. They are not integrated parts of political philosophy.

We can consequently understand the operations by which historicism suppresses 'the fundamental question' between philosophical questions and historical questions, and thus affects forgetting the very meaning of political philosophy. I will retain four of them.

1. Historicism takes as decisive the existence of a dependence of each political philosophy on the historical situation whence it appears. This dependence is decisive principally because it is thought as an essential dependence, that is to say, as a dependence outside of which a political teaching can neither be valued nor even be included. But historicism does not perceive that the relation of a political philosophy in the context within which it appears could be thought in a very different manner. For example, that past philosophers could present what they held for the truth of the political in terms which render it acceptable within the frame of the dominant opinions of their era.

2. It follows from the essential bond that historicism establishes between a philosophy and the historical context within which it appears that every resumption of a political teaching of one context within another profoundly modifies its signification. Consequently, not only the replies but the questions become different according to the moments of history. There are thus no longer perennial questions of political philosophy. The latter is broken into a multiplicity of discourses the contradictions of which historicism enjoys emphasising. To this we could add that the very notion of 'political philosophy' becomes a simply nominal category that refers only to a heterogeneous multiplicity of discourses.

3. Besides all this, the question of the truth of a teaching is found placed in brackets, even destroyed: 'To understand a serious teaching, we must be seriously interested in it, i.e., we must be willing to consider the possibility that it is simply true. The historicist as such denies that possibility as regards any philosophy of the past.'[6]

4. In the end, having thus put into doubt the meaning of the questions of the political best and just, historicism substitutes for these questions of political philosophy some historical questions.

The affirmation of political philosophy's identity thus supposes, according to Strauss, that we re-establish questions, in themselves ahistorical, concerning the nature and value of politics.

Quentin Skinner's approach is precisely opposed. His object is, to all appearances, entirely other. It consists in defining the methodological principles of an historically exact interpretation of past political texts. It is thus a matter of highlighting the characteristics of comprehension within the domain of the history of political thought. However, this enterprise is not without engaging a determination of the status of political texts and their object. We will thus seek to know what remains of political philosophy when we put the proposed type of history of ideas to work.

As Jean-Fabien Spitz recalls in a recent article, the right question with regard to the history of political ideas for Skinner is this: 'What could the author of a text, in writing at the moment when he wrote, in addressing the public which he addressed, have intended to communicate to his readers in using the wording that he used?'[7] Two notions are indeed central: that of intent and that of discursive context. Contrary to a traditional version of the historicism that endeavours to furnish a causal explanation from the way economic-social circumstances determine the intellectual content of a given politics, Skinner elaborates what we could characterise as a more refined form of historicism wherein comprehension of a statement's tenor depends on its inscription within a determined discursive context, where a normative vocabulary and dominant conventions prevail.[8] Indeed, a text is not reduced to a chain of propositions blessed with signification. It also comprises an illocutionary force by which it is simultaneously an act.[9] Now, it is within this illocutionary force that the intention of the author resides. It is thus a matter of a determinant element within the comprehension of the text. The intention must not be understood as 'an intention to do something'. Under this form, intent will designate only the motivations of an author, which inevitably remain at the same time anterior and exterior to the tenor of the text itself. The intention that it concerns must be understood as 'an intention in doing something'. Under this form, it characterises 'the *point* of the action for the agent who performed it',[10] that is to say, the very aim of the action, what the author of a text did by writing it.[11] Yet knowledge of this intention cannot be attained if we stick to the text alone. It additionally supposes that we know the context of the discourse within which it is inscribed, that is to say, what questions it had in view, what type of responses it brings to them, to what extent these responses comply with the prevalent suppositions and conventions of the intellectual and political debate or break from them. The knowledge of the inscription of a text within this context thus furnishes a determinant element for the interpretation of the text itself.

Every question is henceforth of knowing what are the consequences of this conception of the status and object of political philosophy. These consequences reproduce and even reinforce those of the more traditional versions of historicism. And so every statement is conceived as ineluctably left to a particular intention, provoked by some particular circumstances and aiming to bring a response to a particular problem. The opening of the text onto the historico-discursive context has the retroactive effect of containing it within an era and of limiting its stakes. Skinner draws the final consequences of his own approach: (1) the history of thought allows us, according to him, to discover that there are neither atemporal concepts nor even perennial questions of political philosophy; (2) correlatively, there is no essence or truth of politics, there is only an essential variety of presupposed morals and political engagements.[12]

Thus, here is the alternative with which we are confronted. The idea of a non-historicist history of political philosophy could allow us to enter into founding another way of relating political philosophy to its own history. In order to show its possibility, I will here attend to two considerations.

The first concerns the paradoxical status of historicism. It is supposed to found the principle of its validity on history itself. Yet, as Strauss remarked, historicism is not founded on straightforward historical evidence, but on a philosophical thesis: precisely that which affirms the essentially historical character of thought, knowledge, truth, philosophy and political values.[13] In other words, historicism does not rest upon the incontestable observation of a fact, but on the interpretation of a fact. As such, it would not know how to constitute the inevitable result of taking the whole of history into consideration and, in particular, the history of political philosophy. And even less that the interpretation on which it rests is eminently contestable. And so, in order to take only one example, historicism asserts an exact historical comprehension of works of the past and, as we have seen, thinks it has arrived at this in again taking hold of the intention or aim of the author starting from the context (or rather from the reconstitution or reinterpretation of this context), questions which it provoked (or rather some questions that it is supposed to have provoked) and reactions to which it gave rise. This method can certainly allow for making some discoveries that illuminate such and such a passage, such and such particular point of a work. But when an author affirms on several occasions that he does not intend to speak of such and such particular state form but of the state in general, whatever the place and time, is what he says of interpreting truly understood as a function of such and such particular situation? Certainly, we will be able to object that it is not always necessary to take what a philosopher says according to the letter, since his effective intention or his aim is occasionally different from his proclaimed intention. But then it is necessary to admit that we are not doing a history of political philosophy, even of political thought, but a history of ideologies. We can doubt that historicism could recover anything of the properly philosophical stakes of past political philosophical works.

My second consideration concerns the relationship between political philosophy and the history of political philosophy. In this respect, it is necessary to remark that Strauss does not manage to attain the asserted separation between the questions of the one and those of the other. An internal link between the two orders under consideration is in effect re-established by his observation, '"Our ideas" are only partly our ideas',[14] that these are for the most part inherited ideas that demand to be elucidated by means of a philosophical history. This demand for historical explanation is, however, according to Strauss, proper to the modern political philosophy that was established in modifying or in opposing concepts of classical political philosophy. The work of elucidation aims to clarify the basis, henceforth not immediately accessible, starting from which we think. And so modern political philosophy 'is in need of the history of political philosophy or science as an integral part of its own efforts'.[15] It is not a matter of a surreptitious return of historicism, since this reintegration of the history of political philosophy does not at all imply that we relativise the idea of truth or the principle of preference, and that, when all is said and done, we renounce them. The task that the history of political philosophy must fulfil consists in carrying out this special effort which aims to 'transform inherited knowledge into genuine knowledge by re-vitalising its original discovery'.[16] But what Strauss says here, and what we understand with regard to his conception of the relationship between the ancients and the moderns, can be applied to the relationship of political philosophy to itself. The notions of state, sovereignty, government, democracy, etc., which are at the heart of political philosophy, for the most part revive inherited knowledge and require an historical elucidation, starting from which questions of the true and of the false, of the desirable and of the detestable, can be posed clearly. Yet this elucidation can be accomplished only in restoring the philosophical stakes that elevated these notions to the concept. This appears to me to be the task of a philosophical history of political philosophy.

## WHY HOBBES?

This task of philosophical elucidation has animated my research on Hobbes's work. Why Hobbes? For three reasons.

The first comes from this, that his philosophy appears to me to be the bearer of fundamental interrogations which were inevitably masked by an exclusively historico-political interpretation.[17] The fact that his major political works,[18] having been written just before or during the English Civil War, actually seem to definitively determine meaning as a tentative response at the theoretical level to different aspects of the political crisis that his country knew. This is, of course, not false, but it would not know how to take account of the extent of his œuvre's philosophical stakes. In order to detect them, it would thus be necessary to displace the consideration and to replace a historico-political interpretation with an interpretation that would make an effort to take account of the project of the rational re-foundation of knowledge that animates the whole of his philosophy and the politics of which constitutes one of the moments. It thus clearly appeared to me that this philosophy would comprise some unsuspected resources concerning the metaphysical positions that support the political conceptions.

The Hobbesian project of rational re-foundation is indeed made up of two aspects: a rational reconstruction of the science of nature, on the one hand, and a rational reconstruction of ethics and of politics, on the other. Every question would thus be of knowing whether this double reconstruction, which reduces reality to matter in motion, at the same time decisively promoting within the edification of his own social and political world, could be thought as starting from only one principle. Now this seems to me to be the case: Hobbes's logic and first philosophy furnish in effect a critique of the metaphysics of essence and enter into a redefinition of the relationship of knowledge to being, which allows for taking account of the establishment of a new relationship of man to world.[19]

The second reason comes from what Hobbes's political philosophy reproduces under a form of definitions and of purely rational deductions of the concepts that were slowly elaborated from the fourteenth to the beginning of the seventeenth centuries: individual, power, sovereignty, person, state, law, etc. In this sense, it is simultaneously an outcome and a point of departure. It furnishes the version, canonical as it were, that will get modern political interrogations going. Better, it is possible to locate within the internal dynamics by which it is redeveloped from one work to the other the processes by which, for one thing, the concept of the state as institutional order having laws available and a specifically political power supposes the taming of the figure of the prince;[20] for another, the central political question becomes that of knowing how a multiplicity of individual wills can become a unique political will;[21] finally, one of the central juridical questions becomes that of knowing how to found a penal law that does not conflict with ethical individualism.[22]

The third reason comes from what Hobbes perceives, perhaps more clearly than others, of the paradoxical character of politics, always held between language and violence, right and power, reason and passions. Let us begin with the first series: language/right/reason.

The importance of language already appears within the ethics where man is defined not only as a passionate being, but also as a being of speech.[23] This expression is taken in the strong sense: man is not simply a being that speaks; he is a being that becomes what he is by speech. Speech confers on man the most proper dimensions of his existence as simultaneously individual and within his relationship to others. Now the more considerable work of speech is to institute the state by the social pact. The terms of this pact originally found the distribution of rights and of duties, that is to say, define the understanding of sovereignty's political rights and of the subjects' obedience. Speech thus gives being to the state as juridical institution. Better, the state as artificial juridical being is fundamentally tied to language. This is identifiable, for example, at the level of the theory of civil law.[24] The validity of this rests on two things: that it would be the expression of the sovereign will, and that it would be carried to the knowledge of the subjects. Now, it is by speech and, more essentially, by writing that the announcement of law is realised. The theory of the pact and that of civil law thus understood implies a conception of political reason that, when the state follows the internal logic of its maximal function, would not be transcendent and exterior, but simultaneously identical to subjects. Coming out of this first series, we can say that the state is an artificial being of reason.

But there is another series as well: violence/power/passions. Violence is, first, an archaic violence. That to which the passionate dynamics of interhuman relations leads when it does not exist in political power [*pouvoir*].[25] But this violence does not miraculously disappear with the institution of the state. It simply becomes virtual because a new dynamic of the relations between men is established that comes from a coercive power [*puissance*] the state has available. At the end of the second series, the state appears as an artificial being of power [*puissance*].

The state is thus not one or the other, state of reason or state of power [*puissance*], but both. This is precisely what renders it fragile, bearer of the indestructible germs of its crises, experiencing its own dissolution.

These are, briefly outlined, some sites of a journey here within Hobbes's thought. In returning to the work itself, this itinerary aims to furnish some clarifications of the concept of politics, more precisely, of the internal articulations of the modern concept of politics.

It is thus the properly Hobbesian work of the concept within the formation of the fundamental problems and concepts of modern political thought that is the subject of the following pages. This means that I aim neither at establishing a systematic confrontation of Hobbes's major positions with the major political thoughts of his time, nor at determining his inscription within the principal directions of seventeenth-century political thought. My object is more limited: it concerns again taking hold, in some particular places, of the modifications that Hobbes makes subject to some central problems of the ethico-political sphere. These places concern the relationship between individual and state, and between language and power [*pouvoir*], as well as the content of fundamental concepts like war, law, property, state, the right to punish. The work ends with the study of the reflection of Hobbesian thought according to two contemporaries very different from each other: Filmer and Pascal.

## Notes

1. Leo Strauss' work is today much better understood in France. A very significant number of translations have appeared over the last few years. For our purposes, we will refer only to two works, *Natural Right and History* (Chicago, IL: University of Chicago Press, 1953) and *'What is Political Philosophy?' and Other Studies* (Glencoe, IL: Free Press, 1959, reprinted Chicago, IL: University of Chicago Press, 1988), most particularly to this collection's first studies, 'What is Political Philosophy?', pp. 9–55, and 'Political Philosophy and History', pp. 56–77.
2. Quentin Skinner's works have two aspects. The first concerns the history of political thought, see, in particular *The Foundations of Modern Political Thought*, 2 vols (Cambridge: Cambridge University Press, 1978). The second is methodological. A complete enough bibliography is found at the end of the first volume of the work mentioned above. We will reflect in particular on 'Meaning and understanding in the history of ideas', *History and Theory*, 8(1) (1969): 3–53, and on 'Conventions and the understanding of speech acts', *Philosophical Quarterly*, 20(79) (1970): 118–38. Also see the article by Jean-Fabien Spitz, 'Comment lire les textes politiques du passé?', *Droits*, 10 (1989): 133–45.
3. Strauss, 'Political philosophy and history', p. 57.
4. Ibid.
5. Ibid., p. 56.
6. Ibid., p. 40.
7. Spitz, 'Comment lire les textes politiques du passé?,' p. 144. [TN: my translation.]
8. See Skinner, 'Meaning and understanding in the history of ideas'.
9. On Skinner's relationship to Austin, see Skinner, 'Conventions and the understanding of speech acts'.
10. Skinner, 'Meaning and understanding in the history of ideas', p. 44. [TN: in English in the original.]
11. See also Skinner, *The Foundations of Modern Political Thought*, p. xiii.
12. See Skinner, 'Meaning and understanding in the history of ideas', p. 52.
13. See Strauss, 'Political philosophy and history', p. 66.
14. Ibid., p. 71.
15. Ibid., p. 77.
16. Ibid.
17. This first reason directed the writing of Zarka, *La décision métaphysique de Hobbes: Conditions de la politique* (Paris: Vrin, 1987).
18. Let us recall that Hobbes's three principal political works, *The Elements of Law*, *De Cive* and *Leviathan*, date from 1640, 1642 and 1651, respectively.
19. Hobbes's political philosophy began to be elaborated before the

composition of his first political work. See on this point our study, 'First philosophy and the foundation of knowledge', trans. Tom Sorell, in *The Cambridge Companion to Hobbes*, ed. Tom Sorell (Cambridge: Cambridge University Press, 1995), pp. 62–85; also see *De Principiis*, trans. Luc Borot, *Philosophie*, 23 (1989), pp. 5–21. Also see the set of texts touching on first philosophy which precedes the publication of *De Corpore* in 1655, in particular *Thomas White's* De mundo *examined*, trans. H. W. Jones (Bradford: Bradford University Press, 1976).
20. See Chapter 9, 'On the State'.
21. See Chapter 8, 'On Property'.
22. See Chapter 10, 'On the Right to Punish'.
23. See *La décision métaphysique*, pp. 272–92.
24. See Chapter 7, 'On Law'.
25. See Chapter 6, 'On War'.

## *Part I*

# INDIVIDUAL AND STATE

This first part contains two instances. Chapter 2 has the function of bringing to the fore implications of the emergence of a new conception of the individual. In passing from the aesthetics of heroic singularity in Gracián to the universality of the individual in Hobbes, the establishment of a new comprehension of the ethico-political sphere is played out. Chapter 3 furnishes an analysis of the successive phases of the constitution of this new comprehension of the ethico-political sphere in *The Elements of Law*, *De Cive* and *Leviathan*.

*Chapter 2*

# GRACIÁN'S HERO AND HOBBES'S ANTIHERO

### THE SINGULARITY OF THE HERO AND THE UNIVERSALITY OF THE INDIVIDUAL

The theoretical figure of Gracián's[1] work is singular. Indeed, an heir in several of its aspects to Renaissance treatises on the courtier and on the prince and a participant in the theoretico-cultural context of the Counter-Reformation, it shows the traits of a hero who will remain on the margins of the conception of man that organises the dominant currents of moral and political thought in the seventeenth century. We thus cannot fail to be struck by the contrast in the conception of the individual singularity – which subtends the heroic type – to the new notion of the individual that philosophers and moralists elaborate from before the middle of the seventeenth century, and who, precisely, efface that singularity in order to promote a universalisable image of man. This new notion of the individual implies a reinterpretation of the primacy, superiority and excellence that define the hero, a reinterpretation that transforms it into a fiction, the content of which is no longer real but imaginary. Gracián's hero gives way to an antiheroic conception of the individual.

It is this contrast that I would like to interrogate insofar as we cannot bring it back to a pure and simple opposition. Indeed, many of the constitutive elements of the world within which Gracián's hero lives are found again in the anthropological doctrines of authors like Hobbes, Pascal, La Rochefoucauld, etc. as principles that preside over its conduct. On the side of the social world, we again find the distinction, even the separation, between being and appearing, the idea of an inversion of values, the conception of a language and of ciphered conduct that it is essential to decode. On the side of human conduct, we again find that necessity of staying in the background in relation to others, of governing its appearance in order to be placed in a superior situation. Yet Gracián's hero is no longer there. Therefore, it must be that something happened, that the essential determinations of the hero had disappeared and that others were substituted for it. The rules that Gracián conceived within the framework of an instruction manual for the hero's exceptional qualities and capacities are from now on found integrated within the analysis of the behaviour of an individual who is no longer in any way heroic. How to understand this displacement, that is to say, at the same time this recovery and this rupture, whereby that which in Gracián was valuable for a small number is universalised to all men while profoundly changing meaning? What I would like to show is that this displacement is subtended by a modification that intervenes in the conception of the fundamental tendency that defines human behaviour. This modification is, moreover, going to have determinate consequences at the political level. The modern conception of the state in fact draws its anthropological principles from there. The human type of the hero thus enters, at the moral and political level, into a long phase of regression – which is not to say cancellation. Its much later reappearance will coincide with a calling into question of the principles of politics.

## THE PRIMACY OF THE HERO

The first two chapters of *El Héroe* instantly show the framework within which the conception of the heroic type is going to be developed in Gracián's work.[2] This framework is the distinction between being and appearing, reality and mask, the thing and the sign, that is to say, a divided universe where the lure, trap, illusion and deception are constitutive givens.[3] This conception will be developed in all its generality in *El Criticón*.[4] In this text, the universe changes appearance and form according to the vision of it that two characters have who perform a pilgrimage in the great theatre of the world. The world in general, as much natural as social, is a shifting and deceptive façade; it is affected by a general inversion of values.[5] The whole problem for each of them is not to be trapped by fallacious appearances, empty ostentations, indeed even by language that is itself ciphered: when we speak we often say more or something other than what we mean to say.

In this reign of deception which pierces relations between men from top to bottom,[6] the reign of the hero's ongoing conduct will simultaneously mask the understanding of his capacity from others and, inversely, try to penetrate the heart of the other.[7] This reign is not a principle of duplicity which would be proper to the hero, but a means for him to use the universal duplicity to his own ends. We understand the first two maxims of the art of conducting oneself as: (1) render oneself impenetrable, never show oneself entirely; and (2) in particular, hide the affections of one's heart, never show one's passions because without that heroism would suffer a mortal attack. Indeed, to show our passion is to give others the weapons that will be turned against us. These maxims suppose an interpretation of interhuman relations in terms of power [*pouvoir*] and domination: a man who understands another is in a position to dominate him; on the other hand, the one that no one understands escapes from the power [*pouvoir*] of others.

We thus understand that heroism is defined first as a governance of the self which ought to procure an advantage and a superiority over others. This governance of the self takes on two aspects: one is practical, it is a question of a technique of the self which consists in an art of speaking and acting; the other is aesthetic, it is a question of a stylistic manner, of grace, or of that indefinable 'je ne sais quoi' without which all of the world's techniques would remain ineffective. But before discussing certain points of this technique of the self and of this aesthetic style, it is important to say something about the exceptional qualities and perfections that distinguish the hero and that, when they are brought together, make an extraordinary being.

At the origin of all grandeur there is first of all the mind, more precisely the understanding (*entendimiento*). This principal part is composed of two others: a depth of judgement (*fondo de juicio*); and an elevation of mind (*elevación de ingenio*), which, according to Gracián, form a prodigy when they meet.[8] Harmony in these attributes is essential for the hero. Let us note in passing that Gracián gives to this division of the understanding (*entendimiento*) into mind (*ingenio*) and judgement (*juicio*) the aspect of a veritable reform of the philosophical categories of the faculties of the soul.[9] To the multiplication of the faculties of the soul in some philosophers' works, which ultimately results in confusion between mind and will, Gracián opposes the simple distinction between *ingenio*, the finest expression of which is sharpness (*la agudeza*), what is sharpest and most penetrating in the mind, and the judgement that is the basis for prudence.

Mind and judgement supersede nature and art. On the one side, the mind's force, swiftness and subtlety originate from a gift of nature or of God; they are like the sparks or rays of divinity. But the mind also involves art, indeed even artifice. This explains the monumental development in Gracián of an art of the mind or an art of wit (*arte de ingenio*). Which opens rhetoric onto a domain that it had, if not ignored, at least neglected:

> The ancients found some methods for the syllogism, an art for the trope; they stamped sharpness by giving it over, out of respect or out of disinterest, to the sole valour of ingenuity. They were satisfied with admiring it . . . They did not go so far as to analyse it, so that we find in them no reflection and even less definition.[10]

I would retain here only two characteristics of this art of the mind: (1) in Discurso III of his work *Agudeza y arte de ingenio*, Gracián gives himself as an object the sharpness of artifice (*agudeza de artificio*) that relates to subtle beauty, in opposition to sharpness of discernment (*agudeza de perspicacia*) that gives access to complex truths in discovering the most secret; (2) the tropes or figures that are forms for traditional rhetoric become material for the sharpness of the mind in the framework of his analysis. It is thus a matter of treating form or style by taking as matter what, until then, was taken as form:

> Sharpness makes use of tropes and rhetorical figures as well as of instruments for wringing its concepts with refinement, but they restrain themselves from the material foundations of subtlety, and even more, from the ornaments of thought.[11]

The analysis of deceitful sharpness is related to the use of words and to language. It is taken for a constitutive aspect of the hero, because it is often a word, a trait of language, which immortalises a fact or an action.

This first determination of the heroic character suffices to take account of the fact that the type of the hero is applied only to the man of war or to the statesman, but it can equally concern other sorts of men, as they are occupied with literature, erudition or religion. The list of possible activities for the hero is not, however, unlimited. It is indeed always required that the role consist of some excellence. It remains that, in the set of roles likely to give rise to the development of the heroic type, the figure of the prince and that of the warrior preserve a primacy.

However, perfections of the mind are not sufficient to define the hero. It is necessary that they join with qualities of the heart and of taste. The necessity of the hero to have a great heart stems from the fact that action or execution concerns a dimension other than that of the mind. Effects are proportionate to causes, so much so that it is necessary to have an extraordinary heart in order to produce actions of a similar nature. Beyond acquired glory and even excess adversity, the great heart searches for new triumphs. It is thus magnanimity and courage that hold the first place in the order of action. Further, it is necessary that the hero should have excellent taste inasmuch as an elevated mind does not work with mediocre taste. Art also has its role to play here. There is a culture of taste, just as there is a culture of the mind, which completes what nature had begun (*hay cultura de gusto, así de ingenio*). Taste evaluates the right price of things; it accords a proportional esteem to the value of the object.

Such are the three dimensions – spiritual, active and aesthetic – which draw the figure of the hero, who, in a world divided by the ontological and existential difference of being and appearing, accomplishes the great actions and deeds that are preserved in the memory of humanity. The qualities and perfections of the hero are thus such because they are the determinations of his being which shine in the eyes of others. They allow for obtaining eminence in the best, that is to say, this superiority which calls attention to the hero and makes of him a being who never is second or copy from a model, but a being unique in his kind.

Nevertheless, it must very much be that the transition from the hero's qualities to his effects on others be immediate. This transition indeed demands a governance of the self which is deployed, as we have indicated, in a technique and a style. The technology of the hero's self first of all supposes a knowledge of the self and, in particular, of its dominant qualities. This knowledge of the self must escape from the deforming trap of the false mirror that we are to ourselves. In other words, appearance's deceptions are not only exterior but also interior. The hero must first of all decipher himself before piercing the mask of others. This knowledge of the self is required since it allows the hero to hold onto the knowledge of the type of activity at which he can excel, that is to say, of the heroism not to be deceived. But it is insufficient to know oneself; it is also necessary to know fortune. Gracián's hero is in many ways like Machiavelli's prince, elected by fortune. To know fortune is to know the moment when fortune is favourable and the moment when it takes leave.

This triple knowledge of the self, of others and of fortune assure for the hero a mastery of the self that takes the form of an art of the self. We already know that to reveal his passions leads the hero to his ruin. The art of the self therefore intends to hide its interior, its being or its basic lack of power [*pouvoir*] to modify its nature. The principal pitfalls of heroism are paradoxically found in the very qualities that constitute it because they risk at the same time carrying he who possesses them to unchecked anger and to uncontrolled greed. This is why, if the passions necessarily enter into the hero's disposition, they must remain masked, without which courage is transformed into anger and the love of glory into greed.

But the hero attains his full form and truly becomes an artist of himself only when the technique of the self is coupled with a grace, a manner or a style which provides this supplement which is nothing and everything at the same time. Nothing, because it is indefinable and almost imperceptible; everything, because, without it, the maxims for conduct are reduced to an industrious and ineffective exercise. The conception of the hero in Gracián is, finally, an aesthetics. It is that nothing is more difficult than playing with appearances. Appearance is not easily handled, precisely because we must not give to others the feeling that we are making use of it. The principal pitfall of heroism is here the affectation that is a degradation of ostentation, that shows what it must not show, that is to say, is shown as a mute praise of the self. Affectation is an ostentation that reveals itself. Artifice must couple this with a second artifice which masks the first and changes it into nature. Whence the development in Gracián of an aesthetics of style, of the form or the grace that culminates in the notion of *despejo*, which points out a 'je ne sais quoi' that we can recognise without being able to define it. The aesthetics of *despejo* is an aesthetics of the surface, which paradoxically touches the basis for perfections and values, because, without this, nothing could be elevated to excellence.

Thus, such is the figure of the hero in Gracián: he simultaneously supersedes a technique and an aesthetics which has the singular self for its object. This consideration is important since, if, as we have emphasised, political action does not constitute the only domain within which heroism can manifest itself, the statesman nonetheless furnishes the heroic type par excellence to the extent that he combines valour and prudence. Is this to say, for all that, that the conception of the hero founds a politics in Gracián? The numerous references to political or military action as well as to ancient or more recent statesmen who serve to illustrate the conduct and character of the hero could suggest it. The possible parallels to Machiavelli would seem to move in the same direction of an affirmation of the existence of a politics founded on this conception of the hero. Indeed, does Gracián not dedicate a work which is titled *El Politico* to Don Fernando the Catholic?

> I oppose a king to all preceding kings, and I propose a king to all kings to come. This is Don Fernando the Catholic, this grand master in the art of ruling, the greatest oracle of State reason [*el oraculo mayor de la razónde Estado*].[12]

The notion of state reason – quite central in the era's political thought – which appeared from the first lines of the work, seems to prop up the idea of a politics of the hero. Now, it is clear, in this text, that Gracián provides less a political treatise of the art of governing than a treatise of the governance of the self which makes Fernando the Catholic the most perfect and greatest of kings. In addition, the concept of state reason is in no way inscribed here from the perspective of a political Machiavellianism.[13] On the contrary, in the text cited, this concept designates what Gracián's contemporaries name the true state reason and identify with divine law. This true state reason served as a spearhead to fight against Machiavellianism in every class of Spanish thinkers who intended to introduce a subordination of the political to the religious. Less than a political treatise, Gracián's work is an aesthetics for the political hero's religious end. The very status of the work certifies a certain manner:

> This work will be less a body of his [i.e., Fernando's] history than the soul of his politics; it will not be a story of his deeds, but a discourse on his successes; not a panegyric of a single king, but a critique of several others.[14]

This discourse on the soul of politics and the manner of succeeding in it retains from Machiavelli's *Prince* only the aspects which will precisely be set aside by the theoreticians of state reason in order to elaborate on the rationalisation of governmental practice that has the power [*puissance*] of the state, and not that of the prince, for its object.

But the figure of Gracián's hero is untimely for yet another reason: the forming of a theory of the individual which implies its deposing [*destitution*].

### THE DEPOSING OF THE HERO

This deposing of the hero is given in the form of a result in the work of a later author like La Rochefoucauld. The comparison of La Rochefoucauld with Gracián is justified not only by the fact that he is not a systematic thinker but a moralistic author of maxims, but also, especially, because the reinterpretation of the heroic type occupies an important place in his work. The deposing, as the theoretical result, will later be able to be resituated within the perspective of stronger theoretical elaborations. Let us begin with the result:

> The variations to be seen in the courage of myriads of men come from the different ways their imagination presents death to them, more vividly at one time than at another. Thus it comes about that after scorning what they do not know they end by fearing what they know. Unless one is prepared to consider death the direst of all evils, it should never be contemplated with all its attendant circumstances. The wisest and also the bravest are those who find the least shameful pretexts for not contemplating it, but every man capable of seeing death as it really is thinks it a fearful thing ... And we misunderstand the effects of self-love [*amour-propre*] if we believe it can help us to make light of the very thing that spells its own destruction; the mind, in which we think we can find so many resources, is too feeble at such a juncture to persuade us as we would wish.[15]

Three remarks about and on the subject of this text.

1. First, we find again, transposed in La Rochefoucauld, descriptions touching on the social world and human conduct which were figured in Gracián, without this implying the idea of an influence from the second on the first. In particular, the difference between being and appearing, the deceptive power [*puissance*] of appearance, the reinterpretation of the passionate life in this framework, the desire for semi-unlimited

glory that animates certain men and carries them to the domination of others. We also find there certain aspects of the hero's characterisation: 'However great may be the advantages she bestows, it is not nature alone, but nature helped by luck that makes heroes.'[16] However, these descriptions are included in a moral context which reverses the meaning:[17] far from specifying the natural singularity and superiority of an exceptional individual, they re-inscribe the latter within the perspective of a universalisable analysis of human behaviour. In other words, the heroic character is reinterpreted from a principle of valid explanation, from a nearby modal difference, for the human condition in general.

> When great men succumb to long, drawn-out misfortunes they reveal that they had only borne them through strength of ambition, not of soul, and that apart from great vanity heroes are made like everybody else.[18]

The grandeur of the hero thus amounts to the entirely imaginary grandeur of an empty illusion: what it preserves of reality is common with other men. Likewise, in the text cited above, the inequality of courage, wherein the contempt for death is supposed to reside, in reality amounts to the way in which certain men refrain from knowing it. Emptied of its content, heroism persists no less as a figure affected by negativity. The disproportion between great men and common people is no longer only an ironic characterisation in order to qualify two behaviours which differ only in modality:

> The indifference to death shown by great men is turned aside by love of glory, whilst common men are prevented from realising the full extent of their plight by mere lack of understanding, and that leaves them free to think of something else.[19]

2. Three operations are put to work in this deposing of the hero: decentring, devaluation and universalisation.

Let us begin with the decentring. We have seen that knowledge of the self was one of the essential conditions for heroism in Gracián. Better, the specificity of the hero consisted first with arriving at the truth of the self. Now, this is exactly the reverse of what occurs in La Rochefoucauld: all the resilience of heroism henceforth consists in an ignorance of, or a blindness to, the self. The desire for glory is nothing other than the image of an illusory claim to a mastery of the self and of others. The decentring in relation to the self, in one sense, redirects the hero to the common condition of men and, in another sense, captures the process that distinguishes it. It is henceforth self-love that furnishes the double principle of explanation to the extent that it essentially covers an illusive power [*puissance*] over the self and that it can take on different forms:

> We cannot probe the depth, nor pierce the darkness of its ['it' concerns self-love] abyss. There it covered the most penetrating eyes, it takes a thousand imperceptible turns and returns. There it is often imperceptible to itself. It conceived, it nourished and it elevated, without knowing it, a great number of affections and hatreds; it does things so monstrous that, when faced with them today, it misunderstands them or cannot resolve itself to admit to them.[20]

The devaluation of the qualities of the heart and of taste is directly correlative to the decentring of the self. In a symmetry, again striking compared with Gracián's positions concerning the great heart and excellence of taste, La Rochefoucauld places great actions of mediocre passions at the principle and removes from taste the capacity for a just evaluation of things. On the first point:

> Great and glorious events which dazzle the beholder are represented by politicians as the outcome of grand designs, whereas they are usually products of temperaments and passions. The war between Augustus and Antony, attributed to their ambition to seize the mastery of the world, was probably nothing more than a result of jealousy.[21]

On the second point:

> Amid all the different forms of taste noted above, it is very rare, indeed almost impossible, to find the sort of good taste that is really capable of evaluating each thing – that appreciates its full value, and is universally applicable ... When we ourselves are concerned, our tastes no longer have the necessary soundness;

they are disturbed by distracting influences. Everything takes on a different appearance when it relates to us.[22]

We thus understand that heroism can no longer be thought along the lines of primacy but under the form of a particular effect of the universal principle of self-love. Henceforth, hierarchies and distinctions can no longer have any other content than installing, on the basis of a common condition, in its origin (self-love) and in its ultimate test (death), in all men: 'whatever differences there may be between great men and common, thousands of times men of both kinds have been seen to meet their death with the same demeanour'.[23]

3. Desire for glory and contempt for death are two imaginary masks of the couple love of self/fear of death, which define the condition of the deposed hero and redirect him towards fallen man. There is, of course, a theology of sin underlying this antiheroic figure of man in its – second – nature, as well as the political implications. Pascal supplies us with the most significant theoretical elaboration.

One of the major aspects of theological anthropology, which deposes the hero in redirecting it towards fallen man, consists in a reinterpretation of the love of the self and the fear of death. This reinterpretation, profoundly marked by Augustinianism, involves the distinction of the two states of human nature (according to which man is considered in created Adam or in sinful Adam) defined by Pascal in his *Writings on Grace* and in the letter from 17 October 1651.[24] It follows from the two states of man that the love of self and the fear of death can be considered univocally. Indeed, when we pass from the first to the second nature of man, this love and this fear remain identical to themselves as natural and universal tendencies, but are assigned a fundamental modification in their object, their value and their meaning. In created Adam, man is animated from an infinite love for God and from a finite love for himself compared with God. The proportion of the love (infinite or finite) to its object (infinite or finite) is regulated by the just order of man's dependence on God. This order of dependence and this proportion is found again in the horror of death. This, indeed, 'was natural to Adam while he was innocent, because, being very pleasing to God, his life could not be other than pleasing to him as a man. And death was horrible when it ended a life which was in conformity with the will of God.'[25] However, by the reversal of order of dependence (between man and

God) in sinful Adam, the love that man felt becomes a pride which is related only to himself, according to a double modality by which man is made simultaneously the centre of himself and the centre of all that is not him:

> And thus he has loved himself and all things for himself, that is to say, infinitely.
> That is the origin of self-love. It was natural for Adam and appropriate in his state of innocence; but it has become criminal and immoderate as a result of his sin.[26]

The love of self thus becomes concupiscence – in its three forms[27] – related to ignorance of the truly good. Man conceived in the figure of sinful Adam will thus be concerned only to try desperately to ensure the centrality of its self (desire for glory, power [*puissance*] and riches), and to prevent thinking about death (entertainment).[28] The desire for grandeur is henceforth no longer that other face of misery.

The reinterpretation (devaluation) and extension (to humanity as a whole) of the traits which were supposed to characterise the hero allow one to understand the total effacement of the heroic figure in political theory. The political order no longer depends on the virtue or value of the prince. The government of men no longer has the governance of the self for the model and condition of its success. The political order results from the internal dynamics of universal concupiscence. What is necessary to understand is the process by which order emerges from disorder, justice from force, morality from hatred: 'From lust men have found and extracted excellent rules of policy, morality, and justice; but in reality this vile root of man, this *figmentum malum*, is only covered, it is not taken away.'[29] The mechanisms of the establishment of power [*pouvoir*] become the proper object of politics. Torn from the ethico-aesthetic dimension of the governance of the self, politics can be founded in its order (that of concupiscence) as the regulation of the behaviour of men whose generalised desire for pre-eminence is no longer only the result of a removal of the self:

> If they [Plato and Aristotle] wrote on politics, it was as if laying down rules for a lunatic asylum; and if they presented the appearance of speaking of a great matter, it was because they knew that the madmen, to whom they spoke, thought they were kings and

emperors. They entered into their principles in order to make their madness as little harmful as possible.[30]

The central questions of politics are henceforth those of the origin, the justification and the operation of power [*pouvoir*]. The origin of power [*pouvoir*] takes place in the passage from an initial takeover, which establishes a dominant party to the symbolic function which assures the reproduction of acquired power [*pouvoir*].[31] If there is a necessary passage from the strings of necessity to the strings of imagination, political power [*pouvoir*] cannot be founded exclusively on force: it supposes, on the contrary, that war ends and that power [*puissance*] is institutionalised in signs and social codes ('This habit is a force').[32] The problem of justification is completely bound up with that of institutionalisation by signs. Force can be established legitimately only if it does not appear tyrannical. Whence the problem: how to put force and justice together. But lacking the power [*pouvoir*] to rule the political on an ideal of justice[33] or on a natural law,[34] we have justified force: 'Unable to strengthen justice, they have justified might; so that the just and the strong should unite, and there should be peace, which is the sovereign good.'[35] Finally, on the question of the operation of power [*pouvoir*], the political order appears, always at a distance from its own truth, as the reign of inadequacy. We could show it on the question of the people's opinions[36] or on the gradation of points of view.[37] More essentially perhaps, the inadequacy is that the political order consists of a hidden dimension. Thus, the establishment of nobles based on the hidden truth of their natural state;[38] thus also laws and customs holding on to their authority and their appearance of justice only from the fact that the 'fact of usurpation'[39] remains hidden.

However, the demystification of the royal hero attains its climax at the very moment when the idea of a knowledge or of a governance of the prince's self seems to be brought back. Like that man who has been made king by the people's error, nobles are in effect taken to have a double thought:

> If public opinion raises you above the common run of men, let the other humble you and keep you in perfect equality with all men, for that is your natural station.[40]

The knowledge that nobles, princes or kings must have of themselves thus implies a decoupling of the self, which disenchants the grandeurs of establishment and the prestige of appearance through consciousness of men's natural equality.

## THE INDIVIDUAL AS ANTIHERO

The birth of the antiheroic conception of the individual is not, however, exclusively the result of a theological anthropology of man fallen. This conception has a much more general scope, and the dominant political theories of modern thought seem, in their very diversity, to be bound up with it. When we go back, in fact, from La Rochefoucauld and Pascal to Hobbes, who writes his principal works in the same era in which Gracián drafts his own, we also find a reinterpretation of the hero's characteristic traits by their universalisation and their subordination to tendencies common to all humanity. The theoretical scope of the switch from hero into antihero thus largely exceeds a determined current of thought. We can locate in this some of the issues in Hobbes's ethics concerning the theory of the passions, the definition of the desire for power [*puissance*] and the value conception or importance of a man.

In the first place, we know that Hobbes founds his deduction of the passional and relational life of man on two principles: the desire for self-preservation and the fear of (violent) death, which are the two faces of the very same tendency of each individual to persevere in his being.[41] A redefinition of the set of the passions results from this principled position which homogenises the economy of the system of human affects by a reinterpretation of the determinations, which, traditionally, could have the character of aristocratic virtues. We can even follow in Hobbes this work of reinterpretation, for example, in the case of courage and magnanimity. Thus, Hobbes passes from a definition of courage which makes of it 'the absence of fear in the presence of any evil whatsoever' or, in a more restrained sense, 'contempt of wounds and death',[42] to a definition which makes of it a complex passion that combines the aversion to (that is to say, fear of) an evil and the hope to overcome harm from it.[43] In the same way, magnanimity passes from the status of glory very much founded on the certain experience of the possession of a sufficient power [*puissance*][44] to that of simple disdain (without reference to its well-founded character) for assistance and minimal impediments.[45] More generally, there is in Hobbes a suppression of the traditional distinction between concupiscible passion and irascible passion, by a reduction of the second to the first. In the second place, the desire for power [*puissance*], far from being characteristic of a small number of men, is generalised to all humanity: 'In the first place, I put for a generall inclination of all mankind, a perpetuall and restlesse desire of Power after power, that ceaseth onely in Death.'[46] In the third place, the value or importance of a man loses all moral or exemplary character in order to be reduced, just as in the case of things, to his price within a generalised mutual system of exchange of services. Value is thus not 'absolute; but a thing dependent on the need and judgement of another'.[47] Within this context, the universal pretension of men to esteem themselves and to make themselves esteemed at the highest value becomes, paradoxically, the surest sign of their equality.

Thus, the search for power [*puissance*], glory, real or symbolic victory, reinterpreted on the part of the desire to persevere in being, far from characterising the pre-eminence or excellence of a particular type of man, is only the result of an interminable effort to overcome a fear of death which equalises the conditions.

We retain only two of the political consequences of the effacement of the heroic type. First, there is the absence of every distinction likely to characterise the sovereign by natural qualities or by a form of education. The question is entirely displaced from the institution (or education) of the prince to the institution of the state. The founding social contract has the function of furnishing the juridical conditions for the existence of power [*pouvoir*], and not designating the type of man who will be apt to assume it. On the other hand, in the theory of the artificial being of the state, the concepts of sovereignty and of the civilian definitively confer upon the sovereign only a function of mediation in the juridical constitution of the political order.

We can thus say that, in the anthropological doctrines of the seventeenth century, the deposing of the hero figures among the conditions by which political theory displaces itself from a consideration of the prince to a rationalisation of the mechanisms of power [*pouvoir*] and of the institution of the state.

## Notes

1. Baltasar Gracián (1601–58): for the original text of his works, we will refer to the *Obras Completas*, edited by Arturo del Hoyo (Madrid: Aguilar, 1960). The translations used will be indicated as we go along. On Gracián's life

and work, see Miguel Batllori and Ceferino Peralta, *Baltasar Gracián en su vida y en su obras* (Zaragoza: Institución 'Fernando el Católico', 1969).
2. Baltasar Gracián, *El Héroe*, in *Obras Completas*, ed. Arturo del Hoyo (Madrid: Aguilar, 1960), pp. 1–69. [TN: a partial English translation is found in Baltasar Gracián, *A Pocket Mirror for Heroes*, ed. and trans. Christopher Maurer (New York: Currency Doubleday, 1996).]
3. It is a theology of sin that takes account of this scission of being and appearing, and the correlative reign of deception in the world. Gracián's work is inscribed within the framework of the Counter-Reformation's theological thought and fully participates in the baroque aesthetics which is its expression on the plane of art. See Benito Pelegrín, *Ethique et esthétique du Baroque: L'espace jésuitique de Baltasar Gracián* (Arles: Actes Sud, 1985).
4. Baltasar Gracián, *El Criticón*, in *Obras Completas*, pp. 515–1011. [TN: to my knowledge, this book has not been translated into English since 1681.]
5. See Augustin Redondo, 'Monde à l'envers et conscience de crise dans le *Criticón* de Baltasar Gracián', in *L'image du monde renversé et ses representations littéraires et para-littéraires de la fin du XVIe siècle au milieu du XVIIe*, ed. Jean Lafond and Augustin Redondo (Paris: Vrin, 1979), pp. 83–97.
6. Henry Méchoulan, *Individu et société dans la pensée baroque espagnole*, in *Studia Leibnitiana*, Sonderheft 10 (Stuttgart: Franz Steiner Verlag, 1981).
7. See *The Hero*: 'O candidates for fame and for greatness, attend to this first stratagem for excellence. Let all know you and none sound your depths. Thanks to this stratagem, what is moderate will seem much, what is much will seem infinite, and what is infinite, much more' (Baltasar Gracián, *El Héroe*, p. 8; *The Hero*, in *A Pocket Mirror for Heroes*, p. 6).
8. Ibid., p. 9; p. 10. [TN: Maurer translates *ingenio* as 'intellect'. However, this is too specific a term in English to cover what *ingenio* indicates in Spanish. What is more, the standard translation of *ingenio* into French, *génie*, is also insufficient when translated into English as 'genius'. Zarka's choice of *esprit* for *ingenio* is adequate insofar as it can carry connotations of diplomatic finesse, but that is not implied in the standard English translation of *esprit* as 'mind'. At any rate, *ingenio* encompasses more than diplomacy. Because *ingenio* indicates resourcefulness or creative problem-solving, the standard translation into English, 'ingenuity', is what I will use when translating Gracián directly. When Zarka uses *esprit* to translate it into French, I will use 'mind', and when he uses *génie*, I will use 'wit', insofar as these seem to be the best translations into English of what Zarka intends to get across in French. However, it should not be forgotten that, in this section, 'ingenuity', 'mind' and 'wit' are frequently, if sometimes indirectly, translating the same word. I must thank María del Rosario Acosta López for her help with the translations of Gracían in general, and

especially thank her for drawing my attention to these potential confusions surrounding *ingenio*.]
9. See the introduction to Baltasar Gracián, *La pointe ou l'art du génie*, trans. Michèle Gendreau-Massaloux and Pierre Laurens (Paris: L'Age d'homme, 1983), pp. 17–33. [TN: This is a translation of Baltasar Gracián, *Agudeza y arte de ingenio*, in *Obras Completas*, pp. 229–514. To my knowledge, this book has never been translated into English.]
10. Gracián, *Agudeza y arte de ingenio*, pp. 234–5. [TN: my translation.]
11. Ibid., p. 233. [TN: my translation.]
12. Baltasar Gracián, *El Politico*, in *Obras Completas*, p. 37. [TN: my translation. To my knowledge, this book has never been translated into English.]
13. We speak here of Machiavellianism or of the political descendants of Machiavelli and not of Machiavelli himself, since, as everyone knows, the notion of state reason does not exist in the work of the author of *The Prince*.
14. Gracián, *El Politico*, p. 37. [TN: my translation.]
15. La Rochefoucauld, *Maximes*, in *Maximes suivies des Réflexions diverses, du Portrait de La Rochefoucauld par lui-même et des Remarques de Christine de Suède sue les Maximes*, ed. Jacques Truchet (Paris: Éditions Garnier Frères, 1967), pp. 114–15; La Rochefoucauld, *Maxims*, trans. Leonard Tancock (New York: Penguin Books, 1959), pp. 101–2; maxim 504.
16. Ibid., p. 18; p. 44; maxim 53.
17. In his book *Morales du Grand Siècle* (Paris: Gallimard, 1948), Paul Bénichou analysed with great force and clarity under the title, 'La demolition du héros', how the pessimistic moral theology of Augustinian and Jansenist origin that subtends the anthropology of the *Maxims* led to the destruction of the heroic ideal of the aristocracy and, more generally, of 'every form of spiritualism, even Christian, which is not accompanied by an absolute negation of human values, every form of virtue or grandeur suspected of compromising with nature and with instinct' (ibid., p. 127 [TN: my translation.]). Paul Bénichou primarily has in view the hero such as Corneille had conceived of him. Although the author's analyses seem to us to preserve all their force of conviction, we will, however, see less a demolition of the hero in La Rochefoucauld's anthropology than a reinterpretation of its most characteristic determinations, which certainly negates the proper consistency of the heroic type, but also preserves the traits under the aspect of an illusory figure from which certain men imaginarily draw their own life and conduct.
18. La Rochefoucauld, *Maximes*, p. 12; *Maxims*, p. 40; maxim 24.
19. Ibid., p. 115; p. 103; maxim 504.
20. La Rochefoucauld, *Maximes*, Première édition, in *Maximes*, p. 283; maxim 1. [TN: to my knowledge, this has never been translated into English.]

21. La Rochefoucauld, *Maximes*, p. 8; *Maxims*, pp. 37–8; maxim 7.
22. La Rochefoucauld, *Réflexions diverses*, in *Maximes*, pp. 202–3; *Réflexions diverses/Miscellaneous Reflections*, in *Collected Maxims and Other Reflections*, trans. E. H. Blackmore, A. M. Blackmore and Francine Giguère (Oxford: Oxford University Press, 2007), p. 219.
23. La Rochefoucauld, *Maximes*, p. 115; *Maxims*, p. 103; maxim 504.
24. Blaise Pascal, 'Lettre à M. et Mme. Perier à Clermont, à l'occasion de la mort de m. Pascal le père, décédé à Paris le 24 septembre 1651', in *Œuvres complètes*, ed. Louis Lafuma (Paris: Seuil, 1963), pp. 275B–9B; 'Letter from Monsieur Pascal to Monsieur and Madame Perier, at Clermont, on the occasion of the death of Monsieur Pascal, the father, who died at Paris, 24 September 1651', in *Great Shorter Works of Pascal*, trans. Emile Cailliet and John C. Blankenagel (Philadelphia, PA: Westminster Press, 1948), pp. 82–92.
25. Ibid., p. 277B; p. 88.
26. Ibid.
27. See Blaise Pascal, *Pensées*, in *Œuvres complètes*, fr. 545; *Pensées*, trans. W. F. Trotter, in *Great Books of the Western World*, ed. Mortimer J. Adler, vol. 30 (Chicago, IL: Encyclopaedia Britannica, 1990), fr. 515.
28. We find again a textual quasi-identity in Pascal (fr. 597; fr. 455) and La Rochefoucauld on this point (*Maximes*, Première édition, p. 283; maxim 1).
29. Pascal, *Pensées*, fr. 211; fr. 453.
30. Ibid., fr. 533; fr. 331.
31. Cf., ibid., fr. 828; fr. 304.
32. Ibid., fr. 89; fr. 315. [TN: translation modified.]
33. Cf., ibid., fr. 44; fr. 82.
34. Cf., ibid., fr. 60; fr. 294.
35. Ibid., fr. 81; fr. 299; cf. frr. 85 and 103; frr. 878 and 298.
36. Cf., fr. 93; fr. 328.
37. Cf., fr. 90; fr. 337.
38. See Blaise Pascal, *Trois Discours sur la Conditions des Grandes*, in *Œuvre complètes*, p. 366A–B; *Three Discourses by Pascal on the Station of Noblemen [Redaction by Nicole]*, in *Great Shorter Works of Pascal*, pp. 211–13.
39. Pascal, *Pensées*, fr. 60; fr. 294.
40. Pascal, *Trois Discours*, p. 366B; *Three Discourses*, p. 213.
41. See Yves Charles Zarka, *La décision métaphysique de Hobbes: Conditions de la politique* (Paris: Vrin, 1987), pp. 255–309.
42. Thomas Hobbes, *The Elements of Law, Natural and Politic*, ed. Ferdinand Tönnies (London: Simpin, Mardshall, 1889), p. 38; cf., Leo Strauss, *The Political Philosophy of Hobbes: Its Basis and Genesis*, trans. Elsa M. Sinclair (Chicago, IL: University of Chicago Press, 1963), pp. 30–78.
43. See Thomas Hobbes, *Leviathan*, ed. C. B. Macpherson (New York: Penguin, 1986), p. 123.

44. See Hobbes, *The Elements of Law*, p. 47.
45. See Hobbes, *Leviathan*, p. 123.
46. Ibid., p. 161.
47. Ibid., p. 152.

*Chapter 3*

# THE HOBBESIAN IDEA OF POLITICAL PHILOSOPHY

### CRISIS AND PROJECT

What are the terms of Hobbes's political philosophy? In order to understand it, we should first resituate it within the more general framework of his philosophy. The elaboration thereof is situated at the meeting point of a project and a crisis. The project was considerable and, in certain aspects, comparable to those of several of his great contemporaries. Hobbes intended, in fact, to take up a rational reconstruction of the whole of human knowledge so as to introduce order, certainty and truth into it. This rational reconstruction supposed a double approach. The first was analytic; it aimed to achieve, by the application of a resolutive method, the most universal concepts and most general terms, beyond which all human knowledge could not go back. The second was synthetic; it aimed, by the application of a compositive method, to find where to progressively produce, according to a rigorous deduction, all the knowledge which man could attain. Differently from Descartes, whose ambition was also to reach deductive knowledge of all the things that man can know, Hobbes's own special features stemmed, on the one hand, from this, that linguistic concerns again find a prominent place and, on the other hand, from the fact that he intended to reintroduce politics within the field of philosophy. The crisis was of an order other than the project, but just as considerable as it. It concerned the beginning of the English Civil War, the history of which Hobbes himself came to write later in a work titled *Behemoth*. The first lines of this work sufficiently emphasise the importance that this crisis had for philosophy:

> If in time, as in place, there were degrees of high and low, I verily believe that the highest of time would be that which passed

## The Hobbesian Idea of Political Philosophy

between the years of 1640 and 1660. For he that thence, as from the Devil's Mountain, should have looked upon the world and observed the actions of men, especially in England, might have had a prospect of all kinds of injustice, and of all kinds of folly.[1]

The civil war, which shook England's political and social structures deeply, confirmed Hobbes in the idea that it was up to philosophy to found political knowledge afresh to illuminate men on the necessity of the state and its internal structure, in view of avoiding discord, conflict and war. Civil philosophy thus came to theoretically construct a knowledge the function of which would be practical. This is that practical utility of civil philosophy that Hobbes came to emphasise in *Leviathan*, as opposed to the empty philosophy of inventors of utopias:

> Neither *Plato*, nor any other Philosopher hitherto, hath put into order, and sufficiently, or probably proved all the Theoremes of Morall doctrine, that men may learn thereby, both how to govern, and how to obey; I recover some hope, that one time or other, this writing of mine, may fall into the hands of a Soveraign, who will consider it himselfe, (for it is short, and I think clear,) without the help of any interested, or envious Interpreter; and by the exercise of entire Soveraignty, in protecting the Publique teaching of it, convert this Truth of Speculation, into the Utility of Practice.[2]

There was in this claim less naïveté than we might think on first reading it. There was, on the other hand, much faith in reason. Contrary to the caricatured image which has often been given of him, political philosophy's practical efficiency in Hobbes was based on the idea that the use and development of reason, both on the side of the holder of power [*pouvoir*] and on the side of the subjects, was the surest means of maintaining the stability of the state and civil peace, that is to say, ultimately, the being and well-being of individuals.

The two works that we have just cited, *Behemoth* and *Leviathan*,[3] thus define an antinomy: that which opposes the conflictual and miserable existence of men when the state is destroyed, on the one hand, and the peaceful and industrious existence that they lead when the application of justice is guaranteed by the sovereign power [*puissance*] of the state, on the other. The experience of the process of social decomposition that accompanies the dissolution of the state has contributed to the formulation, by our philosophy, of questions that are going to animate his thought from the inside: why are societies and states susceptible to being destroyed? For what reasons are men sometimes led to revolt, sedition and war?

However, this double interrogation would not be new if it had led Hobbes only in the search for the factual causes of the birth and fall of states. Yet such was not the case. Taken up again within the framework of the general philosophical project of English philosophy, the search for causes quite changed meaning: it could no longer be maintained at the level of an analysis of historical facts. It implied, on the contrary, that we should pass from the knowledge of factual causes to that of principle causes, that is to say, from account to deduction, from particular circumstances to universal principles, or, finally, from civil history to civil philosophy. One of the major turns that Hobbes carried out in the domain of political or civil philosophy consisted in giving to it a demonstrative status by discovering principles not in history, but in human nature. Thereby, he invented a new style of thought or, if we prefer, a new manner of posing political problems, which were henceforth of particular circumstances bound to eras, to places or to the morals of peoples. In other words, history became a source of examples from which we could eventually take lessons, but not a source of principles from which we could deduce consequences. And yet it is very much such consequences deduced from principles that must, according to Hobbes, constitute political philosophy. This new style of thought was, of course, going to reflect upon the content of the political problem itself: why are naturally free, equal and independent men led to associate themselves in order to constitute the state? What are the internal causes which weaken and eventually destroy the state? We said that the elaboration of philosophy is situated at the meeting point of a project and a crisis, but the project modifies the meaning of the crisis in order to give birth to a new ethical and political knowledge.

## *THE ELEMENTS OF LAW*: CONSTITUTION OF THE INDIVIDUAL AND FUNCTION OF THE STATE

Hobbes rewrote and re-elaborated his ethical and political doctrine on several occasions. *The Elements of Law* is the first version. Two significant facts, one external, the other internal, allow for introducing the reading of this work.

The external fact is that the work, written in English in 1640, was published ten years later in the form of two separate treatises, the first of which was titled *Human Nature* and the second *De Corpore Politico*.[4] Although the titles of the two treatises were not chosen by Hobbes himself, they designate no less the principal themes broached in the work. Thus, at the moment of transition,[5] Hobbes writes: 'That part of the treatise which is already past, hath been wholly spent in the consideration of the natural power, and the natural estate of man . . . In this part therefore shall be considered, the nature of a body politic, and the laws thereof.'[6] This simple presentation of the plan of the work involves two fundamental decisions which determine its content. On the one hand, the study of the internal constitution of the individual as well as that of the relations that are naturally established between men which will be able to be made independently of any consideration of the state. Better, what Hobbes calls the state of nature designates precisely the condition of men before the existence of political power [*pouvoir*]. On the other hand, the state or political body will no longer be able to be considered as a natural reality produced by a spontaneous tendency, but, on the contrary, as an artificial reality created by the will. This double decision will have consequences that will exceed the work of Hobbes himself: on the one hand, it opens the path to numerous treatises on human nature that will succeed each other in the seventeenth and eighteenth centuries, and, on the other, it traces the line of political theories for which the existence of the state is subordinated to the preservation of the being and the well-being of individuals. But Hobbes is not satisfied with opening paths and tracing lines. He resolutely sets himself about defining the constitution of man's cognitive and passional faculties, in order to then show how the deployment of interhuman relations irresistibly drives towards a universal conflict which puts each man's existence in peril, indeed takes account of the voluntary creation of the state.

On the plane of the affective and cognitive constitution of the individual, man is found characterised as a being of desire and of speech. Man is first of all a being of desire. The six primitive passions (appetite/aversion, love/hate, pleasure/pain) that define his individuality are only modalities or specifications of a primitive tendency: desire. What is desire? Desire is an effort (*conatus*, endeavour[7]) by which we tend to seek that which contributes to the preservation of our being. The object of desire is of course a particular exterior object likely to aid in the maintenance of our being, but it is also, and more fundamentally, our being itself. What we desire above any other thing, or again what founds the desire for exterior things, is the desire to continue to be. Desire is thus first of all a desire of the self. Starting from this fundamental desire of the self, a first differentiation operates as a function of our relations to exterior objects. Depending on whether we seek an object likely to contribute to the maintaining of our being or whether we withdraw from an object that could harm us, we are affected by appetite or aversion, respectively. The first pair of passions are acquainted with two modalities. First, when the object of appetite or aversion is present, when appetite or aversion is considered insofar as whether it produces in us an agreeable or a disagreeable effect, we speak then of pleasure or pain.

This definition of man's affective life as a function of the desire of the self allows for understanding that there can be no final end exterior to human existence itself. Consequently, happiness cannot consist in the rest and satisfaction that the possession of an ultimate object of love would procure, but on the contrary in the constant and constantly renewed pursuit of pleasure: 'Seeing all delight is appetite, and appetite presupposeth a farther end, there can be no contentment but in proceeding . . . FELICITY, therefore (by which we mean continual delight), consisteth not in having prospered, but in prospering.'[8] Thus, man, as being of desire, will be in motion ceaselessly, on the search for new satisfactions and pleasures, so that 'to forsake the course, is to die'.[9] But this dynamic constitution of affectivity does not suffice to define man. It is in fact necessary to add to him a specific element of his cognitive constitution.

Man is not only a being of desire, but also a being of speech. Speech or, more precisely, the power [*puissance*] that gives birth to it, is what fundamentally distinguishes man from animal. Indeed, if we stick to sensation and imagination, nothing allows tracing a line of clear differentiation between animal life and human life. Like the animal, man experiences sensations that result from the action of exterior objects upon sensory organs. Starting from these sensations, some images are formed that persist when the exterior object withdraws or disappears. These images themselves are bound together according to the order that was first presented between the sensations. That which makes man's specificity, and emancipates his mental capacity from that of the animal, is a quite particular power [*puissance*]: an arbitrary capacity whence language is born. 'A NAME or APPELATION therefore is the voice of a man, arbitrarily imposed, for a mark to bring to his mind some conception concerning the thing on which it is imposed.'[10] Speech thoroughly modifies man's mental and affective constitution by uprooting it from the animal condition and by making of him a being for which science, justice or law have meaning. Significantly, Hobbes will say later in *Leviathan* that, without speech, 'there had been amongst men, neither Common-Wealth, nor Society, nor Contract, nor Peace, no more than amongst Lyons, Bears, and Wolves'.[11]

However, one difficulty is obvious immediately: how can speech enter into the definition of man's individual constitution while it supposes the existence of a relation to others? Better still, how could speech explain the existence of society or of the state while it very much itself seems to be a social institution? Does Hobbes not fall under the reproach that we will later say of natural man in describing civil man? The response to these questions is found in a distinction made by Hobbes himself, between the notion of the mark and that of the sign. In other words, even beyond the creation and use of language by which men mutually signify their thoughts to each other, each individual can, by virtue of the arbitrary power [*puissance*] inherent to his nature, use in an entirely private manner some marks as memory aids: 'A MARK therefore is a sensible object which a man erecteth voluntarily to himself, to the end to remember thereby somewhat past, when the same is objected to his sense again. As men that have passed by a rock at sea, set up some mark, whereby to remember their former danger, and avoid it.'[12] Man thus possessing a private capacity to establish marks, it is only as and when the complexity of interhuman relations that this power [*puissance*] of marking will be transformed to a full and complete power [*puissance*] of speaking.

The definition of man as being of desire and as being of speech thus necessarily leads from the constitution of the individual to that of interhuman relations. Hobbes is situated here beyond every historical configuration: it is less a matter of saying what human existence was when the state did not exist or when it no longer exists, than of designing a theoretical model. Yet that which defines the relations between men in the state of nature is a double anxiety. First, each man is worried about having to constantly find new objects likely to allow him to preserve himself in being. Second, each man is equally worried about the intentions of each other. In other words, the presence of others introduces a factor of uncertainty that redoubles the anxiety of the solitary individual. Better, this uncertainty transforms anxiety into fear. Interhuman relations are therefore going to be undermined from within by distrust, rivalry and the mutual search for superiority. What Hobbes calls the state of war is nothing other than that condition wherein men, inwardly torn between the fear of death and the search for glory, inevitably founder in relations of enmity. But this is equally the state wherein the consciousness is awoken in each person of the necessity to institute a political power [*pouvoir*] which, considering them in every respect, will be able to establish the principles of a peace and of a civil concord.

The preservation of the being and well-being of individuals is thus suspended from the voluntary institution of the state or political body. This is defined by Hobbes as 'a multitude of men, united as one person by a common power, for their common peace, defence, and benefit'.[13] The state or political body is thus the union of a multitude previously impoverished and conflictual. What is the nature of this union and how is it realised? The union is the product of an accord between men's wills. It is thus artificial. The state is a comparable artificial being, says Hobbes, 'which is like a creation out of nothing by human wit'.[14] This political artifice, which has for its goal defending the life and goods of individuals, must be endowed with power [*pouvoir*] and must be likely to allow it to fulfil its function, that is to say, an absolute and indivisible sovereignty. Absolute, in the sense where it is independent of every other power [*pouvoir*] or of every other human right, and in the sense where it has a power [*puissance*] of compulsion which, in principle, neither anything nor anyone can resist. Indivisible, in the sense where sovereignty cannot be divided between different persons or different instances without being itself denied. How is this absolute sovereignty instituted? By a contract: a social pact. The terms and modalities of this pact remain largely undecided within the framework of the work that we are analysing. Hobbes simply indicates that each man 'oblige himself to some one and the same man, or to some one and the same council, by them all named and determined, to do those actions, which the said man or council shall command them to do'.[15] Hobbes will re-elaborate his conception of the social pact in his treatise *De Cive*, where it will become a pact of each member of the multitude with each other, and above all in *Leviathan* where it will receive a substantially different content according to a new theory of authorisation.

However, there remains an important question concerning precisely the passage from the state of nature to the civil state. Indeed, we still do not see well what renders this passage possible. How indeed can we pass from a logic of confrontation and war to a social pact that falls under the jurisdiction of a juridical logic. In other words, how to pass from fact to law. It is at this point that finding a way to put effort into the second significant fact, this time internal, likely introduces the study of *The Elements of Law Natural and Politic*. Yet, if it concerns an author other than Hobbes, it would be necessary to translate this title as 'Elements of *right* [droit] natural and politic' and not, as must be done, with 'Elements of *law* [loi] natural and politic'. It is a matter there of a significant internal fact, because Hobbes forces English vocabulary in order to make the notion of *law*[16] match term by term with the Latin term *lex* (law [loi]) and the notion of *right*[17] with the Latin term *jus* (right [droit]), while the meaning of the pair of English words is not entirely superimposable to the pair of Latin words. This terminological question refers, in fact, to an extremely important doctrinal point, which precisely engages the passage from questions of fact to questions of right. Natural right is indeed defined by Hobbes as the 'blameless liberty of using our own natural power and ability'[18] in view of preserving our life. This right is thus rational as long as it has for an end the preservation of our being. However, this same right becomes contradictory within the state of nature because, conferring upon each a right over all things, it justifies the pursuit of the state of war. In order to avoid this contradiction, human reason is led to form the idea of a natural law which has a content wholly different from natural right. Natural law consists indeed in an obligation or an interdiction by which our reason enjoins us to do or not to do something. The precepts of natural law are 'those which declare unto us the ways of peace'.[19] In other words, the key to the passage from the state of nature to the civil state consists not only in the deployment of interhuman passional life, but also the deployment of the capacity to rationally determine that which best suits the preservation of our being.

## *DE CIVE:* RESPONSES TO THREE OBJECTIONS

Despite the sometimes important changes, the content of *De Cive* remains on the whole quite in concord with that of *The Elements of Law*. Let us note that the most massive changes concern, on the one hand, the absence in *De Cive* of the long development of human nature and, conversely, the addition in the same work of a final part concerning religion which does not figure in *The Elements of Law*. It is thus not truly necessary here to take up again the points that we have just examined. On the other hand, what we will retain from *De Cive* is related to the fact that this treatise was the first political work Hobbes published (1642). As the first edition gave rise to some objections, our philosopher felt the need to respond to them in the second edition (1647). The responses to the (anonymous) objections are recorded in some particularly important remarks. It is thus by examining three of them that we will discuss this work.

The content of the first remark[20] consists in a response from Hobbes to an objection focusing on his critique of the Aristotelian definition of man as 'a political animal'. For Hobbes, indeed, the critique of this definition, that is to say, the negation of the presence in man of a natural predisposition to society, is crucial because it controls at once his conception of the state of nature and his conception of the state. However, the objector immediately sees the difficulty: is denying that there is a native predisposition in man to society not to place a stumbling block on the threshold of the civil doctrine? For, indeed, if the natural tendency to society does not exist, is this not to say that solitude suits man by nature, or as man? But, in this case, do we not annul the project of a civil philosophy in its very principle? For the idea of a politics to be meaningful, the objection of solitude must be surmounted. It is in order to resolve this difficulty that Hobbes carries out in his remark a crucial distinction between the desire for society, in the very large sense of a desire for company, that is to say, for assembly or meeting, and the capacity to live in society in the strict sense of political society. It is thus a matter of distinguishing the predisposition to relation with others, that we must suppose even within the state of nature, from the constitutive relation of political society. The basis for the first must take account of the meeting and gathering of men, and the basis for the second of civil union. Now these two bases are different, since, if men are led to gather themselves, it is because their perpetual solitude is tiresome. We can easily verify it both in the case of children who need others in order to help them to live, and in the case of adults who need them in order to live well. Nature thus constrains men to gather together in order to maintain themselves in being or well-being. However, this predisposition to relation cannot be in any way considered like a predisposition to political society. The example of children is again particularly enlightening, since all of them needing others in order to live, they nonetheless ignore all the force of the pacts that constitute civil society. Whence the claim it is not nature, but education – by which knowledge of the evils of the state of nature must be understood – which renders man suitable for society. This distinction allows Hobbes to establish the existence of a natural predisposition to political society, which is voluntarily founded by the social pact.

The second remark concerns Hobbes's claim that, whatever a man may do in the state of nature, he does not commit injustice with regard to others.[21] In order to re-establish against his objector the meaning of this claim, Hobbes again takes up the principle of each one's natural right to preserve himself. Each one being the sole judge of the most proper means to assure his preservation, there is nothing in what a man does that we can humanly (if not divinely) call unjust. But the objection also has another significance, doubtless more profound, clearly explained by the question: '*Si filius patrem interfecerit, utrum patri injuriam non fecerit.*'[22] Beyond the specific response that furnishes the remark, the real stakes of the objection in fact concern man's malice. Is Hobbes's man, as Rousseau will later call him, a 'strange animal . . . that would believe its own good depended upon the destruction of its entire species!'[23] In short, is man naturally malicious? The response to this question must be absolutely unequivocal: no. There is, according to Hobbes, neither hatred for humanity nor rampant desire for power [*puissance*] which results from the internal constitution of man. If the desire for power [*puissance*] and for domination becomes predominant in the state of nature, and if the violence that follows transforms men into each other's enemies, this is not in any way due to the nature of the individual. In other words, enmity is not the result of a spontaneous tendency of human nature. Each man by nature simply desires to persevere in his being. That which renders men aggressive and violent is very much rather the passional dynamics that are established in the context of the state of nature. When political power [*pouvoir*] does not exist, the anxiety that inhabits each individual is inevitably transformed into fear of others, by reason of the general uncertainty that reigns over other men's intentions. This is, why when the state will be instituted, a pacific dynamic of interhuman relations will be able to be established.

The third remark is directly political.[24] It consists indeed of responses to two objections presented against the idea that the power [*pouvoir*] of the state must be absolute. The first objection concerns the consequences of such a power [*pouvoir*] on the conditions of the existence of the men who are subjected to it. Indeed, is conferring an absolute power [*pouvoir*] to kings not to totally unbind them from the hands giving them the liberty and means of submitting their subjects to a very miserable condition? Who will impede them from accomplishing all manner of extortions and violences? But therefore where is this advantage, so strongly emphasised by Hobbes, of the passage from the state of nature to the civil state. Have we truly gained something in substituting the arbitrariness and violence of one whom we cannot resist for the violence of several against whom it would be possible and legitimate to defend ourselves? To the conception of absolute power [*pouvoir*], the anonymous objector thus opposes the existence in some peoples of a solemn procedure by which princes take an oath not to violate the law.

The objection is strong. The response is argued thus: it consists of three arguments. (1) Hobbes first totally assumes his conception of absolute power [*pouvoir*]. Yes, the state must hold an absolute power [*pouvoir*] because, without it, it will not have at its disposal the necessary means for attaining its goal, knowing how to assure the defence and protection of the subjects. Yes, it is true that this conception of political power [*pouvoir*] implies that that which holds it is not itself submitted to the civil laws that it decrees. It thus cannot, whatever it does, commit injustice with regard to the subjects, but only with regard to God. (2) However, why must we fear that kings use this power [*pouvoir*] badly? Why would they form the design to ruin their subjects? In doing so, would they not again bring their own power [*pouvoir*] into question? Hobbes's response to the objection is this: the power [*pouvoir*] of kings is equivalent to what their subjects give them. Consequently, to harm his subjects is, for a king, to be himself harmed. (3) It remains that this response is insufficient, because it supposes that kings always act rationally and that they always see clearly that their power [*pouvoir*] resides in the prosperity of their subjects. Hobbes knows this and emphasises it himself: '*Quin princeps aliquando inique faciendi animum habere possit, negandum non est.*'[25] But the existence of an oath or a limitation on kings' power [*pouvoir*] will change nothing in the risk of an always possible bad use of the power [*pouvoir*] which remains theirs. Indeed, not only does the oath not have in itself proper juridical value, it would be necessary, whatever limitation that we imagine, to leave to the prince enough power [*puissance*] in order to hold the whole of a people under his protection. Yet this power [*pouvoir*] to protect will always be sufficient, when the prince makes bad use of it by diverting it from its legitimate end in order to become an instrument of the people's oppression. The objection is thus largely shaken off, but not completely destroyed. It is true that life in society will always consist of some risks or some inconveniences, but there is nothing there that can be comparable with the state of misery and the permanent risk of death that would prevail in the state of war of all against all. If men would like to avoid these inconveniences, it should have been that they were sufficiently virtuous in order to govern themselves according to the moral laws that their reason dictates to them. As this is not the case, each one must be held as at least partially responsible for the bitterness that civil life can sometimes cause.

The second objection is more historical. It consists in maintaining that there has never existed such an absolute power [*pouvoir*] in Christianity. Hobbes's response is here without nuance: this claim is false. All political power [*pouvoir*], as long as it is sovereign, is, has been, will be absolute, even if this is not explicitly recognised. Without absolute power [*pouvoir*], there is no sovereignty and, consequently, there is no state. This principle is in addition valuable whatever may be the political regime that we consider. Power [*pouvoir*] in a democracy is exactly the same as in an aristocracy or in a monarchy. But beyond this principle, it is necessary to recognise that the state fully assumes its goal only when the sovereign uses prudence, that is to say, when he acts on the basis of knowledge of the rules that govern the political artifice.

## *LEVIATHAN*: AUTHORISATION, DECISION AND INTERPRETATION

In *Leviathan*, Hobbes again takes up and develops several themes that we have already examined. But the whole of the doctrine is rethought, refounded and re-elaborated in view of surmounting some of the difficulties, even contradictions, that figured in the works that we have already considered. We will thus return to the three major points of this monumental writing, because they modify, specify or complete the content of the earlier work.

The first point concerns the theory of the social contract. If *Leviathan* reiterates, and with such force, the idea according to which the state is founded by a voluntary act by means of which every man commits himself to every other to confer to a third (the future sovereign) the right of governing him, the formulation of the pact and its contents are profoundly modified. Here is the new formulation of the social pact: a 'Convenant of every man with every man, in such manner, as if every man should say to every man, *I authorise and give up my Right of Governing my selfe, to this Man, or to this Assembly of men, on this condition, that thou give up thy Right to him, and Authorise all his Actions in like manner.*'[26] One of the central notions of this text, in any case that which will mobilise our attention, is the notion of authorisation. The social pact is indeed a contract of authorisation. What must be understood by that? In order to respond to this question, it is important to specify the type of relation that authorisation establishes between the subjects and the sovereign, along with the status of the sovereign will (that of the state or the republic). Concerning first the relation between the subjects and the sovereign, authorisation allows for resolving a considerable difficulty in *The Elements of Law* and *De Cive*, which consisted in this, that men, in becoming subjects of the state, appeared as passive beings, deprived of all right, submitted to the omnipotence of political power [*pouvoir*]. Henceforth, with the notion of authorisation a whole other type of relation is established, by which the subjects are the authors of a political will the actor of which is the sovereign. In other words, the relation of authorisation implies that the sovereign acts in the subjects' name and the subjects act by the sovereign. The subjects thus can no longer be considered as submitted to a simply passive obedience, not as deprived of all right. Then, concerning the sovereign will, the contract of authorisation allows for conceiving this not as foreign to the wills of the subjects, but on the contrary as their expression. Thereby, Hobbes brings a solution to a central political problem that he had moreover invented himself, that of the formation of a political being the will of which may also be that of all private individuals.[27]

The second point concerns the theory of law, more particularly that of civil law or positive law. A formula for the Latin version of *Leviathan* provides a striking shortcut to grasping the meaning of the law: '*Authoritas, non veritas, facit legem* [It is authority, not the truth, which makes the law].'[28] The law is the expression of the will of the one who has the right to command.[29] As such, it has as criterion for validity neither the reason of private individuals nor that of jurists. Hobbes thus makes the sovereign the unique legislator and, consequently, the sole source of political legality. It is a tradition deeply rooted in English juridical thought which thus finds itself theoretically challenged, that which consisted in making of custom or of common right (*Common Law*)[30] the principal source of a jurisprudence that governs society. But in making the law the product of authority and not of truth, do we not risk making it something irrational? Must we interpret the principle as the expression of a political decisionism opposed to a juridical rationalism? Not at all, Hobbes himself clearly says: 'and therefore it is not that *Juris prudentia*, or wisdom of subordinate judges; but the Reason of this our Artificiall Man the Common-wealth, and his Command, that maketh Law'.[31] Moreover, the notification, that is to say, making it be brought to the subjects' knowledge, is the condition *sine qua non* of the law's obligatoriness. No one indeed can be obliged to what he does not know or to what he does not understand. In other words, far from opening the path to an obscure and dangerous conception of the irrational transcendence of the will of the state, the theory of the law is on the contrary one of the privileged places where it is possible to sense why, in Hobbes, state reason could ultimately be of another nature than that of private individuals.

Finally, the third point concerns a question that occupies a good half of *Leviathan*. It concerns the interpretation of Holy Scripture. Why is so considerable a place accorded to the study of Biblical exegesis in an ethical and a political work? For two reasons: on the one hand, because the Bible includes revealed divine law and because it is necessary to knowing if in obeying the sovereign we act in accordance with divine laws or not. On the other hand, because the Biblical account has been the object of multiple interpretations very divergent from each other, which have raised up the constitution of opposing sects and furnished the pretext for wars of religion in the course of which civil peace was destroyed. We thus understand that the political doctrine of *Leviathan* must include a reflection on the political consequences of religion. But we also understand that Hobbes's intention was in no way to define the truth in matters of faith, but only to submit ecclesiastical power [*pouvoir*] to political power [*pouvoir*].

### Notes

1. Thomas Hobbes, *Behemoth, or the Long Parliament*, ed. Ferdinand Tönnies (Chicago, IL: University of Chicago Press, 1990), p. 1.

2. Hobbes, *Leviathan*, pp. 407–8.
3. 'Behemoth' and 'Leviathan' are two names of animals, the one terrestrial, the other marine, that Hobbes borrows from the Biblical book of Job. The first symbolises in his work civil war's irrational violence, while the second signifies the state's eminent and incomparable power [*puissance*].
4. This Latin title was paradoxically given to a treatise written in English.
5. This moment of transition does not correspond to the place where the publishers from 1650 had divided the original work in order to turn it into two treatises.
6. Hobbes, *The Elements of Law*, pp. 107–8.
7. [TN: in English in the original.]
8. Hobbes, *The Elements of Law*, p. 30.
9. Ibid., p. 48.
10. Ibid., p. 18.
11. Hobbes, *Leviathan*, p. 100.
12. Hobbes, *The Elements of Law*, p. 18.
13. Ibid., p. 104.
14. Ibid., p. 108.
15. Ibid., p. 103.
16. [TN: in English in the original.]
17. [TN: in English in the original.]
18. Hobbes, *The Elements of Law*, p. 71.
19. Ibid., p. 75.
20. Thomas Hobbes, *De Cive: The English Version*, ed. Howard Warrender (Oxford: Clarendon Press, 2002), pp. 42–5.
21. Thomas Hobbes, *De Cive*, in *Opera Philosophica*, ed. William Molesworth, vol. 2 (London: John Bohn, 1839), pp. 164–5.
22. Hobbes, *De Cive*, p. 165. [TN: *'If a Sonne kill his Father, doth he him no injury?'* (Hobbes, *De Cive: The English Version*, p. 48).]
23. Jean-Jacques Rousseau, 'The State of War', in *The Collected Writings of Rousseau*, vol. 2, trans. Christopher Kelly and Judith Bush, ed. Christopher Kelly (Hanover, NH: Dartmouth University Press, 2005), p. 62; 'Que l'état de guerre naît de l'état social', in *Œuvres complètes de Jean-Jacques Rousseau*, vol. 3, ed. Bernard Gagnebin and Marcel Raymond (Paris: Éditions Gallimard, 1964), p. 611.
24. Hobbes, *De Cive*, pp. 224–5; *De Cive: The English Version*, pp. 98–9.
25. Hobbes, *De Cive*, pp. 224–5. [TN: *'But it cannot be deny'd but a Prince may sometimes have an inclination to doe wickedly'* (Hobbes, *De Cive: The English Version*, p. 99).]
26. Hobbes, *Leviathan*, p. 227.
27. On the whole of these points, see Chapter 9, 'On the State'.
28. Thomas Hobbes, *Leviathan*, in *Opera Philosophica*, ed. William Molesworth,

vol. 3 (1841), p. 202. The same idea is taken up again in an extremely important work of Hobbes on the law, that being *A Dialogue between a Philosopher and a Student of the Common Laws of England*, ed. Joseph Cropsey (Chicago, IL: University of Chicago Press, 1971), p. 55.
29. See Chapter 7, 'On Law'.
30. [TN: in English in the original.]
31. Hobbes, *Leviathan*, ed. Macpherson, p. 317. See Chapter 7, 'On Law.

*Part II*

# LANGUAGE AND POWER [*POUVOIR*]

The new comprehension of the ethico-political sphere, the developmental phases of which we are going to consider, grants an absolutely central place to the question of the relation between language and power [*pouvoir*]. Certainly, since Plato and Aristotle, political philosophy has linked the problem of man as speaking being and that of the city. However, what characterises Hobbes's thought is, on the one hand, the re-elaboration of the theory of language that he undertakes and, on the other hand, the considerable place that the notion of the sign (linguistic or otherwise) plays in the constitution of his doctrine of individual power [*puissance*] and of political power [*pouvoir*]. The two chapters that follow relate to studying different aspects of the Hobbesian theory of language and showing that the ethico-political doctrine of power and power [*puissance et pouvoir*] does not fall under the jurisdiction of a physics, but of a semiology.

*Chapter 4*

# THEORY OF LANGUAGE

FROM THE PROBLEM TO THE THEORY OF LANGUAGE

If there is a problem which is found on all levels of Hobbes's work, it is very much that of language. Whether it is a matter of logic, physics, ethics, politics or theology, and whatever the irreducibility of these different domains may be, they are joined by the place and major function that they give to language.

As concerns logic, it suffices to recall that its proper field is deployed in a theory of names, proposition, syllogism and method in order to show its essential relation to the linguistic function right away: logical space is a logico-linguistic space. I say logico-linguistic and not grammatico-linguistic. On several occasions, Hobbes distinguishes logical considerations from grammatical considerations. And so, in *De Corpore*, when it is a matter of distinguishing simple names from compound names, Hobbes takes care to note that in philosophy, unlike what happens in grammar, a name does not necessarily consist in a single word, but in all the words which, by their meeting, form the name of a single thing. It is not the morphological unity, but the unity of designation that makes the unity of the name. Even though, for grammarians, the expression *body animated, sentient*[1] is composed of three words, it constitutes only one for philosophers. The same idea is taken up again in *Leviathan*:

> But here wee must take notice, that by a Name is not always understood, as in Grammar, one onely Word; but sometimes by circumlocution many words together. For all these words, *Hee that in his actions observeth the Lawes of his Country*, make but one Name, equivalent to this one word, *Just*.[2]

In logic, the unity of the name is a function of the unity or identity of the reference. The distinction between simple names and compound names thus cannot have the same meaning in logic as in grammar: the simple name is not distinguished from the compound by the preposition, but characterises that which is the most common or universal in its genre, whereas the compound name is that which becomes least universal by adding other names. It is thus necessary to dissociate logic from the language that considers the semantic and syntactic dimensions of the use of denominations in the formation of propositions and of syllogisms, from the grammar that is proper to each language and comes under historical contingency. The difference between logic and grammar occurs, in Hobbes, even within the linguistic function and not between an art of thinking that we attain in reflecting on the alinguistic operations (at least in right) of the mind and an art of thinking. As it is not possible in philosophy to construct a language where, as in mathematics, the denominations and the expressions would be at once submitted to the exigencies of logic and would not leave room for ambiguities and the equivocations inherent to the current use of historical languages,[3] the function of logic in philosophy will be to furnish us with the principles of a correct use of the usual denominations of languages in view of redirecting the equivocations and permitting reason. Now, one of the principal sources of the equivocations that have affected philosophical discourse is situated in the flexion of grammar and logic: it concerns the verb 'to be'. The logical analysis of the syntax of the discourse will thus have to give us the means for redirecting the illusions produced by the formation of grammatically congruent, but logically incorrect, expressions. Logic is, in Hobbes, indissociably a science of reason and a science of language.

From there, we can understand the considerable place that language occupies in the knowledge of nature. The principles of knowledge in fact make the object of nominal definitions starting from which the science of nature is deployed as a discourse upon the world. This preponderance of language is correlative to the reduction of experience to a simple discriminatory function which permits, to it alone, neither founding nor absolutely guaranteeing the truth of the theories, but simply to vouch for its explanatory value. We already see how the status of the knowledge of nature differs in Hobbes from the status it had in Bacon. While for Bacon it was necessary to forsake words in order to return to things, for Hobbes there can be knowledge of things only by the mediation of words.

However, Hobbes does not envision language only as an instrument of knowledge; he brings its other uses into play. Thus, the beginning of chapter 3 of *De Corpore* distinguishes, on the one hand, the kinds of discourse the common trait of which is articulating something, like interrogations, pleas, promises, threats, wishes, orders and complaints and, on the other hand, the only kind of discourse that is not satisfied with articulating something, but that affirms and negates, namely, the proposition. This last is the only one sensitive to truth and falsity, the only properly philosophical one. However, the first kinds of discourse, far from being neglected, occupy a leading place in ethics. Language is indeed recaptured in an anthropology of passional interhuman life:

> The passions of man, as they are the beginning of all his voluntary motions, so are they the beginning of speech, which is the motion of his tongue. And men desiring to shew others the knowledge, opinions, conceptions, and passions which are within themselves, and to that end having invented language, have by that means transferred all that discursion of their mind . . . by the motion of their tongues, into discourse of words.[4]

If the passions are at the origin of the tongue's movement which produces the voice, it becomes linguistic sign only to the extent that the relation to its signified is subjected to an arbitrary institution: passion makes the voice, the arbitrariness of the institution makes speech. Speech, once constituted, reflects upon the dynamics of the passional life of man and definitively uproots it from the animal condition. Hobbes's ethics confers to man the status of a being of speech.[5] It is a true pragmatic linguistics that is put to work, and that conditions the political theory of the social pact throughout.

Finally, all Hobbes's theology involves a reflection on language, both natural theology, where it is a question of God's natural speech, and revealed theology, where it is a question of the prophetic speech that is accessible to us, in a time when there is no longer prophet, only within the text of the Holy Scriptures. The problem of language is this time that of the text and of its interpretation.

Still, this observation of the leading place that language occupies at every level of the work cannot guarantee, to it alone, that Hobbes possesses a unified and coherent theory of language. Better, the multiplicity of these fields of investment constitute less a response than a problem: that of the existence of a theory of language. It is precisely this theory of language that we will attempt to draw out by the analysis of the semantic, syntactic and pragmatic aspects constitutively linked to the linguistic function. These three aspects appear in a text from *De Corpore*, which concentrates on some very dense lines of the Hobbesian theory of language. The explication of this text will act as a central theme to the whole of this chapter:

> Quoniam autem Nomina, ut definitum est, disposita in oratione, signa sunt conceptuum; manifestum est ea non esse signa ipsarum rerum; quo sensu enim intelligi potest sonum hujus vocis *lapis* esse signum *lapidis*, alio quam ut is qui vocem eam audisset colligeret loquentem de lapide cogitasse?
>
> But seeing names ordered in speech (as is defined) are signs of our conceptions, it is manifest they are not signs of the things themselves; for that the sound of this word *stone* should be the sign of a stone, cannot be understood in any sense but this, that he that hears it collects that he that pronounces it thinks of a stone.[6]

## SIGNIFICATION AND REFERENCE

I will first of all retain the semantic approach to language. This approach is explicitly contained in our text: 'seeing names . . . (as is defined) are signs of our conceptions, it is manifest they are not signs of the things themselves'. The statement is unequivocal – the names that form the discourse imply a double relation: on the one hand, to the thought that they signify and, on the other hand, to the thing or things that they name, denote or designate. This distinction between signification and reference is a major element of Hobbes's semantics.[7] It indicates indeed that this semantics involves a structure at three levels: word, thought and thing. The word (*vox*), as sign (*signum*), signifies thought and, by the mediation of this signification, acquires the status of name (*nomen*) by which it designates things. Certainly, there are some passages where Hobbes uses *significare* where we would expect rather *nominare* or *denotare*,[8] but when he thematises the questions of signification and of denomination, it is in order to relate the first to thought and the second to the thing. Let us begin with signification:

Speech or language is the connexion of names constituted by the will of men to stand for the series of conceptions of the things about which we think. Therefore, as a name is to an idea or conception of a thing, so is speech to the discourse of the mind.[9]

The voice is the material and thus necessary condition for language, but it is not the sufficient condition. In order that use of the voice becomes a language, two supplementary conditions are necessary. (1) That this use not be natural: the voice acquires the status of linguistic sign only in losing the character of natural sign of the passions in order to become arbitrary sign of thought. There is language only in accordance with a will to give to someone something *to understand*. The arbitrariness of signification allows, in addition, taking account of three linguistic phenomena: the historical character of languages (certain words disappear and some new are created); the diversity of languages (if language was thought's natural sign, all peoples would speak the same language); the individual possibility of making use of new words in order to signify inventions or discoveries (as mathematicians and philosophers do). (2) The second condition of language is that the voice does not run empty, as when we repeat a text that we have learned by heart without understanding its meaning. In this last case, there is always a verbal complex but there is not language, because the latter requires an intention, at least partially fulfilled, of signification.

The arbitrary relation between the linguistic sign and its signified explains that the intention of signification could be more or less adequately fulfilled. It is inadequately fulfilled when verbal discourse is equivocal or ambiguous, that is to say, when the words arouse in the mind thoughts other than those for which they have been planned.[10] On the other hand, it is adequately fulfilled when the concomitance of the conception and of the word that signifies this conception ('that signify such conception')[11] confers evidence to the discourse. This evidence is indeed 'meaning with our words'.[12] The evidence of the discourse, that is to say, the adequate fulfilment of the intention of signification, thus appears at the same time as the norm and as a particular case of the use of language. The norm, because the evidence supposes that the terms employed are subject to nominal definitions which fix signification to them; a particular case, because the procedure of definitions is possible only in science. In the ordinary practice of language, not only is the meaning of words not established by the speaker, but, in addition, the signification of any one depends as much on the goal, the occurrence, and the context of the discourse as on the words used.[13] In other words, that ambivalence and misunderstanding can never be totally removed from the everyday exercise of language.

In the same way that the word signifies the idea, verbal discourse signifies mental discourse. But it would be absolutely false to conclude from this the simply instrumental character of language. Indeed, mental discourse, preliminary to verbal discourse, does not have properly linguistic structure: it is constituted of conceptions or representations bound by principles of association (contiguity and resemblance), and not names, propositions or mental syllogisms. Verbal discourse is thus not the simple replica of mental discourse: the use of words inaugurates new approaches of the mind, which are at the foundation of science.

In order to pass from the problem of signification to that of reference, facing the relation of *signum* to *nomen* should be considered. Now, if all names are signs, the inverse is not true; all linguistic signs are not names. Language is not constituted of names juxtaposed one to another. We will return to this more precisely in the examination of the syntax of discourse, but we can already note that the signs of quantity like *omne, quodlibet, aliquod*, which mark universality or particularity, are not names but parts of names.[14] Their function in verbal discourse is not to denominate, but to determine the denotation or the reference of the name to which they are joined, that is to say, to indicate the extent according to which the name is taken. Considered from the point of view of reference, the theory of language becomes a general theory of denomination. Let us note, first of all, that denomination is just as arbitrary as signification. Between names and the things that they designate, there is no resemblance that could give foundation to the idea that the nature of things would have suggested their names. In order to support this arbitrariness of denomination, Hobbes refers to the mythical figure of a first or of first teachers of names: God or men. This conception of an originary imposition of names is sometimes compensated for by the more historical argument of a fixing of usual denominations. But whatever the origin of names would be, designation is always arbitrary; it is supported by a voluntary act. The artifice of designation certifies the entire exteriority of the order of names compared with the order of things.

## Theory of Language

What can be the object of denomination? What is the extent of language's field of reference? This question is addressed in *De Corpore*,[15] where Hobbes puts to work an approach that consists in progressively expanding the field of reference. Indeed, if Hobbes departs from the statement that it is not necessary that every name be the name of some thing, it is in no way in order to put back into question the idea of a referential view of the name, but, on the contrary, in order to extend it beyond the domain of existing things. The field of reference is extended in a first moment, beyond things that exist, to the images or the phantasms of these things, which could be designated by names. Then, beyond existing things and their representations, there are some names like *future* which refer to a thing that not only still does not exist, but of which we do not know if it will exist. If language can refer to future things, all the more so may it refer to past things (although Hobbes does not say so explicitly), that is to say, of things of which we know that they have existed but that no longer exist now. Better, words like *impossible* and *nothing* are also names, although they could not designate a real or even possible thing. Language's field of reference is thus expanded, beyond the designation of present, past or future and even possible objects, to a something that can be simply fictive. It is without doubt in this sense that it is necessary to understand the statement that completes paragraph six of chapter 2, according to which every name has a relation to a named something (*ad aliquod nominatum*), though this named thing may not always be a thing that exists in nature. The referential view is constitutive of the function of the name, but the thing thus designated can as well be truly existing as simply fictive.

The field of reference, thus opened, is structured. A theory of classes of names corresponds to this structure. Hobbes distinguishes four classes of names: denominations of bodies, denominations of accidents, denominations of phantasms and metalinguistic denominations of denominations. Denominations of bodies are concrete names (substantives or adjectives: *body, mobile, figured*, etc.), which refer to a thing insomuch as we think that it exists. Denominations of accidents are abstract names (*corporeity, mobility*), which designate not the thing itself but its properties. The distinction between names of bodies and names of properties does not exhaust the field of reference of language, the denominations of phantasms (*vision, colour*) refer in fact to the conception that we have of a thing and, lastly, the metalinguistic denominations (*universal, particular*) permit language to refer to itself and to thematise its own approach.[16] This theory of the classes of names is of a capital importance when we pass to the proposition. Indeed, the proposition consists in the linkage of two names (subject and predicate) by which we conceive that the second name designates the same thing as what the first designates. The linkage of subject and predicate thus relates the two terms to an identical thing.[17] The general condition for the validity of a proposition supposes, consequently, that the subject and the predicate can have a common field of reference: it is necessary that the predicate designates all this that designates the subject, as in *a man is an animal*. We thus understand that in every true proposition the related denominations must appear in the same class: they must be two names of bodies, two names of accidents, two names of phantasms or two names of names. The principal errors that hinder human knowledge result from the links of denominations of different classes, which lead to false propositions. The principal interest of chapter 5 of *De Corpore*, where the seven cases of fallacious links of denominations are examined, comes from showing that these links are at the origin of commonly accepted propositions in metaphysics or, more generally, in philosophy. Hobbes here furnishes the principle that subtends his critique of Aristotelian metaphysics and of Cartesian metaphysics. This critique consists in a linguistic analysis of signification and of the reference of denominations, of the validity of propositional links and of the necessity of demonstrations. On this point, Hobbes's conclusion is clear: metaphysics as discourse on being or on the essence of things rests upon an abuse of language.

The theory of denominations is followed by a presentation of the distinctions of denominations which is not simply intended to establish a classification, but, more profoundly, to describe the constitution of terms and to take account of new operations that their use permits. The examination of the distinctions envisages denominations from the point of view of their extent. This first distinction is that of positive names and negative names. The first designate the resemblance, equality or identity of the things that we will consider, while the second designate diversity, dissimilarity or inequality. Proper names (*Socrates*) and common names (*man, philosopher*) are part of positive names. Negative names are constructed by adding the negative particle to the positive name (*non-man, non-philosopher*); they cover everything understood of the things to which the positive name is not suitable. The important thing is to notice that negation supposes language. Indeed, there are not more negative ideas than negative things. If we can represent to ourselves the difference that there is between white and black, in contrast we cannot have any specific idea of non-white which covers not only black, but also other colours distinct from white. The condition for negation, language is also that for contradiction: the latter in fact has place neither in things nor in ideas. Only two names, of which the one is positive and the other is negative, can be claimed contradictory. The second distinction is established between names that designate only a single thing and those that designate several of them. According to Hobbes, the first include proper names (*Homer*), definite descriptions (*whoever wrote the* Iliad) and demonstratives (*this one, that one*), the second are common names. There again, only names can be common or universal: they maintain this capacity for what they designate a plurality of individual things, but in no wise a class distinct from the individuals that it collects. Language is thus also the condition for a universality that exists neither in things nor in mental representations. The third distinction concerns the names of primary and the names of secondary intention. The first designates things (*man, stone*), while the second designates other names (*universal, particular, genus, species,* etc.). If language speaks of things, it also opens the possibility of a self-reference by which it can describe its own operations. The other distinctions between absolute and relative, concrete and abstract, simple and composite names suppose this difference between a language of object and a metalanguage which prevents transposing among things that which takes place among the names by which we designate them.

## LOGIC OF SYNTAX

We can from this point forward pass to the syntactic aspect of the theory of language. This aspect has already been suggested by the examination of the status of signs of quantity. In other words, semantics cannot be totally isolated from syntactic analysis. If we return to our original text, we can indeed remark that the indication of syntax intervenes in semantics: 'But seeing names *ordered in speech* (as is defined) are signs of our conceptions, it is manifest they are not signs of the things themselves' (our emphasis). Likewise, in *De Homine*: 'Speech or language is *the connexion of names* constituted by the will of men to stand for the series of conceptions of the things about which we think.'[18] There is language only when there is positioning or a series of denominations.

The distinction between the semantic and syntactic aspects of language is thus only an abstraction necessitated by analysis. On the other hand, these aspects are indissociably bound in the effective exercise of language.

This appears confirmed by the fact that it is by the syntactic structure of language that allows taking account of the passage from the mark (*nota*) to the sign (*signum*), which is presupposed by the semantic relation of the *signum* to the *nomen*. The first function of words is to act as sensible marks in order to recall thought and to facilitate memory. As sensible marks, words can be the object of an individual use. The verbal mark is thus a memory aid, among other possible ones. It allows each to recollect thoughts more easily than he had. On the other hand, words become signs only in a discursive chain. For there to be sign, it is thus necessary that there was a syntagmatic articulation of words.

On the plane of the syntactic organisation of language, it is important to distinguish two categories of terms: categorems and syncategorems. Even though Hobbes does not explicitly make use of this distinction, it subtends his analysis of the linking of words in utterances. Let us recall that categorems are terms that have by themselves a signification, while syncategorems acquire a meaning or a function only by their link to categorems. Signs of quantity, already reported, the negative particle which makes a negative name etc., are examples of syncategorem. All the parts of discourse thus do not have the same status. However, if the syncategorematic status of the terms that we have just indicated does not appear to be a problem, the same cannot be said for this major syncategorem, that is, the verb *to be*. The examination of the status of the verb *to be* occupies a preponderant place in the theory of language and, more particularly, of the proposition. All Hobbes's effort aims to show that this verb has only a function of a sign of connection (*signum connexionis*) which serves to join the subject-denomination to the predicate-denomination. The verb *to be* is thus reduced to its function of copula. He points out:

> the Consequence, or Repugnance of one name to another; as when one saith, *A Man is a Body*, hee intendeth that the name of *Body* is necessarily consequent to the name of *Man*; as being but severall names of the same thing, *Man*; which Consequence is signified by coupling them together with the word *Is*.[19]

The verb *to be*, in linking the two denominations of a proposition, relates them to one and the same thing. Error would be, evidently, to take this verb for a denomination, that is to say, to deny the difference of status of the parts of discourse:

> as when we say, *a Man, is, a living Body*, wee mean not that the *Man* is one thing, the *Living Body* another, and the *Is*, or *Beeing* a third: but that *Man*, and the *Living Body*, is the same thing: because the Consequence, *If hee bee a Man, hee is a living Body*, is a true Consequence, signified by that word *Is*.[20]

To say that the word *to be* is neither a denomination of thing nor a denomination of being is to say that being cannot legitimately become the object of a statement, that it is only the sign of a link of the terms of a propositional utterance. However, there is a quasi-irrepressible tendency of language that leads us to make of being an object of discourse. The verb *to be* is in particular the principal source of metaphysical illusions. Metaphysicians who, in the example of Aristotle, pretend to speak of being are caught in the trap of language. Through ignorance of the syntactic organisation of discourse, they have taken the word *to be* for a categorem by granting it, besides its function of link of denominations, a proper signification that consists in saying being. The word *to be* thus becomes, fallaciously, subject or predicate of metaphysical propositions.

The Hobbesian attempt to hinder the linguistic displacement from being-sign to being-object is composed of two moments. The first is logical; it consists in showing that the function of sign of connection is not a virtue proper to being, but can as well be assumed by an inflection or an ending of the verb employed.[21] And so the proposition *the man is walking* (*homo est ambulans*) is equivalent to that other *the man walks* (*homo ambulat*). The second moment is historical. Hobbes indeed has sought whether there does not exist a language in which the verb *to be* never assumes the function of copula: 'if it were so, that there were a Language without any Verb answerable to *Est*, or *Is*, or *Bee*; yet the men that used it would bee not a jot lesse capable of Inferring, Concluding, and of all kind of Reasoning, than were the Greeks, and Latines'.[22] Now this language, Hobbes believed, was found in Hebrew: 'Since in place of copula, they [the Hebrews] used the *apposition* of two denominations; it is thus there where it is said, in Genesis 1:2: *the earth unformed thing*, what we are obliged to turn according to the following formula: *the earth was unformed.*'[23] This example is, however, not very conclusive, because the Hebrew equivalent of the verb *to be* is not used as copula only in the present tense. Hobbes is thus led to reinterpret certain Biblical expressions where the verb *to be* seems to have a function of a sign of connection. The approach, however, is clear: it aims at attempting to redirect the ambiguities of which the verb *to be* can be the cause by an analysis of the respective function of the different parts of discourse which leads to a radical attempt of thinking the proposition without being.

## ETHICS OF PRAGMATICS

The semantic and syntactic aspects that we have examined up to the present would have been separated from all real discursive practice, if they were not linked to the pragmatic aspect of language. The initial text of *De Corpore* already indicated this: 'for that the sound of this word *stone* should be the sign of a stone, cannot be understood in any sense but this, that he that hears it collects that he that pronounces it thinks of a stone'. Every use of words exercises a function and is rooted within a context. It is this function and this context that define the pragmatic dimension of language.

The function of language is inscribed within the very definition of the linguistic sign: 'many use the same words, to signify (by their connexion and order,) one to another, what they conceive, or think of each matter; and also what they desire, feare, or have any other passion for'.[24] The linguistic sign has the function of communication. But the latter, far from being accidentally re-attached to signification and to the syntax of our verbal discourse, is indissociably linked to them. Thus, the passage from mark to sign that we again grasped earlier on the syntactic plane now intervenes on the pragmatic plane. Linguistic communication does not establish itself with unities without connection. Between the three aspects of language, there is thus no relation at all with anteriority or posteriority. Words signify thought only within the order of discourse and in view of communicating it to someone. The intention of signification of which we formerly spoke is enveloped within the function of communication. To speak is always to speak to a real or possible interlocutor.

This link of pragmatics to semantics and to syntax is found confirmed

## Theory of Language

by the fact that the examination of the function of verbal discourse, which plays a considerable role in ethics and politics, already intervenes in the logic and theory of science. Indeed, the education and growth of the sciences, necessary to the general good of humanity, find their condition of possibility in communication. Language establishes a space of interlocution upon which the elaboration and transmission of knowledge are built: invention no longer perishes with the inventor. Language always being, in Hobbes, spoken or written and never only mental, we understand that it would be impossible to consider the production of utterances outside the existence of a space of interlocution.

However, the study of the function of language remains abstract as long as it is not situated within a context. For example, the space of interlocution which subtends the production and growth of the sciences is possible only within the political context of civil peace. Indeed, within the state of war,

> there is not place for Industry; because the fruit thereof is uncertain: and consequently no Culture of the Earth; no Navigation, nor use of the commodities that may be imported by Sea; no commodious building; no Instruments of moving, and removing such things as require much force; no Knowledge of the face of the Earth; no account of Time; no Arts; no Letters; no Society; and which is worst of all, continuall feare, and danger of violent death; And the life of man, solitary, poore, nasty, brutish, and short.[25]

Science and technology are possible only within the state, where interhuman relations are governed by politico-juridical norms. The type of relations that men maintain between themselves furnishes the context where the discursive function is exercised, and defines what we can call the regime of communication's functioning.[26] It is within ethics that Hobbes places the study of linguistic contexts. Thus, in chapter 13 of *The Elements of Law*, after having recalled that the preceding chapters traced the powers [*puissances*] and acts of the human mind considered in each man independently of others, Hobbes examines the effects of these powers [*puissances*] and these acts in interhuman relations. Now, these effects are from the signs by which we take knowledge of thought, of the will, or of others' intentions. Among these signs, language occupies a privileged place:

Of these signs, some are such as cannot easily be counterfeited; as actions and gestures, especially if they be sudden; wherof I have mentioned some for example sake in the ninth chapter, at the several passions whereof they are signs; others there are that may be counterfeited: and those are words or speech; of the use and effect whereof I am to speak in this place.[27]

The proper character of linguistic signs, in opposition to other signs (gestures, behaviours, attitudes, etc.), is ambivalence. Language can reveal our thoughts and our intentions to others as well as mask them. *Leviathan* insists on the fact that speech, which is proper to man, has a status absolutely different from the use of the voice in animals of the same species: 'these creatures, though they have some use of voice, in making knowne to one another their desires, and other affections; yet they want that art of words, by which some men can represent to others, that which is Good, in the likenesse of Evil; and Evil, in the likenesse of Good'.[28] This ambivalence of language explains that it renders possible in interhuman relations understanding and persuasion, good and bad counsel, promise and threat, appeasement or excitation of the passions.[29] Language is thus not a neutral instrument of communication. On the one hand, recaptured within a determined relational context, the meaning of what is said also depends on the person who speaks, on his intentions or again on his attitude: 'Though words be the signs we have of one another's opinions and intentions; yet, because the equivocation of them is so frequent according to the diversity of contexture, and of the company wherewith they go (which the presence of him that speaketh, our sight of his actions, and conjecture of his intentions, must help to discharge us of): it must be extreme hard to find out the opinions and meanings of those men that are gone from us long ago.'[30] On the other hand, to speak is also to act, not only because our discourse can produce an effect on others who contribute to modifying the original relational context (thus understanding has accord for sign and concord for effect, while persuasion has controversy for sign and discord for effect), but also, and above all, because speech is itself an act when, for example, we promise something or when we threaten someone.

Let us note that chapter 13 of *The Elements of Law* immediately precedes the chapters dedicated to natural right and to natural law.

# Theory of Language

The theory of contracts [*contrats*] and of pacts essentially consists in an analysis of the speech-acts and of the obligations that the simple fact of pronouncing these speeches created or did not create. Thus, to say '*I will that this be thine to morrow*', and to say '*I will give it thee to morrow*', there is a great difference 'For the word *I will*, in the former manner of speech, signifies an act of the will Present; but in the later, it signifies a promise of an act of the will to Come.'[31] In the first case, the meaning of the phrase is in the carrying out of a present act; in the second, its meaning clearly expresses that it is not the accomplishment of a present act: 'therefore the former words, being of the Present, transferre a future right; the later, that be of the Future, transferre nothing'.[32]

However, if a speech-act puts two interlocutors into relation, it cannot be dissociated from a more general regime of communication which involves the whole of interhuman relationships. Now, if we will consider the relationships that prevail between men in the state of nature, where no civil power [*pouvoir*] exists for furnishing the rules of justice and injustice and enforcing them, and where each one has liberty to interpret according to his particular interest the other's speeches, the regime of communication is a truncated space of interlocution where the lie, misunderstanding and suspicion reign.[33] In other words, the intention of communicating there is undermined by an internal and permanent contradiction. Because each person assumes the role of a private interpreter simultaneously of his own discourse and that of the other, each person takes his own reason for universal reason or norm. It is with this contradictory regime of communication together with the means of surmounting it that Hobbes seems to deal when he writes:

> Forasmuch as whosoever speaketh to another, intendeth thereby to make him understand what he saith; if he speak unto him, either in a language which he that heareth understandeth not, or use any word in other sense than he believeth is the sense of him that heareth; he intendeth also to make him not understand what he saith; which is a contradiction of himself. It is therefore always to be supposed, that he which intendeth not to deceive, alloweth the private interpretation of his speech to him to whom it is addressed.[34]

In order to pass from the contradictory regime to a normal regime of communication, that is to say, in order for an authentic space of interlocution to exist, it is necessary to carry out a displacement of the interpretative authority of my discourse: it is necessary that I take the other for measure of the meaning of what I say, and that the other do the same on my behalf. In other words, it is necessary that each one of the interlocutors agree to no longer establish his subjectivity as universal norm. Now, this alternative between unilaterality and reciprocity is no other than the alternative between the right of each over all things, which is the specific form of natural right in the state of war, and the natural laws or moral precepts which prescribe reciprocal recognition as condition for peace. Indeed, the natural right extended to all things that each person gives to himself only returns to the sphere of the self, everything happening as if each was saying to himself: 'For if it be against reason, that I be judge of mine own danger myself, then it is reason, that another man be judge thereof. But the same reason that maketh another man judge of those things that concern me, maketh me also judge of that that concerneth him. And therefore I have reason to judge of his sentence, whether it be for my benefit, or not.'[35] Inversely, the natural laws prescribe the reciprocity that can take place only by a commutativity of the self and the other. And so the principle that summarises the whole of the laws of nature consists in a rule of commutativity: *'That a man imagine himself in the place of the party with whom he hath to do, and reciprocally him in his.'*[36] The condition of the existence of a non-contradictory regime of communication or of an authentic space of interlocution is thus a moral condition. The laws of nature thus furnish ethical norms for the exercise of language. But clearly this ethics has no effectiveness at all in the state of nature. If moral laws are conceived by the reason of each individual and experienced as a practical interior necessity, they cannot effectively regulate interhuman relations and constitute a civil peace. In other words, language maintains a double relation to ethics: in one sense, it finds in it the principles that condition its exercise as much in what relates to the growth of the sciences as everyday communication. But, in another sense, it is language that, as a last resort, is the condition for the realisation of an ethical world, since the existence of the state, without which this world cannot exist, is the product of a speech-act by which each addressing himself to each is made, by his statement, founder of the political authority that must assure respect for the laws of nature. We thus understand that Hobbes could write,

> the most noble and profitable invention of all other, was that of SPEECH, consisting of *Names* or *Appelations*, and their Connexion; whereby men register their Thoughts; recall them when they are past; and also declare them one to another for mutuall utility and conversation; without which, there had been amongst men, neither Common-wealth, nor Society, nor Contract, nor Peace, no more than amongst Lyons, Bears, and Wolves.[37]

This text, which summarises the semantic, syntactic and pragmatic aspects of language, underlines its essential role in the institution of a specifically human ethico-political world. The double relationship of language to ethics, far from revealing a circle, indicates, on the contrary, the privileged character of the moment of the social contract: a privileged moment where men, henceforth conscious of this, that the unilaterality of the right over all things, which consists in setting up its subjectivity in universal norm, leads only to confrontation, misery and death, found themselves periodically placed in an ethical situation of reciprocity and find a common language in order to exercise, in a face-to-face encounter of each person to each other, this protofounding speech-act which carries to being the first and without doubt most considerable of human works: the political edifice. The function of the state, born from this verbal performance, will ultimately perpetuate this privileged but periodic moment, in assuring the effectiveness of the ethical norms without which men can no longer be understood.

After this analysis of the different aspects of language in Hobbes, I believe that it is possible to say not only that we find in him a unified and coherent theory of language, but, in addition, that the unity and coherence of his philosophy depends on this theory.

## Notes

1. [TN: this phrase comes from Hobbes, *De Corpore*, in *Opera Philosophica*, ed. William Molesworth, vol. 1 (London: John Bohn, 1839), p. 73; in *English Works*, vol. 1, p. 83.]
2. Hobbes, *Leviathan*, p. 103.

3. See Hobbes, *The Elements of Law*, pp. 20–1.
4. Ibid., p. 23.
5. For a detailed study of the ethics of man as being of speech, see our book *La décision métaphysique de Hobbes*, pp. 255–356.
6. Thomas Hobbes, *De Corpore*, p. 15; *Elements of Philosophy, The First Section, Concerning Body*, in *English Works*, vol. 1, ed. William Molesworth (London: Routledge/Thoemmes Press, 1997), p. 17.
7. See Michel Malherbe, *Hobbes, ou l'œuvre de la raison* (Paris: Vrin, 1984), pp. 43–4.
8. For example, in the fourth chapter of *Leviathan*, Hobbes sometimes employs the verb 'to signify' [TN: in English in the original] when it is a question of the reference of the name.
9. Thomas Hobbes, *Man*, trans. Charles T. Wood, T. S. K. Scott-Craig and Bernard Gert (Indianapolis, IN: Hackett, 1998), p. 37; *De Homine*, in *Opera Philosophica*, vol. 2, p. 88.
10. Hobbes, *The Elements of Law*, pp. 23–4; *Leviathan*, pp. 109–10.
11. [TN: in English in the original.]
12. Hobbes, *The Elements of Law*, p. 25. [TN: in English in the original.]
13. Ibid., p. 21.
14. Hobbes, *De Corpore*, pp. 19–20; *Elements of Philosophy*, pp. 21–2.
15. Ibid., pp. 15–16; pp. 17–18.
16. Hobbes, *Leviathan*, pp. 107–8.
17. Hobbes, *De Corpore*, p. 27; *Elements of Philosophy*, p. 30.
18. Hobbes, *Man*, p. 37; *De Homine*, p. 88.
19. Hobbes, *Leviathan*, p. 690.
20. Ibid., p. 691.
21. Hobbes, *De Corpore*, p. 27; *Elements of Philosophy*, p. 30.
22. Hobbes, *Leviathan*, pp. 690–1.
23. Hobbes, *Leviathan*, in *Opera Philosophica*, p. 498. In order that the analysis of the Hobbesian theory be complete, it would also be necessary to examine the function of being in the judgement of existence. [TN: my translation.]
24. Hobbes, *Leviathan*, p. 101.
25. Ibid., p. 186; see Hobbes, *De Corpore*, pp. 6–9; *Elements of Philosophy*, pp. 7–10.
26. See Chapter 5, 'The Semiology of Power'.
27. Hobbes, *The Elements of Law*, p. 64.
28. Hobbes, *Leviathan*, p. 226.
29. Hobbes, *The Elements of Law*, pp. 64–8.
30. Ibid., p. 68.
31. Hobbes, *Leviathan*, p. 194. [TN: italicised English in English in the original.]

32. Ibid.
33. See Chapter 6, 'On War'.
34. Hobbes, *The Elements of Law*, p. 69.
35. Ibid., p. 72.
36. Ibid., p. 92.
37. Hobbes, *Leviathan*, p. 100.

*Chapter 5*

# THE SEMIOLOGY OF POWER [*POUVOIR*]

> A signe is not a signe to him that giveth it, but to whom it is made; that is, to the spectator.
>
> Hobbes, *Leviathan*[1]

## LEVELS OF READING FOR THE ETHICO-POLITICAL SYSTEM

Hobbes's ethical and political philosophy can be the target of a reading at different levels. This situation essentially stems from this: that Hobbes did not always keep, in the elaboration of his doctrine, to the principles that he however articulates as being before those of science, namely, the use of a language the nominal definitions of which must assure the univocity of significations. So that I am better understood: I am not at all saying that Hobbes does not put science's procedures to work in the ethical and political domain. On the contrary, the power [*puissance*] of his doctrine stems precisely from his broad overall consistency. I am only saying is that this consistency is studded with analogies that are sometimes presented as schemes of intelligibility. We are thinking, for example, of the analogy present in chapter 10 of *Leviathan* where man's tendency to increase his power [*puissance*] is compared with 'the motion of heavy bodies, which the further they go, make still the more haste'.[2] These are the analogies that have given rise to readings of the whole of the doctrine in terms of mechanistic physics. Certainly, physics very much constitutes the basis starting from which ethics and politics are deployed, but these cannot be reduced to that. The theory of the passions, the relational dynamics that lead to the state of war, the institution and the juridical function of the state cannot be explained in terms of movement and of composition of movements. Thus, the effects of a man's power [*puissance*] or of political power [*pouvoir*] are defined according to a notion that can have no place in physics, that of the sign. The ethics of a man's power [*puissance*] as much as the theory of political power [*pouvoir*] involve at different levels a specific modality of a semiological relationship between a signifier and a signified. This relationship, which it is possible to locate from *The Elements of Law* up to *De Homine*, takes on a frankly systematic character in *Leviathan*. If the physics of *De Corpore* engages a theory of matter in motion, *Leviathan* engages what it is necessary to call, and this without anachronism, an ethico-political semiology. These are the principles of this semiology that we would like to place in evidence here.

## PHYSICS OF FORCE AND SEMIOLOGY OF POWER [*POUVOIR*]

Every power [*puissance*] produces effects, and so Hobbes compares the motive power [*puissance*] of the body and the motive power [*puissance*] of the mind.

> That power of the mind which we call motive, differeth from the power motive of the body; for the power motive of the body is that by which it moveth other bodies, which we call strength: but the power motive of the mind, is that by which the mind giveth animal motion to that body wherein it existeth; the acts hereof are our affections and passions.[3]

However, if the motive power [*puissance*] of the body or force (strength)[4] and the motive power [*puissance*] of the mind (this last constituting the properly human power [*puissance*] that is joined to cognitive power [*puissance*]) both produce effects and can thus be compared, their difference is considerable as much at the level of the effect's status as at that of its mode of production. Indeed, the body's power [*puissance*] falls within the jurisdiction of a physics of matter in motion, while human power [*puissance*], the study of which belongs to ethics, falls within the jurisdiction of a semiology.

From the physical point of view, power [*puissance*] is measured by its future effects, which are all the greater as the *impetus* of a body, that is to say, the instantaneous speed of its *conatus*, is greater. Now there are two sorts of future effect: (1) the impetus that a body is capable of giving to another body by collision; (2) the work that a body is capable of performing. At this level, it is thus not a question of the sign.

From the ethical point of view: 'THE POWER *of a Man*, (to take it Universally,) is his present means, to obtain some future apparent Good. And is either *Originall*, or *Instrumentall*.'[5] Human power [*puissance*] thus produces some specific future effects, which consist in the obtaining of an apparent good. It thus supposes the passage from a first threshold which leads from the quantitative to the qualitative, from the simple physical effect to the obtaining of a good. This threshold is that of the representation where every physiological reaction is transformed into a subjective appearance. The apparent good itself being a projection of desire, the aim which is inscribed within this definition of power [*puissance*] (as means in view of an end) is only the mode under which power [*puissance*] appears subjectively to a man. The final cause can thus, as *De Corpore* would have it,[6] be reduced to efficient cause or to active power [*puissance*].

This active power [*puissance*] of man is thus producer of effects which must permit the conservation of life. Thus, our natural powers [*puissances*] (qualities of body and mind) and our instrumental powers [*puissances*] (wealth, reputation, friends, chance) produce direct qualitative effects. Power [*puissance*] is considered here only in its value for use without reference to exchange, and is measured by its direct effects.

However, to the qualitative threshold is added a second threshold which leads from the production of qualitative effects to the production of signs. This time, power [*puissance*] is envisaged from the point of view of exchange. Its effects are no longer direct but indirect, mediated by signs. Within interhuman relations, that is to say, within communication and exchange, power [*puissance*] can produce effects only in producing signs. Consequently, the passions and human behaviour become exchanges of signs through which man wears himself out manifesting his power [*puissance*].

The mutation from use to exchange, from direct effect to effect mediated by signs, modifies the definition of power [*puissance*]: 'And because the power of one man resisteth and hindereth the effects of the power of another: power is simply no more, but the excess of the power of one above that of another.'[7] Within exchange, a man's power [*puissance*] is not measured by its direct effects, but relatively to others' power [*puissance*]. Consequently, power [*puissance*] is only the signifying excess, that is to say, that which, within power [*puissance*] or by some other means, is sign of power [*puissance*]. Force itself is evaluated less by its physical effects than indirectly inasmuch as these effects are signs: 'actions proceeding from strength of body and open force, are honourable, as signs consequent of power motive, such as are victory in battle or duel; *et à avoir tué son homme*'.[8]

This relationship of power [*puissance*] to signs is such that a power [*puissance*] that is real but is not manifest by signs is only a weak power [*puissance*] reduced to its direct effects (this is the case of science, because its signs can be recognised only by those who already possess them, and by relation to which it does not constitute a superiority) and, inversely, the appearance of a power [*puissance*] to which the reality of this power [*puissance*] does not correspond is a power [*puissance*] (this is the case of the eloquence which presents the noticeable signs of science without real possession of knowledge).

In other words, not only do signs signify power [*puissance*], but a power [*puissance*] has reality – when we consider it in interhuman relations at the level of its indirect effects and not in itself at the level of its direct effects – only as signified. The theory of value only expresses this necessity of the link of power [*puissance*] to signs, and so: 'The *Value*, or WORTH of a man, is as of all other things, his Price; that is to say, so much as would be given for the use of his Power.'[9] Power [*puissance*] exists, within exchange, only inasmuch as it is capable of making a spectacle of itself through signs under the gaze of others, which expresses the evaluation that it makes by other signs – the signs of honour: 'according to the signs of honour and dishonour, so we estimate and make the value or WORTH of a man'.[10] These signs are acts, gestures, behaviours and speeches. The value of a man caught in the network of exchange is neither a moral absolute nor the value that he brings to himself, but is simply his price.

We can take any of our natural or instrumental powers [*puissances*]. We will see that it exists as power [*puissance*] only by the signs that signify it in exchange. In this regard, the example of wealth is remarkable: 'riches are honourable; as signs of the power that acquired them. – And gifts, costs, and magnificence of houses, apparel, and the like, are honourable, as *signs* of riches.'[11] Hobbes does not say that wealth is a power [*puissance*] by itself, but inasmuch as it is a sign of the power [*puissance*] that has acquired it or inasmuch as it manifests itself by signs like gifts, expenditures or clothes. Wealth is thus at the same time signifier and signified. It is in this relationship to the sign that it is a power [*puissance*]. On the other hand, when the liberty that transforms it into sign errs, it 'expose[s] men to Envy, as a Prey'.[12]

On the ethical plane, power [*puissance*] is very much the signified of signs or signifiers, signifiers that make it exist as power [*puissance*] and produce themselves from the signified since power [*puissance*] is by itself a power [*puissance*]. It is thus very much a semiology that raises Hobbes's ethics.

In the same way, when we pass from the ethics of human power [*puissance*] (*potentia*) to the politics of the state's power [*pouvoir*] (*potestas*), this power [*pouvoir*] belongs to the political domain only because it is neither solely nor essentially overt violence, that is to say, because it is founded and deployed itself within a network of symbolic relations.

Thus, the power [*pouvoir*] of the state is instituted by the verbal performance of the social pact, and even when it is acquired by force: 'It is not therefore the Victory, that giveth the right of Dominion over the Vanquished, but his own Covenant', which is expressed by the vanquished 'either in expresse words, or by other sufficient signs of the Will.'[13]

These are again the signs that reign over its functioning, so that, for example, a violence inflicted by the sovereign to a subject has political character only if it is codified in the signs of right: 'that the evil inflicted by publique Authority, without precedent publique condemnation, is not to be stiled by the name of Punishment; but of a hostile act; because the fact for which a man is Punished, ought first to be Judged by publique Authority, to be a transgression of the Law'.[14] Power [*pouvoir*] is political only as producer of signs codified by right. In this sense, *potestas* is at the same time *potentia* and *jus*, the dimension of right falling entirely within the jurisdiction of the symbolic function.

It is thus indeed a semiotics and not a physics that raises ethics and politics. This does not mean that the physical dimension disappears – it is present each time that it is a question of the use of force – but this means only that, by their very essence, individual power [*puissance*] and political power [*pouvoir*] are not reduced to the simple use of force but are given to see, to understand, to write. It is thus now a question of studying the first aspect of this semiology which is constituted by a taxonomy of signs.

## TAXONOMY OF SIGNS

Envisaged from the point of view of the relationship of signifier to signified, signs are arranged into three categories: natural signs, conventional signs and supernatural signs.

## Natural Signs

> When a man hath so often observed like antecedents to be followed by like consequents, that whensoever he seeth the antecedent, he looketh again for the consequent; or when he seeth the consequent, he maketh account there hath been the like antecedent; then he calleth both the antecedent and the consequent SIGNS one of another, as clouds are a sign of rain to come, and rain of clouds past.[15]

We find this definition of the sign simultaneously in *The Elements of Law*, *Leviathan* and *De Corpore*. Six remarks on the natural sign.

1. In the case of the natural sign, the link from the sign to its signified is a relation of consecution between an antecedent event and a consequent event. But this link must not be simply unique or accidental. In order that there may be a sign, it is necessary that the link have been the object of several anterior perceptions. The aptitude for distinguishing and recognising signs thus depends on experience.

2. The consequent or the antecedent can equally be sign of one another. That which is the object of an actual perception is sign of the other. Thus, a visible antecedent can temporarily be the sign of an invisible consequent. This is the case in conjecture of the future. And a visible consequent can be the sign of a definitively invisible antecedent. This is the case of conjecture of the past.[16]

3. The reading of natural signs, being founded on experience, does not at all cover absolute certainty, for 'If the signs hit twenty times for once missing, a man may lay a wager of twenty to one of the event; but may not conclude it for a truth.'[17] The reading of natural signs thus falls only within the jurisdiction of conjecture, and the value of conjectures will depend on acquiring more or less great experience.

4. Hobbes speaks of antecedent and consequent, and not of cause and effect. The first pair depends indeed on the imagination, while the second depends on reason and covers certainty. What's more, men – Spinoza will remember this in the *Theologico-political Treatise* – are all the more inclined to search for signs the less they know natural causes. Such is the origin of superstition; lacking knowledge of the causes of their good and their bad fortune, men have a tendency to make the attribution to 'things Casuall for Prognostiques'.[18] Another example, beauty is a sign of the good without being the cause of it; on

the other hand, utility is a cause of the good without being the sign of it.[19]

5. There are some natural signs of a man's power [*puissance*] and of his passions. Thus, the eminence of the faculties of the body or of the mind is a sign of power [*puissance*]; for example, the beauty or the force of the body and the intellectual qualities (save science, which is artificially acquired) or morals of the mind. There are natural signs of the passions: facts and gestures. For example, redness of the face is a natural sign of shame, laughter is a natural sign of a sudden glory. In the *Treatise of Man*, Descartes also considered this type of sign: 'As for other external movements, ones which serve neither to ward off the evil nor to produce the good, but which merely bear witness to the passions – such movements as those of laughing and weeping – these occur only by chance . . .'[20] We again find some similar considerations in Gerauld de Cordemoy's *Discours physique de la parole* concerning the signs of the passions.[21] Cartesian physiology is a semiophysiology because it puts into correlation the mechanical functions of the body and their biological signification.

For Hobbes, there are additionally some natural signs of civil honour and some natural signs of religious worship: 'There be some signes of Honour, (both in Attributes and Actions,) that be Naturally so; as amongst Attributes, *Good, Just, Liberall,* and the like; and amongst Actions, *Prayers, Thanks,* and *Obedience.*'[22]

6. Natural signs can be deceptive because they can be counterfeited in order to give the illusion of the existence of the passion that they usually signify.[23]

### Conventional Signs

This second category of signs is itself constituted of two subcategories: arbitrary signs and signs of institution.

#### ARBITRARY SIGNS

A MARK therefore is a sensible object which a man erecteth voluntarily to himself, to the end to remember thereby somewhat past, when the same is objected to his sense again. As men that have passed by a rock at sea, set up some mark, whereby to remember their former danger, and avoid it.

*The Semiology of Power* 79

> In the number of these marks, are those human voices (which we call the names or appellations of things) sensible to the ear.[24]

1. Any object, provided that it be perceptible, can be used as mark. The absence of all natural relation between the mark and what it has the function of marking implies the detachment of the object that serves as mark. However, one mark can be better than another according to whether it fulfils more or less well the function that is assigned to it.

2. Any object becomes mark only in virtue of a voluntary decision. There is thus arbitrariness of the assignation of an object as mark. The relation between signifier and signified is neither of resemblance nor of consecution observed in experience. This possibility of arbitrariness is proper to man. Arbitrariness is thus the threshold that permits distinguishing man from animal, and starting from which will be possible the simultaneously intellectual and passional mutation which makes the singularity of man.

3. The utilisation of the mark is individual, man thus voluntarily establishes marks for himself (*to himself*).[25] Marks thus do not suppose in any way interhuman or social contract. On the contrary, it is starting from them that every interindividual contract is possible.

4. The function of the mark is to enable memory. Thoughts within mental discourse are in fact vanishing. The memory of them disappears as soon as time passes and as other affections strike our senses. The mark is thus a reminder which makes it possible to extend the field of memory by the facility with which it recalls a distant memory. The mark is mark of a thought and not of a thing; language is first of all only a particular form of it.

> the first use of names, is to serve for *Markes*, or *Notes* of remembrance. Another is, when many use the same words, to signifie (by their connexion and order,) one to another, what they conceive, or think of each matter; and also what they desire, feare, or have any other passion for. And for this use they are called *Signes*.[26]

1. The human voice, like every mark, is perceptible by the senses, in this case by hearing. Within its function of marking for the individual's memory, it is distinguished however in this, that it frees man from a simply actual and immediate impression of the world. By terms man can himself recall his thoughts in all circumstances.

2. Every voice does not thus constitute a language in its current form: 'Moreover the signification that does occur when animals of the same kind call to one another, is not on that account speech, since not by their will, but out of the necessity of nature these calls by which hope, fear, joy, and the like are signified . . .'[27] In order that the voice be a mark and not the natural sign of a passion, it must in no way be composed of natural relation to its signified. Thus, the cry is a voice without being a mark: 'these calls are not speech since constituted by the will of these animals, but burst forth by the strength of nature from the peculiar fears, joys, desires, and other passions of each of them; and this is not to speak, which is manifest in this, that the calls of animals of the same species are in all lands whatsoever the same, while those of men are diverse'.[28] The arbitrariness of the institution of the human voice as mark implies the dissimilarity of the voices of individuals, while nature imposes the resemblance of animal voices. The natural movement of the tongue (*the motion of his tongue*)[29] is a necessary physical condition, but not intellectually sufficient for speech.

3. Besides the voluntary act of institution, the verbal mark supposes that what is signified be a thought: 'That Understanding which is peculiar to man, is the Understanding not onely his will; but his conceptions and thoughts, by the sequel and contexture of the names of things into Affirmations, Negations, and other formes of Speech.'[30] Comprehension of speech is comprehension of a thought that cannot be linked in any way to the *hic et non* of actual circumstances.

4. The function of verbal marks is thus recalling (*to recall*)[31] our thoughts, in transferring our mental *discursion* into verbal discourse. There is thus juxtaposition of a mental chain and a verbal chain, which permits the linking of vanishing thoughts to be fixed and to be ordered. The use of words thus has a constituent function in thought, so that 'ratio . . . is but oratio'.[32] Thus, the differences between concrete names and abstract names, names of things and names of discourse, particular names and universal names, render possible the constitution of the universal significations of science.

But if reason is oration, if there is no rational thought without verbal discourse, this does not imply that all speech conveys a signification. Verbal discourse, once constituted, can run empty: 'As it is with beggars, when they say their *paternoster*, putting together such words, and in such manner, as in their education they have learned from their nurses, from their companions, or from their teachers, having no images or conceptions in their minds answering to the words they speak.'[33] Thus, language, which, on the one hand, renders science possible, on the other, will be a factor of uncertainty concerning its signification.

5. The verbal mark becomes sign when it passes from an individual use to a function of communication. The sonorous aspect of the voice finds here its principal application. But the very arbitrariness of the linguistic sign makes this communication problematic: 'Because, however, I would say that names have arisen from human invention, someone might possibly ask how a human invention could avail so much as to confer on mankind the benefit speech appears to us to have. For it is incredible that men once came together to take counsel to constitute by decree what all words and all connexions of words would signify.'[34]

How to pass from the mark to the sign of communication? Is language conditional on society or society on language? It is because Hobbes makes speech and verbal communication the condition of society, and not the inverse, that his political philosophy is a semiology of power [*pouvoir*] and not a sociology of power [*pouvoir*].

6. Communication was constituted bit by bit, from one man to the other 'as need (the mother of all inventions) taught them; and in tract of time grew every where more copious'.[35] The state of nature furnishes the ahistorical model of such a constitution, which is developed in a process of recognition. Language is in fact cause of bringing men together and cause of their conflict before being cause of their union in the state. The first effort of communication renders a second necessary, and that from others, without which we would need to suppose a collective convention from the beginning, since the state of nature is precisely that of suspicion and truncated communication. The first linguistic collective act will be the social contract. The function of political power [*pouvoir*] will be rendering a univocal communication possible.

7. Words become signs for communication not one by one, but within the order and relationship of discourse. The wording, the syntagmatic articulation of words alone makes it possible to communicate thought. From the political point of view, the constitution of a universality or a static generality that is a product of language responds to the nominalist theme, according to which the universal is not in things but in language.

8. Speech is not the simple natural expression of the passions. However, the passions introduce new inflexions or new forms of discourse. The

ways of speaking that express the passions are partly the same as those that express our thoughts, and partly different. Thus: 'all Passions may be expressed *Indicatively*; as *I love, I feare, I joy, I deliberate, I will, I command*: but some of them have particular expressions by themselves, which neverthelesse are not affirmations, unlesse it be when they serve to make other inferences, besides that of the Passion they proceed from'.[36] Deliberation expresses itself in the subjunctive; desire in the imperative, under the form of a command, a counsel or a prayer, depending on whether the interlocutor is obliged to obey or not; empty glory, indignation, pity and rancour in the optative; desire for knowledge expresses itself in the interrogative mode. Speech-acts thus raise a pragmatics.

INSTITUTED SIGNS

Instituted signs form the second subcategory of conventional signs.

> It is therefore necessary, to consider in this place, what arguments, and signes be sufficient for the knowledge of what is the Law; that is to say, what is the will of the Sovereign, as well in Monarchies, as in other formes of government.[37]
>
> The Law of Nature being excepted, it belongeth to the essence of all other Lawes, to be made known, to every man that shall be obliged to obey them, either by word, or writing, or some other act, known to proceed from the Soveraign Authority.[38]
>
> Nor is it enough the Law be written, and published; but also that there be manifest signs, that it proceedeth from the will of the Soveraign.[39]

1. Instituted signs are as arbitrary as the marks or verbal signs of which individuals make a private use. But, unlike the latter, the first presuppose the social contract and thus the institution of sovereign power [*pouvoir*]. These signs are produced exclusively by the political authority, that is, by the state, and more precisely, by its representative: the sovereign. These are thus civil or political signs. All the others are only private signs produced by particular individuals. To the production and to the private interpretation of signs is superimposed within the state a production and a political interpretation of signs.

2. Instituted signs are arbitrary since the relation of signifier to signified depends on the will of the sovereign. However, they are

distinguished from arbitrary private signs because this relation must always be adequate and manifest. Thus, while an individual can speak without saying anything, or say a thing other than what he thinks, the instituted sign requires an exact coincidence of the political will signified and of the sign.

3. The sign belongs to the very essence of the civil law because it belongs to that essence of being known and communicated explicitly. Thus, the notion of sign appears within the definition of the civil law: 'I define Civill Law in this manner. CIVILL LAW, *Is to every Subject, those Rules, which the Common-wealth hath Commanded him, by Word, Writing, or other sufficient Sign of the Will, to make use of, for the Distinction of Right, and Wrong; that is to say, of what is contrary, and what is not contrary to the Rule.*'[40] Every theory of right is founded on the double determination of the instituted sign as adequate and manifest.

4. The instituted sign is first of all an adequate sign (*sufficient sign, signum idoneum*).[41] The notion of adequate sign belongs to the theory of authorisation. The sovereign, authorised by the subjects in the social contract, authorises the laws in his turn. The law is an act of will, that is to say, a commandment expressed orally or in writing. The law is thus essentially an act of verbal or graphic language. Adequacy characterises the relation of signifier to signified. It thus affects the relationship between the will of the sovereign and the signs that express it. More precisely, adequacy plays out at the very heart of the civil law in the relationship between the letter and the meaning. Yet the letter and the meaning are one only in the literal sense of the written text, to which the subordinate judge must necessarily refer himself. So that although the law could be expressed by writing or speech, writing finds itself privileged because it is only within the written text that there is a literal sense, and thus adequacy of signifier to signified, even if the materiality of the text can sometimes present some difficulties of interpretation. This adequacy allows the civil law to be explicit and universally communicable.[42]

5. The instituted sign is then a manifest sign (*manifest sign*).[43] The manifest sign redoubles, without repeating, the adequate sign. The manifest sign is indeed sign of authentication and not of authorisation. This time the sign makes it possible to recognise that a text issues directly from the sovereign: 'The difficulty consisteth in the evidence of the Authority derived from him; The removing whereof, dependeth on the knowledge of the publique Registers, publique Counsels, publique Ministers, and publique Seales; by which all Laws are sufficiently

verified.'⁴⁴ The manifest sign redoubles the adequate sign in authenticating it, is a sign of sign, a writing of writing.

6. Writing is thus the model of the adequate sign and of the manifest instituted sign. Now, if it makes the explicit and universally communicable character of the law possible, it also guarantees its permanence. Writing is essential to the existence of civil law, in opposition to the law of nature, and thus to the juridical function of the state. Thus, when the people is illiterate, it is necessary to find a substitute for writing: 'in ancient time, before letters were in common use, the Lawes were many times put into verse; that the rude people taking pleasure in singing, or reciting them, might the more easily reteine them in memory'.⁴⁵ The law supposes a permanence for which writing furnishes the model. The absence of writing is not exempt from the necessity of an inscription within memory: learning the commandments by heart, linking them to the fingers of the hand (as Solomon prescribed), repeating them in all circumstances, inscribing them on doorjambs (as Moses prescribed). All things that constitute other ways of writing. The permanence of the law is essential to the existence of a civil right and a penal right. Without writing or one of its substitutes, the existence of the state is, if not impossible, at least precarious.

We can finally add, in order to confirm the status of writing as the model of the adequate sign, the constant argument in Hobbes according to which custom and tradition do not make right. Yet the absence of writing tends to return the law to custom, that is to say, right to fact. Writing is thus linked to the essence of the state.

7. If writing is the model of the instituted political sign, it is not the only kind. There are additionally, on the one hand, the signs of civil honour, like badges, coats of arms, armorial bearings and, above all, 'Titles of *Honour*, such as are Duke, Count, Marquis, and Baron.'⁴⁶ Titles of nobility heighten from the institution and not directly from heredity. On the other hand, some signs of the official worship of God exist: 'those Attributes which the Sovereign ordaineth, in the Worship of God, for signes of Honour, ought to be taken and used for such, by private men in their publique Worship'.⁴⁷

SUPERNATURAL SIGNS

God declareth his Lawes three wayes; by the Dictates of *Naturall Reason*, by *Revelation*, and by the *Voyce* of some *man*, to whom

*The Semiology of Power* 85

by the operation of Miracles, he procureth credit with the rest. From hence there ariseth a triple Word of God, *Rational, Sensible,* and *Prophetique*: to which Correspondeth a triple Hearing; *Right Reason, Sense Supernaturall*, and *Faith*.[48]

Therefore, we are to interpret Gods speaking to men immediately, for that way (whosoever it be), by which God makes them understand his will: And the wayes whereby he doth this, are many; and to be sought onely in Holy Scripture: where though many times it be said, that God spake to this, and that person, without declaring in what manner; yet there be again many places, that deliver also the signes by which they were to acknowledge his presence, and commandement; and by these may be understood, how he spake to many of the rest.[49]

By *Miracles* are signified the Admirable works of God: & therefore they are also called *Wonders*. And because they are for the most part, done, for a signification of his commandement, in such occasions, as without them, men are apt to doubt, (following their private naturall reasoning,) what he hath commanded, and what not, they are commonly in Holy Scripture, called Signes, in the same sense, as they are called by the Latines, *Ostenta*, and *Portenta*, from shewing, and fore-signifying that, which the Almighty is about to bring to passe.[50]

1. There are three ways for God to speak to men: the natural speech of reason, sensible supernatural speech, prophetic supernatural speech. Only the last two interest us here, for natural speech does not suppose the intervention of supernatural signs. By contrast, the doctrine of supernatural signs concerns, on the one hand, the revelation of God's commandment to a singular individual: the prophet and, on the other hand, the works by which God accredits a prophet to men: miracles.

2. The doctrine of supernatural signs thus falls within the jurisdiction of a Biblical exegesis, where it concerns, by an interpretation simultaneously external (historical critique) and internal (cross-referencing texts), knowing what signs those signs are and what their functions are, for: 'Seeing therefore Miracles now cease, we have no signe left, whereby to acknowledge the pretended Revelations, or Inspirations of any private man; nor obligation to give ear to any Doctrine farther than it is conformable to the Holy Scriptures, which since the time of our

Saviour, supply the place, and sufficiently recompense the want of all other Prophecy.'[51]

3. Let us note first of all that supernatural signs constitute a separate category, they are indeed neither natural nor arbitrary. Supernatural signs are opposed to natural signs. Thus, in order that there may be miracle, two conditions are required: (a) that the event be unusual, that is to say, very rare. The first rainbow was a miracle 'because the first; and consequently strange; and served for a sign from God, placed in heaven, to assure his people, there should be no more an universall destruction of the world by Water'.[52] By contrast, in our day rainbows are frequent and are thus no longer miracles, both for those who know the natural causes of them and for those who do not know them. (b) It is equally necessary that, for the event 'we cannot imagine it to have been done by naturall means, but onely by the immediate hand of God'.[53]

Supernatural signs are no longer arbitrary, for if they depend only on the will of God who signifies himself by them, their goal being to give some credit to God's prophet to men, they can fulfil this function only if they arouse by them, and not in virtue of a prior contract, the idea that they are the immediate effects of divine omnipotence. There is thus a specific status of supernatural signs. The relation of signifier to signified is unexplained in terms of experiential connection or human institution, because supernatural signs come under a particular and extraordinary will of God.

4. Among the supernatural signs, there are those by which God speaks immediately to a particular man in a personal revelation. Thus, a dream, an apparition or a vision are signs: 'that is to say, somewhat, as a sign of Gods presence'.[54] In the same way, in the case of angels: 'For it is not the shape; but their use, that makes them Angels. But their use is to be significations of Gods presence in supernaturall operations.'[55]

Sensible supernatural signs signify an immediate presence of God. But these signs are always particular, for they are revealed only to a singular individual, and are produced in accordance with the opinions and particular status of the prophet. Spinoza remembers this. Consequently, for Hobbes, no other man can know with certainty if God really appeared to the prophet, or if it is a question only of an imposter who takes his dreams for reality.

5. For want of certainty that the prophet's speech is indeed the word of God, miracles have the function of giving rise to the belief it is indeed

thus, that is to say, giving credit to the prophet's speeches. Only miracles do not constitute a sufficient guarantee for believing a legitimate faith, for, as Scripture itself attests, the miracles of a false prophet can deceive a true prophet, and thus much more easily the community of men naturally carried, by fault of knowledge of causes, to see miracles everywhere. A second sign is consequently necessary, namely, the instruction of established religion. Thus, Moses had prescribed the rule according to which it is not necessary to 'take . . . any for Prophets, that teach any other Religion, than that which Gods Lieutenant, (which at that time was Moses,) hath established'.[56]

## LANGUAGE: PARTICULAR SYSTEM AND GENERAL EFFICIENCY

The taxonomy of signs makes it possible to reveal the double status of language. Indeed, language is constituted by a particular category of signs, arbitrary signs, different specifically from natural signs and supernatural signs. These signs form a system of communication distinct from other systems constituted by the natural signs of the passions and behaviours or by the signs which God used in order to speak to men supernaturally. However, it is within its very specificity that language establishes the principle of its general efficiency.

1. As we have seen, language's signs are distinguished by a fundamental trait: the arbitrariness of the relationship of the phonic signifier to the mental signified. Yet this arbitrariness makes all the ambivalence of language. For if it allows, on the one hand, recording and communicating thought, we also know that, once constituted, it can run empty or be utilised for expressing a thing other than what we think. Hobbes sums up this ambivalence in a sentence: 'as men abound in copiousnesse of language; so they become more wise, or more mad than ordinary'.[57] Thus, speech has an ambiguous status, because the arbitrariness of its relation to thought makes of it the place of contraries, that is to say, of truth and of error, of sense and of nonsense, of avowal and of misrepresentation, of fair play and of trespass. To the four legitimate uses of speech – the recording of thought, education, the expression of intent and of will, seduction – four abuses correspond term by term – the bad recording of thought by the abuse of words the signification of which is floating, the error that follows the use of metaphorical terms, the fact of giving for its will what is not, the fact

of wounding others: 'a tragedy affecteth no less than a murder if well acted'.[58] Thus, verbal signs are those that can be most easily counterfeit. But the same goes for writing:

> Though words be the signs we have of one another's opinions and intentions; yet, because the equivocation of them is so frequent according to the diversity of contexture, and of the company wherewith they go (which the presence of him that speaketh, our sight of his actions, and conjecture of his intentions, must help to discharge us of): it must be extreme hard to find out the opinions and meanings of those men that are gone from us long ago, and have left us no other sigification thereof but their books.[59]

The text of Holy Scripture will be there in order to testify to the difficulty in finding again the meaning that it conveys. Writing is thus itself a place of ambivalence. It furnishes, on the one hand, the model for the adequate and manifest instituted sign, but it can also be the place of an insurmountable difference between letter and meaning. This internal ambivalence in the proclaimed or written linguistic sign at the same time takes account of its general efficiency.

2. This general efficiency of language affects the natural sign first of all. Indeed, if the passions introduce new inflections within speech, in return speech modifies the passions: 'These formes of Speech, I say, are expressions, or voluntary significations of our Passions: but certain signes they be not; because they may be used arbitrarily, whether they that use them, have such Passions or not.'[60] Speech establishes the dimension of comedy within the passions and interhuman relations. Thus, facts and gestures, although they lend themselves to forgery with more difficulty, become equivocal. Speech thus introduces its own ambivalence within the natural signs of the passions. It affects the natural sign of arbitrariness and introduces uncertainty within nature itself. We understand therefore that: 'by speech man is not made better, but only given greater possibilities'.[61] Speech will play a fundamental role in the inflationary dynamics of the sign in the state of nature.

On the other hand, if speech introduces uncertainty in the natural sign, it alone permits the establishment of political order: 'For without this [language] there would be no society among men, no peace, and consequently no disciplines.'[62] Speech maintains a double relationship to the state.

On the one hand, the institution of the state effects a mutation within language, in making us cross the threshold that leads from the equivocal and truncated speech of the state of nature to the adequate and manifest writing of the civil state. From arbitrary private signs to instituted public signs, the question of language is resumed here within the political problematic.

But the inverse is also true, because the production of the state is the result of a linguistic and more particularly verbal performance which engages a specific function of signs: 'The way by which a man either simply Renounceth, or Transferreth his Right, is a Declaration, or Signification, by some voluntary and sufficient signe, or signes, that he doth so Renounce, or Transferre; or hath so Renounced, or Transferred the same, to him that accepteth it. And these Signes are either Words onely, or Actions onely; or (as it happeneth most often) both Words and Actions.'[63] The contract [*contrat*] is an exchange of signs, it consequently implies a capacity to produce them, to receive them and to recognise them. This signifies that the beings with which such an exchange is impossible are not capable of contracting [*contracter*]. For example, brute beasts, 'because not understanding our speech, they understand not, nor accept of any translation of Right; nor can translate any Right to another',[64] or God, with whom we do not have direct relation, save in the case of supernatural revelation.

Thus, the sign intervenes in the definition of the contract [*contrat*], in the characterisation of its object, and in the delimitation of the conditions for its validity. Even though verbal signs are not the only ones to make a contract [*contrat*] possible, linguistic capacity is always presupposed, and so the forms of the contract [*contrat*] are studied in their verbal formulation: 'Expresse, are words spoken with understanding of what they signifie: And such words are either of the time *Present*, or *Past*; as, *I Give, I Grant, I have Given, I have Granted, I will that this be yours*: Or of the future; as, *I will Give, I will Grant*: which words of the future, are called PROMISE.'[65] Language is presupposed by every juridical relationship. The social contract is itself subtended by a theory of the performative utterance.

Language also plays a fundamental role in the juridical functioning of the state. This time, it is writing that defines civil law, in opposition to the law of nature which only falls under the jurisdiction of speech (thus the law of nature has a universality only *in foro interno*, without effect *in foro externo*): 'Civill, and Naturall Law are not different kinds, but different parts of Law; whereof one part being written, is called Civill, the other unwritten, Naturall.'[66] To the particular individual, imagining, in virtue of natural right, the means of his own conservation, the civil law substitutes a universal rule of differentiation of the just and the unjust, of the good and the bad, of yours and mine. But the universal validity of civil law supposes that in the state each individual would be able to be acquainted with it. Writing belongs to the essence of civil law because to this essence belongs the property of being known and explicitly communicated. If everyone knows who the sovereign is in virtue of the act of establishing the state, it is additionally necessary to know what his will is. Writing thus founds, simultaneously and correlatively, the universality of the law and its communicability. Those who cannot understand the signs of the law (animals, children, the mad, etc.) are excluded from this universality. In order that a being fall under the jurisdiction of a juridical relation, it must be, we know, in a position to understand arbitrary signs. It is on this capacity of speaking that is founded the theory of the juridical person (the child is a juridical person only virtually, in accordance with its impending acquisition of speech). In order that a being may appear to a state, it is necessary, at least in right, that it know how to read.

There is thus not a universality of civil law that will pre-exist the writing by which it is communicated, any more than there is universal thought without the use of speech. Linguistic signs, in the theory of right as in the theory of knowledge, do not have a simple instrumental function but a constituent function.

The efficiency of language is exercised again at the level of supernatural signs, since these are not given to us immediately within a supernatural revelation, but mediately within the text of Holy Scripture. The interpretation of visions, dreams or miracles must thus be exercised upon a text, that is to say, on some linguistic signs. Interpretation is here exegesis, for 'the question is not of obedience to God, but of *when*, and *what* God hath said'.[67] Here it will be necessary to distinguish what in the text exceeds our understanding from what can receive an assignable meaning. Thus, the word *mind* is taken most often in Scripture in the metaphorical sense; on the other hand: 'I find the KINGDOME OF GOD, to signifie in most places of Scripture, a *Kingdome properly so named*, constituted by the Votes of the People in Israel in a peculiar manner; wherein they chose God for their King by Covenant made with him, upon Gods promising them possession of the land of Canaan.'[68]

3. Finally, the general efficiency of language also plays out on another field: language is in fact the general interpreting of all the other categories of signs. This is here the proper function of nominalism, which consists in determining the signification of the words that we employ in order to speak of the other categories of signs. Thus, it is necessary to distinguish the definition of a denomination from what does not belong to it and what falls only under the jurisdiction of a judgement of value that we carry on a speech, an opinion, a gesture, an action: 'And therefore in reasoning, a man must take heed of words; which besides the signification of what we imagine of their nature, have a signification of the nature, disposition, and interest of the speaker; such as are the names of Vertues, and Vices; For one man calleth *Wisdome*, what another calleth *feare*; and one *cruelty*, what another *justice*; one *prodigality*, what another *magnanimity*; and one *gravity*, what another *stupidity*, &c.'[69]

In the same way, from the political point of view, care must be taken in the interpretation of the notion of *unique act of a people*, in this regard, only the unity of the representative (of the sovereign) makes the unity of the person and thus of the act. In other cases, if the act of multiple men seems to contribute to a unique end, or if this multitude acts at the instigation of one of them, it is not there a question in any way of the sign of a unique act, but it is a question only of multiple acts of a disparate multitude.

Finally, the lack of comprehension of the word *heresy* can make us take for a sign of the latter what is not it. Indeed, heresy only signifying a private opinion to which is added our indignation, no religion is thus in itself heretical. However, within the state, heresy designating a private opinion condemned by the head of the Church, that is to say, the sovereign, we can thus without absurdity ask the sovereign to condemn the speeches and acts of a heretical doctrine.

If language is the general interpreting of all other signs, it is not necessary to project in these what simply falls under the jurisdiction of a displacement of the linguistic function.

## REGIMES OF FUNCTIONING

We call regime of functioning the simulation of a general system in which all the categories of signs enter into a dynamics of production, interpretation and exchange. A regime of functioning must thus have a consistency, that is to say, that it must obey some general principles of production, interpretation and exchange of signs. A regime of functioning is thus defined, on the one hand, by the centre (or centres) of production and by the centre (or centres) of interpretation, which are able to be according to identical or different cases, and, on the other hand, by the general principles that preside over the generation of signs. We distinguish in Hobbes's ethico-politico-theological system three regimes of functioning: inflation (state of nature), self-regulation (civil state), interpretation (kingdom of God).

### Regime of Inflation

1. The state of nature is a regime of functioning of signs characterised, on the one hand, by the multiplicity of centres of production and of interpretation of signs, and, on the other hand, by the identity of these two types of centre. Each individual in fact engages in a production of signs by which he signifies his power [*puissance*], and also engages in the interpretation of signs that issue from others. The state of nature is thus characterised by the absence of a hierarchically dominant centre as political power [*pouvoir*] will be. It is thus that we can interpret individuals' equality of fact and equality of right. Equality of fact: 'NATURE hath made men so equall, in the faculties of body, and mind; as that though there bee found one man sometimes manifestly stronger in body, or of quicker mind than another; yet when all is reckoned together, the difference between man, and men, is not so considerable, as that one man can thereupon claim to himselfe any benefit, to which another may not pretend, as well as he.'[70] Equality of right or of liberty 'each man hath, to use his own power, as he will himselfe, for the preservation of his own Nature; that is to say, for the preservation of his own Life; and consequently, of doing any thing, which in his own Judgement, and Reason, hee shall conceive to be the aptest means thereunto'.[71] This double equality characterises a situation in which each individual is just like the others, an autonomous centre of production and of interpretation of signs. The centres are thus in the state of nature simultaneously multiple and autonomous.

2. But the equal autonomy of the individual centres of production and interpretation of signs, far from assuring a stability of the regime of functioning, on the contrary, is the source of a permanent *rivalry*: 'From this equality of ability, ariseth equality of hope in the attaining of

our Ends. And therefore if any two men desire the same thing, which neverthelesse they cannot both enjoy, they become enemies.'[72] The autonomous and multiple centres are thus in *competition*.

3. From the fact of the uncertainty that the arbitrary sign (speech) introduces within the natural signs of the passions and behaviours, every message (speech, fact, gesture, comportment) is ciphered, without which the cipher is never given, or at least, each individual deciphers only in the uncertainty of others' signs. In other words, the state of nature is necessarily that of suspicion, misrepresentation and truncated communication. This is the reign of misunderstanding, for lack of existence of a natural and universal code of interpretation of signs. Generalised uncertainty and misunderstanding this time imply the mutual *distrust* of the multiple and autonomous centres in competition.

4. The issue of the production and interpretation of signs in the state of nature, is, for each individual, the preservation of his existence, because the surest means of this preservation is the reproduction and accumulation of power [*puissance*]: 'So that in the first place, I put for a generall inclination of all mankind, a perpetuall and restlesse desire of Power after power, that ceaseth onely in Death. And the cause of this, is not always that a man hopes for a more intensive delight, than he has already attained to; or that he cannot be content with a moderate power: but because he cannot assure the power and means to live well, which he hath present, without the acquisition of more.'[73] This general inclination of humanity is thus not an innate tendency. It is therefore necessary to know how individuals can reproduce and accumulate their power [*puissance*]. The response is clear: 'every man looketh that his companion should value him, at the same rate he sets upon himselfe: And upon all signes of contempt, or undervaluing, naturally endeavours, as far as he dares . . . to extort a greater value from his contemners, by dommage; and from others, by the example'.[74] The reproduction and accumulation of power [*puissance*] thus occurs only by the growth of the signs of recognition, and the subjective feeling that provokes this growth is *glory*.

5. Competition, distrust and glory: such are the three causes of war, such are equally the three characters of the relation between the multiple and autonomous centres of the production and interpretation of signs. War is in fact, in its essence, an uncontrolled inflation of signs, even if there is no overt battle or violence: 'For WARRE, consisteth not in Battell onely, or the act of fighting; but in a tract of time, wherein the Will to contend by Battell is sufficiently known.'[75]

6. It remains to be seen what the general principles which command the generation of signs in the regime of inflation are. We can determine two of them: (a) a circular principle of intensification; (b) a centrifugal centre of expansion. These two principles are implied in the status of value: 'The *Value*, or WORTH of a man, is as of all other things, his Price; that is to say, so much as would be given for the use of his Power: and therefore is not absolute, but a thing dependent on the need and judgement of another.'[76]

In the regime of inflation, the imaginary affects value. A thing or a person has value as far as the buyer grants it to him: 'as in other things, so in men, not the seller, but the buyer determines the Price. For let a man (as most men do,) rate themselves as the highest Value they can; yet their true Value is no more than it is esteemed by others'.[77] In other words, the more value we attach to a man's power [*puissance*], the more this power [*puissance*] appears as desirable and useful, the more his value increases.

Yet the estimation of value is made by signs, signs of honour: 'The signs of honour are those by which we perceive that one man acknowledgeth the power and worth of another.'[78] The growth of a man's value thus coincides with the growth of the signs by which others recognise his power [*puissance*]. Such a growth is itself possible only by a parallel growth of the signs of worthiness: 'And HONOURABLE are those signs for which one man acknowledgeth power or excess above his concurrent in another.'[79] Signs of honour/signs of worthiness, such is the inflationary spiral of signs. This spiral is determined by a double principle of growth of signs: (1) a principle of accumulation restricted by circular intensification of the couple signs of honour/signs of worthiness; (2) a principle of accumulation widens by centrifugal expansion of the same pair of signs to a greater number of men.

7. Such is thus the inflationary spiral of the signs which explain how the state of nature collapses into war, and that this war would be universal. Power [*puissance*] is signified in signs or signifiers, and, as signified, it is reproduced by the reproduction and accumulation of signifiers.

## Regime of Self-regulation

1. The institution of the state, in order to constitute the necessary and sufficient condition for peace, must transform the regime of inflation

of signs into a regime of self-regulation. This self-regulation is defined first by the existence of a hierarchically dominant centre of production and interpretation of signs. This centre, political power [*pouvoir*], does not suspend the production of signs by particular individuals become subjects of the state, but is superimposed on it.

2. The dominant character of the political centre of production of signs implies an inequality of this centre with the individual particular centres which prevents it from being itself taken in the inflationary spiral. The unity of the political authority is necessary for founding the unity of a juridico-political code. The state is essentially one, but this unity is not necessarily that of an individual (monarchy). It can also be that of a council (aristocracy, democracy). The unity of the civil person is thus juridical, it is the unity of an artificial will produced by the social pact.

3. The dominant political centre founds the unity of the state because it produces adequate and manifest signs, that is to say, signs that function simultaneously as a type of particular sign and as a universal and univocal code of interpretation of the signs produced by the subjects. We have seen that it was precisely there the character of writing instituted the civil law, where, on the one hand, letter and meaning coincide in the literal sense, and which, on the other hand, serves as norm for the interpretation of the signs produced by individuals. The juridical code constituted by adequate and manifest instituted signs is self-interpreting, and, in return, serves as norm in the interpretation of the private signs of the subjects. The value and meaning of the signifier, for instituted signs, are ruled by the signified (the will of the sovereign) and not by other individuals, whether simple subjects, legislators or subordinate judges.

4. The regime of inflation was the reign of misunderstanding. To resolve misunderstanding is to speak aright. The signs produced by the subjects are henceforth interpreted by the political authority for what, in them, concerns the public domain, that is to say, what touches society and the state. In other words, if the individuals become subjects guard the liberty of producing signs, none of them can pose as universal centre of interpretation. Interpretation henceforth falls only under the jurisdiction of the political authority. Social communication is possible by the separation that inserts the state between the production of signs by private individuals and the interpretation that henceforth falls under the jurisdiction of the political.

5. In order to assume their function, instituted political signs must not be able to contradict each other. Yet contradiction is avoided because the political authority alone henceforth remains free and autonomous, that is to say, without obligation with regard to itself. That which implies that each new sign expressing the will of the sovereign cancels out an anterior sign if it is contradictory to it.

6. In the regime of self-regulation, the dynamics of signs is such that it compensates for the deficiency or for a weakness of the individual or council that holds political power [*pouvoir*]. For example, a sign proceeding from an error of the sovereign is an insufficient sign (*unsufficient signe*)[80] of his will: 'the grant were either voyd, as proceeding from Errour, commonly incident to humane Nature, and an unsufficient signe of the will of the Granter [here it is about the sovereign]'.[81] In the same way: 'consequences of words, are not the signes of his will, when other consequences are signes of the contrary; but rather signes of errour, and misreckoning; to which all mankind is too prone'.[82] There is thus an institutional logic of signs which overcomes the insufficiencies of the individual who holds sovereignty.

7. Writing once instituted reacts to the dynamics of signs issued by subjects. Indeed, in the same way that the theory of instituted juridical writing introduced a logic of the institution from the political point of view, likewise, from the anthropological point of view, it makes a new logic of human behaviours in the state possible. Social affects are produced by a new *mimesis* of desire, which is not that of the state of nature and which produces a reversal in the reading of signs. For example, the excess of glory that in the regime of inflation was a sign of worthiness becomes in the state a sign of legitimate suspicion.

8. However, the regime of self-regulation of signs in the state is put back into question when, within the political power [*pouvoir*] (*summa potestas*), power [*puissance*] (*potentia*) is separated from right (*jus*). Thus, it is possible that the sovereign himself puts the state into danger by the production of signs the signified of which is only power [*puissance*]. For example: in condemning the innocent, in making a non-legitimate use of force in acts of hostility with regard to subjects, or again in conferring to a subject advantages that can harm the Republic. In all these cases the signified is not the civil person of the sovereign, but his person and his simply natural power [*puissance*]. The state enters into contradiction with itself by this dissociation of power [*puissance*] and right, because the sovereign is again found at the same level as the subjects, and thus

risks being carried away by the resurgence of the regime of inflation of signs.

### Regime of Interpretation

1. The regime of interpretation concerns God's royalty over his particular people. There is here a political regime of interpretation because the centre of production of supernatural signs, namely God, is distinct from the centre of interpretation of these signs, namely, the prophet. Or more exactly, the same centre is held between two poles, the one theological and the other political. This is why Moses is considered at times as the simple lieutenant of God (God is represented by Moses as prophet) and sometimes as a sovereign in his own right (Moses as sovereign, represents the people).

2. This double point of view is that the political pole of interpretation of signs is dependent on the theological pole of production in the relation of prophet to God-sovereign, but that it becomes in its turn dominant by relation to the theological pole in the relation of the prophet-sovereign to the people. There is indeed always an uncertainty on the subject of sensible supernatural signs and on the subject of miracles, which grant pre-eminence to the political pole of interpretation. Only the prophet-sovereign is authorised to distinguish truth from deception. This means that divine laws become laws for the people only when they are invested with a political character by the prophet-sovereign. Religion makes law for the Republic only to the extent that supernatural signs receive endorsement from instituted signs. The theological is thus always of the theologico-political, for the particular kingdom of God (where politics is a part of religion) as well as for the civil kingdom (where religion is a part of politics). Holy Scripture is thus a political text, but written in language often equivocal and metaphorical. Scripture thus falls under the jurisdiction of political writing; Moses is a state founder.

Hobbes's ethico-politico-theological system is thus very much a transformational dynamics of the regimes of the functioning of signs. The transformation, that is to say, the passage from one regime to another, is made possible by this particular symbolic system, but the efficiency of which is general, that is, language: speech, writing, Holy Scripture.

## CODE OF READING OF SIGNS

Hobbes's semiology thus distinguishes three great categories of signs which are placed into a system within three regimes of functioning. Yet it is not possible to make the categories of signs and the regimes of functioning correspond term by term.

Thus, the regime of the state of nature's inflation is not composed only of natural signs, but also of arbitrary signs (speech). Indeed, there would not be inflation of signs without the existence of speech. This is why the animals that do not have speech know neither the state of nature – 'men are continually in competition for Honour and Dignity, which these creatures are not; and consequently amongst men there ariseth on that ground, Envy and Hatred, and finally Warre; but amongst these not so'[83] – nor the civil state, since without speech, 'there had been amongst men, neither Common-wealth, nor Society, nor Contract, no more than amongst Lyons, Bears, and Wolves'.[84]

Likewise, the regime of self-regulation of the civil state's signs put to work not only instituted signs, but also natural signs and supernatural signs. For natural signs we can take the example of the succession of power [*pouvoir*]. Indeed, if a late sovereign has not designated his successor by express speeches or by testament, it is necessary to resort to natural signs for what his will must have been: 'But where Testament, and expresse Words are wanting, other naturall signes of the Will are to be followed: whereof the one is Custome. And therefore where the Custome is, that the next of Kindred absolutely succeedeth, there also the next of Kindred hath right to the Succession; for that, if the will of him that was in possession had been otherwise, he might easily have declared the same in his life time.'[85] In the absence of established custom, the presumption of natural affection for the closest parent (first of all, the child of masculine sex) must be taken as a natural sign of the sovereign's will. For supernatural signs, it is necessary to remark that the sovereign also exercises a priestly function, and that he is the sole representative of God on earth, thus: 'as none but Abraham in his family, so none but the Soveraign in a Christian Common-wealth, can take notice of what is, or what is not the Word of God. For God spake onely to Abraham; and it was he onely, that was able to know what God said, and to interpret the same to his family: And therefore also, they that have the place of Abraham in a Common-wealth, are the onely Interpreters of what God hath spoken.'[86]

Finally, within the regime of interpretation of signs, besides supernatural signs, some natural signs and some instituted signs are also involved. The theory of sacraments, for example, concerns instituted signs of the admission and of the commemoration of this admission into the kingdom of God: 'A SACRAMENT, is a separation of some visible thing from common use; and a consecration of it to God's service, for a sign, either of our admission into the Kingdome of God, to be of the number of his peculiar people, or for a Commemoration of the same. In the Old Testament, the sign of Admission was *Circumcision*; in the New Testament, *Baptisme*.'[87]

The impossibility of identifying the three categories of signs in the three regimes of functioning requires a middle term likely to make us pass from the one set to the other. This middle term is constituted by the modalities of relation of signifier to signified. We name these modalities of the relation of the sign to its signified a code of reading of signs. Hobbes does not thematise this code under the form of a systematic theory, but we can draw it out from the passages where the modalities of the relationship of sign to signified are defined. We will be satisfied here with bringing out this code's three rules illustrated by some examples.

FIRST RULE: *Signs are either certain, conjectural, or insufficient*
Within the regime of inflation of signs (state of nature), the signs of power [*puissance*] are only conjectural or insufficient: 'Of these signs, some are such as cannot easily be counterfeited; as actions and gestures, especially if they be sudden; whereof I have mentioned some for example sake in the ninth chapter, at the several passions whereof they are signs; others there are that may be counterfeited: and those are words or speech.'[88] The natural signs of the passions are the best signs, without being for all that certain signs. On the other hand, arbitrary signs are always insufficient because they can be easily counterfeited.

Within the regime of self-regulation (civil state), there are certain, conjectural and insufficient signs. Certain signs are adequate and manifest instituted signs, and it is only by relation to them that probable signs (for example, the natural signs of the late sovereign's will concerning his succession) and insufficient signs (for example, a sign proceeding from an error of the sovereign is an insufficient sign of his will) are determined.

Within the regime of interpretation (kingdom of God), signs are certain only for those who receive supernatural revelation, but for others they are either conjectural (when there is a miracle and preaching of the official religion), or insufficient (when there is a miracle without preaching or vice-versa). Conjectural signs become certain only by the addition of political instituted signs.

SECOND RULE: *Signs are either direct or indirect.*
Within the regime of inflation, there are direct signs and indirect signs of power [*puissance*]. Direct signs of power [*puissance*] are those that signify the possession of a natural power [*puissance*] (physical beauty, force, eminence of intellectual and moral qualities) or instrumental (gifts and expenditures = direct signs of wealth; friends and servants = direct signs of power [*puissance*] over others; good fortune = direct sign of God's favour). Indirect signs are those that manifest consciousness or the opinion that we have of possessing a power [*puissance*], for example: 'to adventure upon great exploits and danger, as being a sign consequent of opinion of our own strength: and that opinion a sign of the strength itself'.[89] Indirect signs of power [*puissance*] are therefore signs of signs.

Within the regime of self-regulation, there are also direct signs and indirect signs of sovereign power [*pouvoir*]. Direct signs: those that signify the possession of political power [*pouvoir*] (that is to say, adequate and manifest signs). Indirect signs: all the attributes attached to the civil person of the sovereign and that distinguish him from the subjects (for example, the persons attached to his public service).

Within the regime of interpretation, supernatural signs are the direct signs of the kingdom of God over his particular people. On the other hand, the things set apart for divine service that we call holy or clean (in opposition to profane and common things), like the holy house – that is to say, the temple – or becoming holy – that is to say, tithes, sacrifices and offerings – are indirect signs of this kingdom.[90]

THIRD RULE: *Signs are either joined to the signified or separated from the signified.*
Within the regime of inflation of signs, the signs of power [*puissance*] that merge with this power [*puissance*] are joined to the signified. For example, victory is a sign joined to force, the large number of friends and servants is a sign joined to the power [*puissance*] that they

constitute for us. On the other hand, eloquence is separated from the science of which it, however, can be the sign.

Within the regime of self-regulation of signs, adequate and manifest signs are joined to the political power [*pouvoir*] that they express, as long as acts of hostility against subjects and the condemnation of the innocent are separated from the signified.

Within the regime of interpretation of signs, the vision revealed to the prophet is joined to the presence of God that it signifies, as long as the prophet, who consists in speaking in the name of God, is disconnected from his signified.

We see that these three rules of the code of reading signs permit passing from taxonomy to regimes of functioning. It is only within the regime of political self-regulation that we find signs simultaneously certain, direct and joined to signifieds: the adequate and manifest signs of power [*pouvoir*].

Such are the principles of a semiological reading of Hobbes's ethico-political work.

## Notes

1. [TN: in English in the original.]
2. Hobbes, *Leviathan*, p. 150.
3. Hobbes, *The Elements of Law*, pp. 27–8.
4. [TN: in English in the original.]
5. Hobbes, *Leviathan*, p. 150.
6. Hobbes, *De Corpore*, in *Opera Philosophica*, vol. 1, p. 117; *Elements of Philosophy*, in *English Works*, ed. William Molesworth, vol. 1, pp. 131–2.
7. Hobbes, *The Elements of Law*, p. 34.
8. Ibid., p. 35.
9. Hobbes, *Leviathan*, p. 151.
10. Hobbes, *The Elements of Law*, p. 35.
11. Ibid. [TN: Zarka's emphasis.]
12. Hobbes, *Leviathan*, p. 150.
13. Ibid., pp. 255–6.
14. Ibid., p. 354.
15. Hobbes, *The Elements of Law*, p. 15.
16. See Hobbes, *Leviathan*, p. 98.
17. Hobbes, *The Elements of Law*, p. 16.
18. Hobbes, *Leviathan*, p. 172.
19. See Hobbes, *Man*, pp. 51–2; *De Homine*, p. 101.
20. René Descartes, *Treatise of Man*, trans. Thomas Steele Hall (Amherst,

NY: Prometheus Books, 2003), p. 106; in Œuvres de Descartes, vol. 11, ed. Charles Adams and Paul Tannery (Paris: Lépold Cerf, 1909), p. 194.
21. Gerauld de Cordemoy, Œuvres philosophiques, avec une étude bio-bibliographique, ed. Pierre Clair and François Girbal (Paris: PUF, 1968), pp. 207 and 209. [TN: to my knowledge, this book has never been translated into English.]
22. Hobbes, Leviathan, p. 400.
23. See Hobbes, The Elements of Law, p. 64; cf. also Geraud de Cordemoy, Discours physique de la parole, in Œuvres philosophiques, ed. Pierre Clair and François Girbal (Paris: PUF, 1968), p. 209.
24. Hobbes, The Elements of Law, p. 18.
25. [TN: in italics in English in the original.]
26. Hobbes, Leviathan, p. 101.
27. Hobbes, Man, p. 37; De Homine, p. 88.
28. Ibid., pp. 37–8; pp. 88–9.
29. [TN: in English in the original.]
30. Hobbes, Leviathan, pp. 93–4.
31. [TN: in English in the original.]
32. Hobbes, The Elements of Law, p. 23
33. Ibid.
34. Hobbes, Man, p. 38; De Homine, p. 89.
35. Hobbes, Leviathan, p. 101.
36. Ibid., p. 128.
37. Ibid., p. 318.
38. Ibid., p. 319.
39. Ibid.
40. Ibid., p. 312.
41. [TN: italicised English in English in the original.]
42. See Chapter 7, 'On Law'.
43. [TN: italicised English in English in the original.]
44. Hobbes, Leviathan, p. 320.
45. Ibid., p. 319.
46. Ibid., p. 158.
47. Ibid., p. 406.
48. Ibid., p. 396.
49. Ibid., p. 459.
50. Ibid., pp. 469–70.
51. Ibid., p. 414.
52. Ibid., p. 470.
53. Ibid.
54. Ibid., p. 459.
55. Ibid., p. 437.

56. Ibid., p. 476.
57. Ibid., p. 106.
58. Hobbes, *The Elements of Law*, p. 68.
59. Ibid.
60. Hobbes, *Leviathan*, p. 129.
61. Hobbes, *Man*, p. 41; *De Homine*, p. 92.
62. Ibid., pp. 39–40; p. 91
63. Hobbes, *Leviathan*, pp. 191–2.
64. Ibid., p. 197.
65. Ibid., p. 193.
66. Ibid., pp. 314–15.
67. Ibid., p. 415.
68. Ibid., p. 442.
69. Ibid., p. 109.
70. Ibid., p. 183.
71. Ibid., p. 189.
72. Ibid., p. 184.
73. Ibid., p. 161.
74. Ibid., p. 185.
75. Ibid., pp. 185–6.
76. Ibid., pp. 151–2.
77. Ibid., p. 152.
78. Hobbes, *The Elements of Law*, p. 35.
79. Ibid.
80. [TN: in English in the original.]
81. Hobbes, *Leviathan*, p. 277.
82. Ibid., p. 275.
83. Ibid., pp. 225–6.
84. Ibid., p. 100.
85. Ibid., pp. 249–50.
86. Ibid., p. 501.
87. Ibid., p. 450.
88. Hobbes, *The Elements of Law*, p. 64.
89. Ibid., p. 35.
90. Hobbes, *Leviathan*, pp. 449–50.

# Part III

# FUNDAMENTAL CONCEPTS OF POLITICS

We have just seen the considerable place that language and, more generally, the notion of sign occupy within Hobbes's ethico-political system. The examination of the re-elaboration of the fundamental concepts of politics is going to confirm it for us. The essential issue of this third part is to show how the reorienting, transformative and innovative work operated by Hobbes upon the concepts of war, law, property, state and penal right put into place the terms of a problematic which is going to become one of political thought's major currents up to the end of the eighteenth century. Naturally, this examination could be completed by the study of other concepts, but the concepts that we have retained have a structuring function around which the majority of others can be at least indirectly approached.

*Chapter 6*

# ON WAR

THE STATE OF NATURE: MISINTERPRETATION OR MODEL?

The specific contribution of Hobbes's philosophy for a thought of war stems from what it creates with the concept of the state of war and, for close to two centuries of political thought, a tradition that is simultaneously distinguished from the theologico-juridical tradition of just war and from the tactical and strategic tradition of the art of war. However, the historical repercussion of a concept cannot single-handedly guarantee semantic value. Better, we can legitimately ask ourselves if the Hobbesian concept of state of war does not cover a misinterpretation, both the specious character – 'there is no war between men: it is only between states'[1] – and the function of justification – 'Who could have imagined without shuddering the insane system of natural war of each against all? What a strange animal this is that would believe its own good depended upon the destruction of its entire species! . . . Nevertheless, that is where the desire or rather the rage for establishing despotism and passive obedience have led one of the finest geniuses that ever existed'[2] – of which Rousseau will vehemently denounce. Certainly, Rousseau does not reject the concept of state of war as such, but the form of a war of all against all that Hobbes gives to it. It is thus the pertinence and the originality of the Hobbesian concept that it is a question of re-establishing. For, on the one hand, if it is true that the state of war defines first of all the contentious relations between men in the state of nature, it constitutes above all a model for rendering account of every kind of war, interindividual war as much as international war and subversive war. On the other hand, the state of interindividual war is far from being reduced to a state of pure violence. The act of violence is always temporary, the state of war is permanent,

Hobbes says before Rousseau. Yet this distinction can be justified only because the dynamics of human behaviours within the state of nature is a dynamics of signs, and not only of force, or the act of violence: '*To kill his man*' itself appears as a sign.

## THE MODEL FOR THE STATE OF WAR AND THE THREE KINDS OF WAR

The problem of war is found at three levels in the œuvre. The first concerns interindividual relationships within the state of nature, which, as we know, characterise the condition of some men apart from the existence of a political power [*pouvoir*], that is to say, of a public power [*puissance*] invested with right, alone likely to guarantee interior peace and exterior defence. The state of nature does not correspond to a historical moment for humanity, but consists of a theoretical simulation of human behaviour, either when the state does not yet exist or when it is destroyed: 'Hereby it is manifest, that during the time men live without a common Power to keep them all in awe, they are in that condition which is called Warre; and such a warre, as is of every man, against every man.'[3] There, it is a question of a state of war and not of simple conflicts or temporary battles because 'WARRE, consisteth not in Battell onely, or the act of fighting; but in a tract of time, wherein the Will to contend by Battell is sufficiently known.'[4] War is thus a permanent state where the dynamics of interindividual relations leads to a showdown. This tendency recognised in confrontation supposes, on the one hand, the existence of an indefinite desire for power [*puissance*] and, on the other hand, the unlimited natural right of each over everything, including over others.

But we must be clear about this desire for power [*puissance*] and this natural right. For, first, if Hobbes makes much of the 'perpetuall and restlesse desire of Power after power, that ceaseth onely in Death',[5] the general inclination of all humanity, this desire has no innate tendency or natural aggressiveness. Contrary to what Rousseau says of it, this desire does not belong to the internal constitution of the individual. Indeed, the cause is not 'always that a man hopes for a more intensive delight, than he has already attained to; or that he cannot be content with a moderate power: but because he cannot assure the power and means to live well, which he hath present, without the acquisition of more'.[6] It is the dynamics of interindividual relationships, and not the internal constitution of the individual, that transforms, for security reasons, the desire to persevere in being into an indefinite desire for power [*puissance*] from which the three causes of war result: rivalry, distrust and glory. Second, natural right rationally justifies the desire for power [*puissance*], but only as far as it remains rooted in the desire to persevere in being.

There is a third determination of the state of interindividual war, the equality of the belligerents. From this equality results its contradictory character in fact and in right. In fact, because the natural equality of men, which is essentially an equality of maximal power [*puissance*], renders all victory precarious and all domination uncertain: the weakest man can always kill the strongest because of the fragility of the human body.[7] The equality of power [*puissance*] has for its correlate the equality of reciprocal fear and generalised insecurity. In right, because the equality of liberty or of natural right, which justifies each of the belligerents' desire for power [*puissance*] in the name of his desire to persevere in being, enters into contradiction with itself by leading to violent death. We subsequently understand that 'he therefore that desire to live in such an estate, as is the estate of liberty and right of all to all, contradicteth himself. For every man by natural necessity desireth his own good, to which this estate is contrary, wherein we suppose contention between men by nature equal, and able to destroy one another.'[8]

The state of interindividual war is thus defined by three properties of man's reciprocal relation: (A) the desire for indefinite accumulation of power [*puissance*]; (B) the natural right over all things; (C) the equality which renders it contradictory. We could thus retain these three properties – (A), (B) and (C) – that we will also find in the two other kinds of war as constitutive of the general model for the state of war.

The second inscription of the problem of war concerns international war. If Hobbes does not formulate a particular theory about this, it is that he presupposes that the relationships between states do not differ from the relationships between individuals in the state of nature. The state of international war is even taken as the best historical example of the state of interindividual war: 'But though there had never been any time, wherein particular men were in a condition of warre one against another; yet in all times, Kings, and Persons of Soveraigne authority, because of their Independency, are in continuall jealousies, and in the state and posture of Gladiators; having their weapons pointing, and their eyes fixed on one another; that is, their Forts, Garrisons, and Guns upon the Frontiers of their Kingdomes; and continuall Spyes upon their neighbours; which is a posture of War.'[9] Is there, for all that, a perfect identity of the two forms of state of war? Which of the three properties distinguished above are also applied to international war?

Property (A) finds an integral application in the logic of fact of the relation between states. Thus: 'Kings, whose power is greatest, turn their endeavours to the assuring it at home by Lawes, or abroad by Wars.'[10] The dynamics of states' accumulation of power [*puissance*] is animated by the same concern as that of particular individuals: security. States, like individuals, are moved by a desire to persevere in being. This desire presupposes that each state guard against the causes of internal destruction and external destruction. Compared with its own subjects, the state must enforce laws from a power [*puissance*] disproportionate to that of each of the subjects. Its simple conservation thus must be sufficient in principle, but in principle only, that is to say, provided that the rules that govern the political artifice to protect it against civil war be respected. However, this state is not alone; it faces other states. From this point of view, the power [*puissance*] it has is only relative. Its desire to persevere in being thus necessitates that it [the state] augment it [power] in order to protect itself. States thus enter in a logic of accumulation of power [*puissance*], that is to say of war, with the aim of 'rendering more sure' the power [*puissance*] that they already possess over their subjects. The accumulation being reciprocal, it is pursued indefinitely. The desire to persevere in being becomes indefinite desire for power [*puissance*] for states as for individuals, and for the same reasons.

Property (B) also finds an integral application in the state of international war: 'For as among masterlesse men, there is perpetuall war, of every man against his neighbour; no inheritance, to transmit to the Son, nor to expect from the Father; no propriety of Goods, or Lands; no Security; but a full and absolute Libertie in every Particular man: So in States, and Common-wealths not dependent on one another, every Common-wealth, (not every man) has an absolute Libertie, to doe what it shall judge . . . most conducing to their benefit. But withal, they live in the condition of a perpetuall war, and upon the confines of battel, with their frontiers armed, and canons planted against their neighbours round about.'[11] This full and absolute liberty available to states like individuals within the state of nature is none other than natural right. States enjoy a complete independence vis-à-vis each other; their right to persevere in being implies the right to the means of this perseverance, these last dependent on the sole judgement of the sovereign, this thus leads for each of them to an unlimited right over all things. States thus have available in their reciprocal relationships an unlimited natural right, here also for the same reasons as individuals in the state of nature.

On the other hand, property (C) is not applied to the state of international war. There is no principle of natural equality of maximal power between states. Whatever the fragility of political bodies may be, we cannot say that the weakest can destroy the strongest because we cannot destroy a state like we kill a man, even the sovereign of a monarchy. Indeed, if within a monarchy (this is again more evident in states where political power [*pouvoir*] is held by a council) the natural person of the sovereign bears the juridical artificial person of the state. It is however impossible to identify them. Thus, it is only accidentally that the natural death or the violent death of the sovereign can bring about the destruction of the state. The cause of this destruction is not the death of the natural person of the sovereign, but the impossibility or the absence of application of the juridical procedures which must assure the succession of power [*pouvoir*]. In the same sense, when the sovereign of a state is held captive by another state, this does not *ipso facto* bring about the loss of sovereignty and the destruction of the state. Indeed, the sovereign is captive as natural person and not as public person. However, if the capacity of the political institution to protect the subjects is added to this captivity, or if the sovereign, without being captive himself, renounces sovereignty in submitting to the victor, then the state is dissolved: 'If a Monarch subdued by war, render himself Subject to the Victor; his Subjects are delivered from their former obligation, and become obliged to the Victor. But if he be held prisoner, or have not the liberty of his own Body; he is not understood to have given away the Right of Soveraigntie; and therefore his Subjects are obliged to yield obedience to the Magistrates formerly placed, governing not in their own name, but in his.'[12]

Additionally, the state of international war does not have the same consequences as the state of interindividual war. First, when it is not yet a question of victor and vanquished, each state protects the industrious activity of its subjects; the state of international war does not imply miserable existence for individuals. Next, when one state is conquered by another, the death of the first does not bring about the death of the individuals who make it up, but the substitution of one subjection for another. This substitution is equally valid for the captive soldier whose life the victorious state will spare. The state is an artificial being whose desire to persevere in being is not an end in itself, but is subordinated, as means, to the individuals' desire to persevere in being. We thus understand why the state of international war does not enter into contradiction with itself. This state of war thus does not necessitate the institution, moreover perfectly inconceivable in Hobbes's system, of an international state. For property (C) must thus be substituted, in the case of international war, property (C'): no natural equality and no contradiction.

The third inscription of the problem of war concerns the relation of the sovereign to the rebel. The rebel is a subject who deliberately refuses the authority of the established republic. His offence does not fall under the jurisdiction of penal law, but of an act of hostility. Thus, the evil inflicted upon the subjects who have broken their allegiance comes under the right of war because, in challenging their subjection, they also challenge the penalty provided by the law, and suffer as enemy of the republic 'because the nature of this offence, consisteth in the renouncing of subjection; which is a relapse into the condition of warre, commonly called Rebellion; and they that so offend, suffer not as Subjects, but as Enemies. For *Rebellion*, is but warre renewed.'[13] What are those relational properties that justify the application of the concept of state of war to the relation of the sovereign to the rebel?

Property (B) is applied without too many problems. Indeed, in renouncing his subjection, the rebel is himself excluded from the state: they mutually become enemies, and each of them again finds his natural right unlimited. Thus, 'all men that are not Subjects, are either Enemies, or else they have ceased from being so, by some precedent covenants. But against Enemies, whom the Common-wealth judgeth capable to do them hurt, it is lawfull by the originall Right of Nature to make warre.'[14] On the other hand, the application of property (A) seems to present more difficulties. How can the state and the rebel, who belong to two different orders of reality, enter into a relational dynamics of accumulation of power [*puissance*]? On the side of the rebel, first of all, we can conceive a process of accumulation, to the extent that the rebellion is always a beginning for subversion the stakes of which is the capture of power [*pouvoir*]. On the other hand, on the side of the state, the destruction of the rebel does not seem to constitute a direct means for increasing its power [*puissance*], but only for conserving what it already possesses. However, because the example of the kind reserved for the rebel is apt to incite other subjects to not follow the same path, and to redouble obedience, we can also conceive that the repression of rebellion is an indirect, although not indefinite, means for increasing the state's power [*puissance*]. Finally, property (C) cannot be applied, on account of the absence of every species of equality between the belligerents. The state's power [*puissance*] is, in principle, disproportionate in relation to that of the rebel(s). But, for all that, it does not follow that property (C') is suitable, since not only can the rebel not reasonably hope to take it, but, additionally, his defeat brings about his death. The third kind of war is thus contradictory, but only on the rebel's side: 'And for the other Instance of attaining Sovereignty by Rebellion; it is manifest, that though the event follow, yet because it cannot reasonably be expected, but rather the contrary; and because by gaining it so, others are taught to gain the same in like manner, the attempt thereof is against reason.'[15] For property (C) and for property (C') must thus be substituted property (C'') in the case of the third kind of war: no natural equality, contradiction only on the side of the rebel.

We can thus say that the two properties (A) and (B) define the general model for the state of war, while properties (C), (C') and (C'') signify interindividual war, international war and subversive war, respectively.

Although the Hobbesian distinction of the three kinds of war recalls the classification that Grotius gives in chapter 3 of the first book of *De jure belli ac pacis*, in distinguishing private war, public war and mixed war, Hobbes's perspective is very different. Indeed, for the latter, it is impossible to define the conditions of a just war or those of an unjust war. At whatever level it is situated, war falls short of the just and the unjust. The use of the notion of natural right changes nothing in the matter, since this right in the state of war is ultimately up to the simple exercise of power [*puissance*], that is to say, to fact. It follows for our model for the state of war that property (B) will be reduced to property (A). Natural right rationally doubles the desire for accumulation of power [*puissance*] and is contradicted when the desire is contradicted, that is to say, when the desire for power [*puissance*] contradicts the desire to persevere in being which was at its origin. Consequently, in order that there be state of war, it is necessary and it suffices that some other elements (individual or state) reciprocally enter into a relational

## THE POSSIBILITY OF WAR AND THE THREE CAUSES OF WAR

Why is man a being capable of war? Hobbes himself asks this question: 'Why therefore may not men, that foresee the benefit of concord, continually maintain the same without compulsion, as well as they?'[16] Why is man a wolf to man?

The response is nearly identical in *The Elements of Law, De Cive* and *Leviathan*: (1) Because there is a rivalry between men regarding honour and dignity, which created envy, hatred and war. (2) Because, unlike the animal, for which private good does not differ from common good, man compares himself with others, and 'can relish nothing but what is eminent'.[17] Whence it follows that he seeks others' superiority and domination. (3) Because men judge themselves each one wiser than the others, and more fit to govern the *res publica*. (4) Because man has at his disposal 'the art of words, by which some men can represent to others, that which is Good, in the likeness of Evill; and Evill, in the likenesse of Good; and augment, or diminish the apparent greatnesse of Good and Evill; discontenting men, and troubling their Peace at their pleasure'.[18] These first four fundamental reasons are completed by two others which derive from them: the capacity of man to distinguish a wrong from an injury, and the artificial character of the political bond, opposed to the natural character of animal concord.

Now the first three reasons correspond to the three causes of war: rivalry, mistrust and glory. On the other hand, the fourth reason can appear strange: what relation can speech have with war? This relation is fundamental, not so much because speech would be itself one cause of war among others, but because it makes it possible to take account of this essential ambivalence of human existence which makes of man a being capable simultaneously of war and of civil peace.

Indeed, if the animal can make a natural use of the voice in order to express its affections and its present desires, it lacks the capacity to utilise and to understand arbitrary signs, that in which speech is properly comprised. Yet speech is precisely what gets man out of the immediacy of affections and present circumstances, in facilitating memory, and what allows him to communicate to others not only his affections, but also his thought, his questioning, to formulate promises and orders. Without it being necessary to enter here into an examination of the origin and of the effects of speech, we will note that this is fundamentally ambivalent.

Speech is the best and the worst of things. The best: 'the most noble and profitable invention of all other, was that of SPEECH, consisting of *Names* or *Appellations*, and their Connexion; whereby men register their Thoughts; recall them when they are past; and also declare them one to another for mutuall utility and conversation; without which, there had been amongst men, neither Common-wealth, nor Society, nor Contract, nor Peace, no more than amongst Lyons, Bears, and Wolves'.[19] The worst: 'when they use them to grieve one another: for seeing nature hath armed living creatures, some with teeth, some with horns, and some with hands, to grieve an enemy, it is but an abuse of Speech, to grieve him with the tongue'.[20] But the abuse of speech, far from being only accidental, is the other face of use: just as speech has the considerable advantage of permitting man to institute civil peace by a verbal performance, likewise this is what makes of him a being capable of error, lie, discord and, finally, war. Speech is a double-edged sword. Place of contraries: of truth and error, of meaning and nonsense, of avowal and misrepresentation, of fair play and foul, speech puts each man in the anxious uncertainty of the real designs of others. Because his relation to thought is arbitrary, because it is always possible to say a thing other than what we think, and to verbally give to an evil the appearance of a good, speech, as we have seen, inaugurates within interhuman relationships the dimension of a comedy which is going to turn into tragedy. Within the state of nature, where each individual has no other concern than the preservation of his existence, and where he is sole judge of the proper means to assure it, each one finds himself in relation to the other in the situation of a cheat who knows only his own interest. Each one will have to decipher the intentions of the other through his concealments and his feints. That words would be 'wise mens counters' and 'the mony of fooles'[21] not only concerns knowledge: 'by speech man is not made better, but only given greater possibilities'.[22]

If speech takes account of the possibility of controversy and of disagreement, the three causes of war allow for defining the object.

The first is rivalry: 'if any two men desire the same thing, which neverthelesse they cannot both enjoy, they become enemies; and in the way to their End, (which is principally their owne conservation, and sometimes the delectation onely,) endeavour to destroy, or subdue one an other'.[23] The first cause of war is economic. We can legitimately think that this mutual desire for an identical thing, the enjoyment of which cannot be shared, presupposes scarcity [*rareté*]. Supposing that nature would be miserly in useful goods or in things necessary to the conservation of life, we then understand that the desire to persevere in being could bring each man to attack the other who has it in possession, or to defend those that he himself possesses. Additionally, this scarcity seems confirmed by the precariousness of human work in a time where its products can at any moment be usurped. But the scarcity of goods and the economic war that results from it cannot take account of the state of war's universality and the permanence. Scarcity gives rise to a war of need, not of desire; it can explain a local rivalry, not a universal rivalry; it can provoke a temporary conflict, which lasts as long as hunger or thirst and which passes once the satisfaction obtained, not a perpetual conflict, whereby 'the invader again is in the like danger of another'.[24] Additionally, if scarcity was the state of war's sole principle, this would suppose that the hypothesis of an abundance of goods would do away with rivalry. Yet it is exactly the reverse that occurs, for, as opposed to beasts, which do not feel offended by their companions as long as they enjoy their pleasures, 'Man is then most troublesome, when he is most at ease.'[25] The Latin version of this same passage of *Leviathan* clarifies: '*Homo autem tunc maxime molestus est, quando otio opibusque maxime abundat.*'[26] Scarcity alone thus cannot take account of the permanent will to mutually harm; economic war is not enough for the state of war.

This is why the first cause of war is completed by a second: mistrust. '[F]rom this diffidence of one another, there is no way for any man to secure himselfe, so reasonable, as Anticipation; that is, by force, or wiles, to master the persons of all men he can, so long, till he see no other power great enough to endanger him: And this is no more than his own conservation requireth, and is generally allowed.'[27] The second cause of war gives place to an offensive war of prevention, which applies violence and cunning and which concerns security. In one sense, mistrust – opinion according to which a man is not truthful – follows from rivalry over useful goods or things necessary to the conservation of life. Each one, seeing in the other an aggressor, anticipates this real or imaginary aggression in order to master the potential adversary. Let us note that the best means to assure one's own security is not to destroy the other but 'to make themselves Masters' of him [the other].²⁸ The desire to persevere in being becomes desire for domination. But this domination cannot be satisfied from a single victory. As soon as it begins, it is necessary that it expand and expand again, until this, that the growth of our own power [*puissance*], to which those whom we dominate contribute, shelters us from danger, that is to say, no longer encounters obstacles. In principle, there is a limit; in fact, this limit does not exist. There will always be an obstacle, there will always be danger, whether it comes from our enemies, our servants or our friends. Whoever lent me a hand today can turn against me tomorrow. It is thus necessary that I always continue to increase my power [*puissance*] to 'master the persons of all men he can'. This is not madness but necessity, at least as long as the motive is the conservation of oneself. And if this is necessary, then it is permitted; we have the liberty or the right to it.

In another sense, mistrust reveals the truth of rivalry, for if this was first of all about a thing immediately useful to the conservation of life, its issue henceforth is of another order: power [*puissance*] over others. And rivalry over power [*puissance*] gives rise to a war of desire. Certainly, the desire for power [*puissance*] still remains rooted in the desire to persevere in being, since it is a question of assuring its security. Power [*puissance*] over others is not straightaway sought in itself, but only as a useful means or an instrument. Only the course to domination procures pleasure for itself, so much pleasure that certain men forget the first object of rivalry: the thing necessary to the conservation of self, and taking 'pleasure in contemplating their own power in the acts of conquest, which they pursue farther than their security requires'.²⁹ The pleasure of power [*puissance*] carries the desire for domination to expand to the entire world. The place of rivalry having thus changed, the useful good is henceforth almost forgotten, in favour of the pleasure of power [*puissance*]. The state of war is universal because all men are brought to desire an identical thing that all are not able to have. Pascal understood this: 'for there must be different degrees, all men wishing to rule, and not all being able to do so, but some being able'.³⁰ The third cause of war is going to assure the reproduction of the state of universalised war.

This third cause of war is glory: 'every man looketh that his companion should value him, at the same rate he sets upon himself: And upon all signes of contempt, or undervaluing, naturally endeavours, as far as he dares ... to extort a greater value from his contemners, by dommage; and from others, by the example'.[31] Glory is a reflexive passion; it is a specification of joy in the relation to others. It consists in that exultation of the mind that provokes the image of our power [*puissance*]. Glory is thus the pleasure of power [*puissance*]. Yet the first chapter of *De Cive* showed at length that glory cannot be shared by all men. One's glory necessarily has for its correlate the other's unhappiness. But, at the same time, glory demands, in order to be real, that our power [*puissance*] be recognised by others, without which it would be only empty glory. And so men seek to obtain this recognition by wars of prestige 'for trifles, as a word, a smile, a different opinion, and any other signe of undervalue'.[32] The glory that is first a subjective effect, becomes the specific cause of a war that relates to anything, and that assures the state of war's permanence.

The state of war thus very much resulting from a relational dynamics that transforms the desire to persevere in being into indefinite desire for accumulation of power [*puissance*], it remains to be shown that this accumulation is essentially thought in terms of signs, the ordeal of force itself having a function of sign.

## THE LOGIC OF WAR

A man's power [*puissance*] 'is his present means, to obtain some future apparent Good.'[33] Thus defined, human power [*puissance*] can be considered, as we have seen in the preceding chapter, under two relations: in its use-value and in its exchange-value. Under the first relation, each individual puts his natural faculties and his instrumental means to work with the aim of acquiring some things necessary to his being. The use-value of power [*puissance*] is then measured by the quantity of goods that it procures in order to assure the reproduction of a man's existence, not only in the present, but also, and above, all in the future. Considered under the second relation, a man's power [*puissance*] becomes this time a means for obtaining power [*puissance*] over others. The determination of its value in exchange thus depends on its relation to the power [*puissance*] of others: 'And because the power of one man resisteth and hindereth the effects of the power of another: power simply is no more, but the excess of the power of one above that of another.'[34] Power [*puissance*] consists henceforth only in the excess of power [*puissance*], this is why power [*puissance*] must be eminent. The manifestation of this excess or of this eminence of our natural or instrumental faculties is the sign of our superiority over others. Power [*puissance*] thus resides in the signifying excess: 'The signs by which we know our own power are those actions which proceed from the same; and the signs by which other men know it, are such actions, gesture, countenance and speech, as usually such powers produce.'[35] In inter-human relationships, relations of power [*puissance*] are necessarily mediated by signs not only because signs render our power [*puissance*] visible, but also because signs permit the reproduction and growth of power [*puissance*]. Because its value depends on the opinion and on the need of others, a man's power [*puissance*] exists only if it is manifest or is exposed to the eyes by the speeches, acts, gestures or behaviours which are its signs. The other expresses in its turn that it recognises our excess or our lack of power [*puissance*] by other speeches, acts and gestures which are signs of recognition or of contempt.

The accumulation of power [*puissance*] implies a strategy of communication. Such is the status of the dialectic of signs of worthiness and signs of honour. Two rivals are in competition: the one manifests, by relation to the other, signs of an excess of natural power [*puissance*] of body (beauty, force, etc.) or of mind (eloquence, persuasion, gravity, authority, etc.); or, again, signs of an excess of instrumental power [*puissance*] (wealth, friends, reputation, luck). A third party regards them: the signs of worthiness are those by which he recognises in the one an excess of power [*puissance*] over the other. This third himself produces signs with regard to each of the rivals: to the first, signs of honour (giving way to, exalting, imploring, listening to advice, etc.); to the other, dishonourable signs (passing ahead of, mocking or taking pity on, not listening while he speaks, etc.). Why the third? Because rivalry is universal and because any third party is always, directly or indirectly, engaged in every temporary competition which seems firstly to concern others than him. The third party's point of view is that of the universality of the state of war.

We see at such point the state of war distinguishing itself from a state of pure exercise of force or of overt violence which would render it on the contrary unthinkable. This does not mean that violence is absent from it, but that it itself [violence] intervenes only as sign: 'actions proceeding from strength of body and open force, are honourable, as signs consequent of power motive, such as are victory in battle or duel; *et à avoir tué son homme'*.³⁶ Thus, do not confuse power [*puissance*] (*power, potentia*) with force (*strength*),³⁷ which is only one of many forms, and the manifestation of which by a physical effect is at the same time sign for a third.

We can draw three consequences: first, the state of war is a theatre – in the double sense of place where spectacles are given and of the place of military operations – where all speech, every gesture, every attitude falls less under the jurisdiction of direct function of use than an indirect function of spectacle. Second, the growth of power [*puissance*] is an accumulation of signs, and not of objects; or at least an object can enter there only as a sign. Man does not spontaneously desire power [*puissance*]. He desires it only because others, really or imaginarily, desire it. Men's desires imitate each other. It is that imitation that brings them towards the same thing. It is also what renders them indefinite. Third, rivalry is not straightaway desire for the other's destruction, but, on the contrary, desire to dominate him. War is cunning before being violence. The desire for domination begins by trying to make of the other a friend or a servant. This is why war begins by seduction and gives place to violence only when seduction fails.

The true stakes for the *libido dominandi* unveils the motivation for war: each of the belligerents 'naturally endeavours, as far as he dares . . . to extort a greater value'.³⁸ The desire for domination of rivals is shared by a desire for recognition. But this desire is contradictory because it is at the same time refusal of recognition: the one desires to be recognised as superior by the other, and reciprocally, but both are at the same time unaware of the resemblance of their reciprocal desire for superiority. Without being conscious of it, they install themselves as equals in the same moment when they are mutually affirmed unequals. This contradiction penetrates the individual and shakes his existence, henceforth separated between the fear of death and the desire for glory. But glory lives down fear; it leads men to put their life in peril for trifles. Thus, glory introduces irrationality in the human desire to persevere in being, in making it risk this being for 'a word, a smile, a different opinion'.³⁹ War is not in itself irrational. Quite to the contrary, it is rational as long as it is rooted in the desire to persevere in being, as when it relates to a good necessary to the conservation of the self or when it leads to taking the offensive for the safeguarding of the self. On the other hand, it becomes irrational when we seek victory only for the pleasure that it procures, that is to say, for glory.

# On War

The state of interindividual war is contradictory. This is why it demands to be overcome by the institution of a political order, which is essentially a juridical order. The state's existence, in giving univocal norms to communication, has the function of preventing the exchange of signs from turning into war. Peace does away with neither disagreement nor controversy. It only permits solving conflict by law and not by acts of private violence. The passage from war to peace makes the law a central question.

## Notes

1. Jean-Jacques Rousseau, 'Que l'état de guerre naît de l'état social', in *Œuvres complètes de Jean-Jacques Rousseau*, vol. 3, ed. Bernard Gagnebin and Marcel Raymond (Paris: Éditions Gallimard, 1964), p. 604. [TN: my translation.]
2. Rousseau, 'The state of war', pp. 62–3; 'Que l'état de guerre', p. 611.
3. Hobbes, *Leviathan*, p. 185; cf. Thomas Hobbes, *De Cive: The English Version*, in *The Clarendon Edition of the Philosophical Works of Thomas Hobbes*, vol. 3, ed. Howard Warrender (Oxford: Clarendon Press, 2002), pp. 49–50; *De Cive*, in *Opera Philosophica*, vol. 2, p. 166; *The Elements of Law*, pp. 72–3.
4. Hobbes, *Leviathan*, p. 185.
5. Ibid., p. 161.
6. Ibid.
7. Cf. Hobbes, *De Cive: The English Version*, pp. 45–6; *De Cive*, p. 162.
8. Hobbes, *The Elements of Law*, p. 73.
9. Hobbes, *Leviathan*, pp. 187–8.
10. Ibid., p. 161.
11. Ibid., p. 266.
12. Ibid., pp. 273–4.
13. Ibid., pp. 360–1.
14. Ibid., p. 360.
15. Ibid., p. 205.
16. Hobbes, *The Elements of Law*, p. 102; see also Hobbes, *De Cive: The English Version*, pp. 93–4; *De Cive*, pp. 211–13; *Leviathan*, pp. 225–7.
17. Hobbes, *Leviathan*, p. 226.
18. Ibid.
19. Ibid., p. 100; see also Hobbes, *The Elements of Law*, pp. 17–18; *Man*, pp. 39–40; *De Homine*, pp. 90–1.
20. Hobbes, *Leviathan*, p. 102.
21. [TN: Ibid., p. 106.]
22. Hobbes, *Man*, p. 41; *De Homine*, p. 92.

23. Hobbes, *Leviathan*, p. 184.
24. Ibid.
25. Ibid., p. 226.
26. [TN: Hobbes, *Leviathan*, in *Opera Philosophica*, p. 130. My translation: 'Man is then most troublesome when leisure and wealth most abounds.']
27. Hobbes, *Leviathan*, p. 184.
28. [TN: Ibid., p. 185.]
29. Ibid., pp. 184–5.
30. Pascal, *Pensées*, fr. 828/304.
31. Hobbes, *Leviathan*, p. 185.
32. Ibid.
33. Ibid., p. 150. Human power [*puissance*] is either natural or instrumental. Under its first form, it is constituted by the faculties of the body or the mind, like force, beauty, prudence, eloquence, etc.; under its second form, it is constituted by the exterior elements of the individual, like wealth, friends, reputation and luck.
34. Hobbes, *The Elements of Law*, p. 34.
35. Ibid.
36. Ibid., p. 35. The expression emphasised by Hobbes is in French in the text.
37. [TN: Italicised English in English in the original.]
38. Hobbes, *Leviathan*, p. 185.
39. Ibid.

*Chapter 7*

# ON LAW

Law, properly, is *the word* of him, that by right hath command over others.[1]

Hobbes, *Leviathan*, ch. 15

Lex est *mandatum ejus personae, sive hominis sive curiae, cujus praeceptum continet obedientiae rationem.*

*De Homine*, ch. 14, 1

## THE LAW IN GENERAL AND ITS SPECIFICATIONS

'Law, properly, is the word of him, that by right hath command over others.'[2] Such is the unified concept that Hobbes gives of the law in general.[3] The difference between laws, in particular the difference between natural law and civil law, derives from the specification of the term left undetermined in the general definition. In order to pass from this definition to particular laws, it is in fact sufficient to specify the name of the legislator. Thus, natural law is characterised as 'the word of God, that by right commandeth all things',[4] and civil law considered as adding nothing to the general concept of the law other than 'the name of the person Commanding, which is *Persona Civitatis*, the Person of the Common-wealth'.[5] *The Elements of Law* already indicated it – 'From the difference of the authors, or lawmakers, cometh the division of law into divine, natural, and civil'[6] – before recalling in the following paragraph that natural law and divine law are a single law.

The definition of the law in general is composed of two principal determinations: on the one hand, the notion of a right to command which belongs to a legislator; on the other hand, the indication of a mode of signifying. To these two general determinations is added a third, the specification of the legislator, who intervenes in order to specify the kind of law.

First, in the definition of the law, the notion of command is fundamental. It is what assures the unity of the concept but also its limitation. The law returns to a relation of obligation between persons. It is thus neither, in an old sense, a principle of action that immanently governs beings,[7] nor, in a modern sense, a necessary relation between phenomena.[8] As command, the law is indeed the declaration of one person's will to another who must obey him. In order to become aware of this, it is necessary to throw out imperative locutions like *Do this* or *Do not do this*, which can express a command as well as a counsel, and to wonder 'who it is that speaketh, and to whom the Speech is directed, and upon what occasion'.[9] The passing of the linguistic dimension indeed allows for understanding, on the one hand, that there is command only if 'the party is obliged to do, or forbeare',[10] and, on the other hand, that this interlocutor 'without expecting other reason than the Will of him that sayes it'.[11] The law thus always supposes a relation of obligation, while counsel is indifferent to it and the promise does not suppose it but creates it.[12] Thus conceived, the law necessarily includes reference to the legislator. It drives, beyond its matter and its form, to its source: the legislator who founds it in its form and its matter. Generally, the legislator (divine or human) founds the law and transcends it. Such and such utterance acquires the character of a law only as expression of his will. Better, the kind of law is, as we saw, relative to the status of the legislator.

Second, the definition of the law involves a mode of signifying: 'Law, properly, is the word of him, that by right hath command over others.' The law of nature is thus *the word of God*,[13] and civil laws 'are to be signified by sufficient Signs; because a man knows not otherwise how to obey them'.[14] The mode of signifying does not come under an exterior consideration. It is internally bound to the question of knowing what the law says: *quid ipsa lex dicat*.[15] Without knowing it, we would not know to whom we are obliged. The mode of signifying is thus implicated in the essence of the law: 'To rule by Words, requires that such Words be manifestly made known; for they are no Lawes: For to the nature of Lawes belongeth a sufficient, and clear Promulgation, such as may take away the excuse of Ignorance.'[16]

As Hobbes indicates at the beginning of the chapter on God's prophetic speech, the term *word* and its corresponding Latin *verbum*, utilised in the expressions *word of man* and *verbum hominis*, *word of God* and *verbum Dei*, have the meaning of *speech* or of *sermo* and not that of *vocabulum*.[17] In other words, they do not designate, as in grammar, a part of the discourse isolated from the relationship to others which renders it significative as a noun, a verb or an isolated word, but a complete discourse or speech, '*a perfect speech or discourse*'.[18] The law is thus a discourse, a speech or an utterance, '*speech, discourse, or saying*', by which he who speaks orders something to someone.[19]

Third, the specification of the legislator allows for differentiating (if we start from God's prophetic speech, that is to say, the positive divine laws) natural law from civil law. On the one side, the irresistible and eternal power [*puissance*] of God founds the immutability and universality of the laws of nature. On the other, the artificial will of the sovereign, as power [*pouvoir*] to make and to break the law, simultaneously assures the existence of civil laws and the possibility of their change. The difference between natural law and civil law proceeds, in this sense, from the difference between the will of the eternal God and the will of the mortal god.

Additionally, the specification of the legislator makes it possible to specify the two general determinations of the law, namely, the foundation of the right to command and the mode of signifying. On the side of God, the foundation of the right to command resides in 'The Right of Nature, whereby God reigneth over men, and punisheth those that break his Lawes',[20] and its mode of signifying is its natural speech. On the side of the civil legislator, the foundation of the right to command resides in the social contract that institutes it, and its mode of signifying consists in a promulgation that, in principle, can take several forms: it can be exercised orally, in writing or by some other adequate sign of his will, '*by Word, Writing, or other sufficient Sign* [in Latin *signum idoneum*] *of the will*'.[21] Thus, *The Elements of Law*, after having distinguished the laws following the legislator, introduces a second distinction which stems from the mode of promulgation: 'From the difference of promulgation, proceedeth the division of laws into written and unwritten.'[22]

Yet the divine foundation of the natural law and the political foundation of the civil law raise some difficulties. On the side of natural law, we in fact know that this has a double character, in the sense where its content can be held either for a simple conclusion to a simple theorem of reason or for a command of God. It is in the second case that it receives the status of law properly said. Better, considered as a precept of reason, natural law is experienced along the mode of an internal obligation or of conscience, all the force of which resides in the reasons that lead there.[23] Commentators have dedicated a considerable number of pages to this problem: does the foundation of obligation reside in human reason alone or in the command of God?[24] On the side of civil law, we know that Hobbes revises his theory of the social contract in order to assure a valid juridical foundation to the right to command for the sovereign legislator.[25] We are not here counting these questions first, but displacing interest at the level of the mode of signifying. First, if, as divine command, the natural law is signified by God's immediately present speech in man as simple theorem of reason, it refers to the exercise of human speech, and that along a mode entirely other than that of command. Natural law appears here at the flexion of two speeches: man's speech and God's speech. On the other hand, if the political mode of signifying civil laws always consists in a promulgation, the theory of promulgation is subjected to an absolutely significant evolution from *De Cive* to *Leviathan*. Suffice it to say for now that this evolution concerns the status of writing. While this is assigned a subordinate function in *De Cive*'s theory of civil laws, it acquires a preponderant place in *Leviathan*'s theory of the promulgation, authentication and interpretation of the laws.

In other words, approached by the study of natural law and civil law, the relation between language and politics is the reverse of that which prevails from the point of view of the social contract. If the social contract, in its dual status of event and of structure, makes the state the product of an express or a tacit speech-act, on the other hand, the examination of the status of natural law and of civil law seems to make the state the condition for an event within language, the appearance of a writing of power [*pouvoir*]. The institution by the state of a code of positive rules requires a juridico-political writing of power [*pouvoir*]. In order to try to show it we will take up three points: first, the natural law: man's speech and God's speech; then, civil law and the writing of power [*pouvoir*]; finally, the interpretation of the law: the letter and the meaning of the law.

## THE NATURAL LAW: MAN'S SPEECH AND GOD'S SPEECH

Hobbes approaches the treatment of natural law from two points of view: ethical and theological. What characterises the ethical point of view is that natural law is considered there, at least provisionally, without reference to the will or to God's speech. Thus, in chapters 15–17 of *The Elements of Law*, 2 and 3 of *De Cive*, and 14 and 15 of *Leviathan*, natural law is related only to man. In its ethical definition, natural law is thus not strictly speaking a law, that is to say, a command, but, as Hobbes says, a theorem, a conclusion or a precept of reason concerning action and which man can attain by a true reasoning on what favours his preservation. The reference to the legislator thus suspended, natural law is thus related to human reason,[26] to *recta ratio*, that is to say, ultimately to the rational use of speech.

> A LAW OF NATURE, (*Lex Naturalis,*) is a Precept, or generall Rule, found out by Reason, by which a man is forbidden to do, that, which is destructive of his life, or taketh away the means of preserving the same; and to omit, that, by which he thinketh it may be best preserved.[27]

Without pretending to give an exhaustive explanation of this definition, I will mention two points:

1. Natural law is what dictates to us the reason concerning what we have to do or to neglect to do in order to assure our conservation. Yet what dictates reason is nothing other than a conclusion drawn from a reason founded on true principles.[28] Consequently, on the one hand, natural law draws its force from the only reasons which lead there. Each feels compelled to desire that the law of nature take effect, independently of the reference to a divine command. On the other hand, it has meaning and value only for a being of reason, that is to say, in virtue of what specifies human nature and distinguishes it from the animals. 'Reason is not less of the nature of man than passion, and is the same in all men, because all men agree in the will to be directed and governed in the way to that which they desire to attain, namely their own good, which is the work of reason. There can therefore be no other law of nature than reason, nor no other precepts of NATURAL LAW, than those which declare unto us the ways of peace.'[29] Natural law, as it leads to man's proper good, is also 'the work of reason'.[30]

2. Natural law is fundamentally distinguished from natural right, which is defined by liberty. 'Law, and Right, differ as much, as Obligation, and Liberty; which in one and the same matter are inconsistent.'[31] We thus understand that natural right and natural law can

form the two branches of a rational alternative which is presented to each man: *'That every man, ought to endeavour Peace, as farre as he has hope of obtaining it; and when he cannot obtain it, that he may seek, and use, all helps, and advantages of Warre.'*[32] This alternative between the first law of nature and the right over all things is an alternative between the unilateral perspective of the individual self which subtends the state of war and the required reciprocity as condition *sine qua non* for peace. From the point of view of the unilateralism of its self, each says in some way to itself: 'if it be against reason, that I be judge of mine own danger myself, then it is reason, that another man be judge thereof. But the same reason that maketh another man judge of those things that concern me, maketh me also judge of that that concerneth him. And therefore I have reason to judge of his sentence, whether it be for my benefit, or not.'[33] The right over all things rests, and we will return to this, on a soliloquy of the self. On the other hand, the unique content that the laws of nature merely specify are reduced to a demand of reciprocity: *'Do not that to another, which thou wouldest not have done to thy selfe.'*[34] This reciprocity rests on the principle of a commutativity of the self and of the other, condition of any agreement: *'That a man imagine himself in the place of the party with whom he hath to do, and reciprocally him in his.'*[35]

The two fundamental properties of natural law that we are going to draw out: (1) its character of precept for reason; (2) the demand for reciprocity that it includes, revealing the double relation that it maintains with human speech. In one sense, indeed, to the same extent that natural law is a conclusion of reason, discovered by a valid reasoning from true principles, it finds its condition in speech. Let us recall, if need be, the claim from *Leviathan*: 'Reason is not as Sense, and Memory, borne with us; nor gotten by Experience onely; as Prudence is; but attained by Industry; first in apt imposing of Names; and secondly by getting a good and orderly Method.'[36] There is no place to introduce difference between theoretical reason and practical reason. The precept of reason is clearly defined by Hobbes as a conclusion, a theorem or a general rule. Theoretical reason and practical reason are a single reason. A conclusion from theoretical reasoning becomes a practical precept when it concerns the desire to persevere in being. We do not see how man could discover without speech a general rule that neither sense nor simple experience, which he shares with animals, is sufficient to constitute. To the same extent that natural law imposes itself upon man as man, it has meaning and value only for man as being of speech.[37]

However, if there is no reason without speech, the reverse is not true: there can be a speech denuded of reason, an insane speech, a foolish speech [*une parole insensée, une parole d'insensé*]. In this sense, the precept of right reason that furnishes the condition for agreement with the demand for reciprocity, also furnishes, by the same demand for reciprocity, the condition of a shared meaning, reactivatable by two or several interlocutors. In other words, if the law of nature has meaning and value only for a being that speaks, it appears retroactively as the ethical norm without which communication cannot take place. It is the very demand for reciprocity that, on the one hand, opens the possibility of a life in common and, on the other hand, the possibility of a common language. Moreover, Hobbes himself transposes the demand for reciprocity inscribed within the law of nature to the level of speech: 'Forasmuch as whoever speaketh to another, intendeth thereby to make him understand what he saith; if he speak unto him, either in a language which he that heareth understandeth not, or use any word in other sense than he believeth is the sense of him that heareth; he intendeth also to make him not understand what he saith; which is a contradiction of himself. It is therefore always to be supposed, that he which intendeth not to deceive, alloweth the private interpretation of his speech to him to whom it is addressed.'[38] If each one makes of himself the unique interpretive authority of his own discourse, if discourse has only the private meaning that the speaker gives it, the exercise of speech contradicts the intention of communication which nevertheless presides over it. In order that speech escape from the contradiction of soliloquy, it is necessary that I make of the other a constitutive authority of my own discourse's meaning. Likewise, in order to get out of the state of war, it is necessary that I content myself with as much liberty as I concede to others. From one side as from the other, it is necessary that there be reciprocity.

It is thus in the same movement that man discovers natural law as moral norm for coexistence and as ethical regulating principle for interlocution. In the test of existential and linguistic contradiction, moral reciprocity is recognised as a universal and immutable demand for the establishment of a consensus and for a shared meaning.[39]

We can give two confirmations of this double function of the moral law. The first can be drawn from the moment where the social pact comes to pass. This moment is at the same time that of a reciprocity of will and of a reciprocity of speech. The second is brought to us by the analysis of the discourse of the fool [*insensé*][40] that Hobbes begins in treating of the natural law of justice: 'The Foole hath sayd in his heart, there is no such thing as Justice.'[41] The fool speaks, he claims first to himself in an interior soliloquy that there is no justice. If he stopped himself there, this would not be too serious. But if he stopped himself there, he would not be insane [*insensé*]. As he is insane, he does not stop himself there; he says it to others:

> sometimes also with his tongue; seriously alleaging, that every mans conservation, and contentment, being committed to his own care, there could be no reason, why every man might not do what he thought conduced thereunto: and therefore also to make, or not make; keep, or not keep Covenants, was not against Reason, when it conduced to ones benefit. He does not therein deny, that there be Covenants; and that they are sometimes broken, sometimes kept; and that such breach of them may be called Injustice, and the observance of them Justice: but he questioneth, whether Injustice, taking away the feare of God, (for the same Foole hath said in his heart there is no God,) may not sometimes stand with that Reason, which dictateth to every man his own good; and particularly then, when it conduceth to such a benefit, as shall put a man in a condition, to neglect not onely the dispraise, and revilings, but also the power of other men.[42]

This text alone would merit a long study. It is a question, if we can say so, of a public soliloquy of the self. The fool is the one who speaks in the name of reason against reason. He presupposes reciprocity and denies it at the same time. This fool is thrice insane. Once because what he says is contradictory. Twice because his claim [*son dire*] contradicts everything he says [*son dit*]; the statement [*énonciation*] contradicts the terms [*énoncé*]. Thrice because he needs cooperation from others and his remarks exclude him from all society, even from a society of bandits: 'He therefore that breaketh his Covenant, and consequently declareth that he thinks he may with reason do so, cannot be received into any Society, that unite themselves for Peace and Defence, but by the errour of them that receive him; nor when he is received, be retained in it, without seeing the danger of their errour.'[43] The fool can enter with others neither in a common language, nor in a common life or action. He is outside the common. The discourse of the fool is the negative of contractual [*contractuelle*] interlocution.[44]

This is not all, since the discourse of the fool has another interest. In order to become aware of it, it is sufficient to remark that the fool, who has said in his heart and to others that there is no injustice, has also said (as in Psalm 14), 'in his heart, *There is* no God'. The fool is, dare we say, going to the limit of his logic, or rather of his contradiction. In refusing the law of nature as precept of reason, he also rejects it as command of God. This is an atheist: he removes himself simultaneously from all human community and from the kingdom of God. The fool thus reveals, at least negatively, the correlation between the ethical definition and the theological definition of natural law.

In chapter 18 of *The Elements of Law* as in chapter 4 of *De Cive*, the law of nature is identified with divine law. From precept of reason that is imposed upon the being of speech, both as norm for coexistence and as regulating principle for interlocution, natural law becomes word of God. It becomes command signified by God's speech. If the law of nature is well situated at the flexion of man's speech and of God's speech, every question is henceforth of knowing what is the status of the God's speech and the relationship that is established between the precept of reason and divine command.

The identification of natural law with divine law is made, more or less in the same terms, in *The Elements of Law* and *De Cive*, with two exceptions, however: on the one hand, *De Cive* is more systematic; on the other hand, it is more peremptory as the title of chapter 4 indicates: '*Quod lex naturalis est lex divina*'. Then again, *The Elements of Law* proceeds to this either by way of explicit confirmation or by the negative way of non-invalidation. But in substance the approach of the two texts is similar: the identification of natural law with divine law is takes place by the mediation of Holy Scripture. Here is how Hobbes announces his approach in *The Elements of Law*:[45]

> The laws mentioned in the former chapters, as they are called the laws of nature, for that they are the dictates of natural reason; and also moral laws, because they concern men's manners and conversation one towards another; so are they also divine laws in respect of the author thereof, God Almighty; and ought therefore to agree, or at least, not to be repugnant to the word of

God revealed in Holy Scripture. In this chapter therefore I shall produce such places of Scripture as appear to be most consonant to the said laws.[46]

This text clearly indicates that the passage from the ethical point of view to the theological point of view takes place by the consideration of the author of natural laws. Natural law becomes divine law by scriptural confirmation. Holy Scripture thus tells us that God inscribes his law in the heart of men[47] and that the law is God's speech.[48] The law is thus God's speech 'wherein he governeth as many of Mankind as acknowledge his Providence, by the naturall Dictates of Right Reason'.[49] Scripture also attests that the search for peace and the principle of reciprocity are divine prescriptions.[50] The chapter closes the identification of natural law with divine law through the claim that it is God who 'hath given reason to a man to be a light unto him'.[51] We see that Hobbes carries the identification of natural law with divine law to its ultimate consequences. All that which seemed to proceed from man alone seems now to find its foundation and its source in God.

How to take account of the relation of the precept of reason to the command of God? It is quite necessary to recognise that the reference to the divine legislator is possible only by the intervention of a heterogeneous element in the deployment of the ethical doctrine: scriptural reference. This is without doubt the reason why *Leviathan* no longer immediately redirects the deduction of the laws of nature through a confirmation drawn from Holy Scripture, but postpones the latter to the end of the political theory. Additionally, the identification of the law of nature with divine law has as a goal, as a reading of *Behemoth* can attest, hindering those who, in the name of a private interpretation of Scripture and thus of a fallacious consideration of divine law, contradict the principle of reason that founds civil obligation. That means that the identification results from a principle essentially exterior to the body of the ethical doctrine. It remains that the internal obligation or conscience that binds us to the law of nature can be completely founded only as correlate of a command that, as it happens, can be imposed upon us as such neither by our own reason, nor by others, but by a being who transcends the series of reciprocal relationships between men, that is to say, by God. Moreover, in making the law of nature a divine command, Hobbes assures his normative character with regard to the civil legislator: 'For the civil law cannot make that to be done *jure*, which is against the law divine, or of nature.'[52]

We can thus pass to the examination of civil law which, we are going to see, maintains another relation to language.

## CIVIL LAW AND THE WRITING OF POWER [*POUVOIR*]

The mode by which God signifies natural laws is immediate, since we recognise them in the immanence of our reason. In this God's natural speech is distinguished from his prophetic speech which cannot be signified without signs. Natural laws keep, of course, the same status within the state, where they become civil laws without needing to be promulgated: 'if it be a Law that obliges only some condition of men, or one particular man, and be not written, nor published by word, then also it is a Law of Nature'.[53] This character fundamentally distinguishes the law of nature from the positive civil law, which is politically instituted 'by word, or writing, or some other act, known to proceed from the Sovereign Authority'.[54] The theory of positive civil laws thus demands a theory of the political mode of signifying the sovereign's will. We are going to see that Hobbes was progressively inclined to grant not an exclusive, but a leading place to writing. Let us first of all go back over the definition of civil law:

> CIVILL LAW, *Is to every Subject, those Rules, which the Common-wealth hath Commanded him, by Word, Writing, or other sufficient Sign of the Will, to make use of, for the Distinction of Right, and Wrong; that is to say, of what is contrary, and what is not contrary to the Rule.*[55]

Hobbes distinguishes four points in this definition of the law and deduces from it a certain number of conclusions. We will attempt to assemble the conclusions in the examination of the definition's four points.

1. Civil laws can be general or particular. They can be addressed to all the subjects, but also to such or such province, such or such profession, even to a particular individual. Unlike Rousseau, for Hobbes the sovereign will is not necessarily general.

2. Civil laws furnish the rules of the just and of the unjust. They thus define a civil and penal rule based on which each subject can distinguish what he has liberty to do from what is forbidden to him, what

belongs to him from what does not belong to him. These regulations of action and of property suppose a juridico-political definition only from terms like the just and the unjust, yours and mine.[56]

3. Only the republic can make civil laws. Whence Hobbes deduces, on the one hand, that the sovereign is the sole legislator since it is only by him that the republic has the capacity to do whatever it may, and, on the other hand, that the legislator is not submitted to civil laws. He has, in order to again take up an expression from Bodin, the power [*pouvoir*] 'of making and repealing law'.[57] In his *Exposé du droit naturel*, Bodin gives this definition of the law: the law 'is nothing other than being the highest power imposed or decreed. To impose is certainly to decree and to ordain.'[58] Between Bodin and Hobbes, there is Bacon who also makes the law depend on the sovereign in opposition to Coke, for whom the *Common Law*[59] is the supreme law of the kingdom.[60] It is on this principle that Bacon can develop, in *De Dignitate et augmentis scientiarum*,[61] a treatise on universal justice or the sources of right. The two major principles of this treatise will be taken up again by Hobbes in his definition of the good law: the first merit of laws, for Bacon as for Hobbes, is the certainty or the clarity, that is to say, the absence of equivocation, ambiguity or obscurity; the second merit of laws stems from this, that they must be necessary for the good of the people, that which implies the rejection of their excessive accumulation. Bacon's treatise is thus composed of the idea of a rewriting of laws into a single healthy and active body, the application of which falls under the jurisdiction of the legislator. We will also refer, in this regard, to the proposition from Bacon to James I concerning the general revision of English laws and their merging into a single body.[62] As far the relation of judges to the sovereign is concerned, Hobbes also agrees with Bacon who writes in his *Essays*: 'Let judges also remember, that Salomon's throne was supported by lions on both sides: let them be lions, but yet lions under the throne; being circumspect that they do not check or oppose any points of sovereignty.'[63] But Hobbes radicalises what nuance and precaution there could be in Bacon's approach. The opposition to jurists of the *Common Law*[64] is reduced in Hobbes to two principles of universal application: first, it is not duration or use that confers authority to laws, but the will of the sovereign. If a custom can be as good as law, it is only to the extent that it is rendered such by the sovereign's silence, which, as it happens, is a sufficient sign of his will. Silence is, we know, sign of contentment. Second, it is not sufficient to

say that the law can never be opposed to reason. It is still necessary to recognise that the sole reason that must be taken for law is that of the sovereign, and not the *jurisprudentia* of the jurists. In order to interpret the law, the judge will thus come to refer to the reason that has led the sovereign to make this law.

4. The theory of civil law is composed of a theory of the political modes of signifying laws: 'Commands, are to be signified by sufficient Signs; because a man knows not otherwise how to obey them.'[65] The essential notion here is that of *sufficient sign*,[66] *signum idoneum*, sufficient sign or adequate sign. Several signs can have this status: the speech, writing or even any other act of the sovereign, even, as we have indicated, silence. This plurality of the modes of signifying is supported by two principles: first, just as the sovereign transcends the laws that he establishes, likewise he transcends the modes by which he signifies law. Second, neither the sovereign being able to foresee everything nor the laws to envisage all possible cases, it is thus necessary that the subordinate judge be able to rely on a sign either express or by inference of the sovereign's will or intention.

However, on this point Hobbes's doctrine evolves between *De Cive* and *Leviathan*. The status of writing in the theory of the promulgation of the laws is going to change from one work to the other. In *De Cive*, Hobbes notes that it is necessary to the essence of the laws that the subjects know two things: (1) who the person is to whom the right to make laws belongs; (2) *quid ipsa lex dicat*, what the law itself says.[67] The first question is quickly settled. Knowledge of the legislator depends on the subjects who have themselves either expressly instituted or tacitly recognised him as sovereign.[68] The second question is the object of a longer response. Hobbes first recalls that it is up to the legislator to promulgate civil laws, without which the subjects would not know to whom we oblige them and could not obey.[69] He then develops a theory of promulgation where writing plays an absolutely subordinated role. Certainly, the mode of the law's promulgation justifies the distinction between *lex scripta* and *lex non scripta*, but the notion of *lex scripta* does not necessarily imply writing: 'Non ergo *legi scriptae* intelligo eam, sed vox'.[70] It is thus not writing, but the voice that is necessary in the written law. The voice belongs to the essence of the written law, while writing has the function only of recalling memory. Obviously, Hobbes here wants to take account of the fact that laws have existed before the appearance of writing. Thus, the example of illiterate or uncultivated peoples is utilised in *De Cive* in order to show the contingent character of a writing of civil law.

This theory of the oral essence of promulgation is not secondary; it affects the whole structure of the state. If promulgation is oral, it is indeed necessary to explain how, once the moment of declaration passed, citizens can consult the law. Does memory suffice to conserve its knowledge? Hobbes would doubtless not agree, since he develops a conception of oral publicity continued from the law.[71] In order to take account of this publicity, *De Cive* distinguishes two cases: that of democracy, on the one hand, that of aristocracies and monarchies, on the other. In a democracy where each can participate in the establishment of the law, those who were absent at the time of promulgation must gain knowledge of the law by the intermediary of the people present. Absentees must thus believe what the people present tell them. The case is more complex in a monarchy or an aristocracy, because only a small number of persons can this time hear, in the presence of the king or of the sovereign council, the declaration of sovereign will. It is thus necessary that some of these persons be charged with doing publicity, either verbally or in writing. The original promulgation by the sovereign must be followed by a series of small, second promulgations. We easily see the drawbacks of such a system for the state such as Hobbes conceives it: knowledge of the law is based on *the habit* that subjects take hold of to see the same persons carrying out the promulgation and on *the belief* or the confidence that they grant to these persons. The law can thus be at any moment the subject of falsifications. Hobbes furthermore envisages the case: when the men charged with the promulgation of laws substitute their own will for that of the sovereign, what must the subjects do? They must, of course, obey, since they are not informed of the usurpation, but this ignorance excuses in advance the illegal acts that they could commit. We easily conceive the uncertainty that this system of the law's publicity is going to introduce within the state. More, save in the case of a democracy – and we know that for Hobbes democracy is not a truly viable political regime – oral promulgation brings about a growth of the number of intermediaries between the sovereign and the subjects, thus an increased risk of falsification. In other words, speech, far from assuring a greater proximity between subjects and sovereign, distances them from him all the more. The state of *De Cive* is essentially, although not exclusively, a state of speech. It is precisely in order to overcome the drawbacks that are associated with it that *Leviathan* re-elaborates the theory of promulgation and of authentication:

> the Law is a Command, and a Command consisteth in declaration, or manifestation of the will of him that commandeth, by voice, writing, or some other sufficient argument of the same, we may understand, that the Command of the Common-wealth, is Law onely to those, that have means to take notice of it.[72]

*Leviathan*'s whole theory of promulgation is elaborated around the notion of sufficient or adequate sign (rendered in our text by that of *sufficient argument*[73]). The expression is already found in *De Cive*, but it is in *Leviathan* that it is systematised. What are the sufficient or adequate signs for the promulgation of a civil law? Hobbes first of all seems to go back over *De Cive*'s doctrine since he establishes an equivalence of principle between speech, writing and other acts of the sovereign. However, despite this equivalence of principle, writing acquires a preponderance of fact: it becomes *in fact* the model of the adequate sign of promulgation.

The relation of the sovereign will to writing is double. On the one hand, this will transcends all modes by which it is signified: writing is here put on the same plane as speech. The sovereign is not bound to the code that he establishes. On the other hand, as the subjects and subordinate judges must clearly and permanently know what the sovereign's will is, writing appears this time like the mode of promulgation that guarantees the best certainty on the content of the law, even though it itself gives rise to difficulties of interpretation.

Indeed, writing allows for surmounting the difficulties linked to the law's oral promulgation in furnishing as much to subjects as to subordinate judges a common reference on what the present will of the sovereign is, independently of the more or less distant moment where this will was declared. On the side of the subjects, written laws allow them to be adequately informed at any moment. Certainly, they will always need to be interpreted. It will always be necessary to climb back from the text to the will of the sovereign. Writing does not thus annul the existence of intermediaries or interpreters, but it makes it possible to reduce their number and, correlatively, reduce the risks of falsification. Better, we will see, it is writing that makes it possible to authenticate intermediaries. On the side of subordinate judges, writing precisely makes it possible to delimit their function, which is to apply the law, not to make it. If the sovereign transcends the written code, the subordinate judge is bound by its meaning. To this we can add another fundamental argument: writing alone is in a position to assure a true distinction between law and custom – it assures the autonomy of civil law compared with past examples or use.

One could certainly object to us that writing is not so essential to civil laws, since in *Leviathan* Hobbes himself goes back over the example of illiterate or uncultivated peoples who live in a state and under laws without having the art of writing available: 'in ancient time, before letters were in common use, the Lawes were many times put into verse; that the rude people taking pleasure in singing, or reciting them, might the more easily reteine them in memory'.[74] But the example of these illiterate peoples seems to me to have in *Leviathan* a different meaning from what it had in *De Cive*. Indeed, in *Leviathan*, it is less a question of drawing an argument from it in order to show that writing is not essential to civil law than of indicating, on the contrary, the necessity of a substitute for writing. Thus, learning the laws by heart, binding commandments to his hand's digits (as Solomon prescribed), repeating them in all circumstances and writing them on doorposts (as Moses prescribed) are so many means for overcoming the absence of writing. The function of writing is assured by other voices. This means that, without writing, the state is certainly not impossible, but precarious. In the internal logic of its maximal functioning, the state of *Leviathan* is not an ignorant people's state; it is a state of writing. It is enough, in this regard, to recall the essential function that the subject's education plays there. Civil law has a privileged relation to instituted political writing because it makes it possible to assure the clarity and universality of the rules that subjects must know in order to conform there. Indeed, if it is true that, when the people is uncultured, writing constitutes a factor of separation between those who hold power [*pouvoir*] and the subjects, on the other hand, when the people is educated, it constitutes a factor of regulation of civil communication.

The privilege of fact – not of right – of writing is confirmed by the theory of authentication, which has the function of resolving the difficulty linked to the theory of the law's oral publicity from *De Cive*. Hobbes indicates this difficulty right away: 'For private men, when they have, or think they have force enough to secure their unjust designes, and convoy them safely to their ambitious ends, may publish for Lawes what they please, without, or against the Legislative Authority.'⁷⁵ The problem to which the theory of authentication must respond is that of the highlighting of the sovereign's authority: 'Nor is it enough the Law be written, and published; but also that there be manifest signs, that it proceedeth from the will of the Soveraign.'⁷⁶ Hobbes distinguishes authentication from authorisation: the latter resides in the sovereign's will, the former concerns the certification that what is given as the sovereign's will is properly such. Yet authentication is assured by the recording of the law in official collections or its certification by public seals. The writing of the law thus takes part in the process that allows for recognising it as such. Certainly, the law can also be authenticated by official persons: councils or ministers. Intermediaries, we have said, will never be totally removed. However, with writing, a common reference exists on which subjects could directly or indirectly rely: 'But when the question is of injury, or crime, upon a written law; every man by recourse to the Registers, by himself, or others, may (if he will) be sufficiently enformed, before he doe such injury, or commit the crime, whither it be an injury, or not'.⁷⁷ Better, when a dispute concerns obedience to a public functionary, *Leviathan* no longer makes, as *De Cive*, habit and belief intervene but writing once more: the authority of the functionary is henceforth 'To have seen his Commission, with the Publique Seale, and heard it read; or to have had the means to be informed of it, if a man would, is a sufficient Verification of his Authority. For every man is obliged to doe his best endeavour, to informe himself of all written Lawes, that may concerne his own future actions.'⁷⁸ Writing authenticates the intermediary.

Model for the manifest sign of promulgation, writing also becomes model for the manifest sign of authentication. Everything thus happens as if the existence of the Hobbesian state must produce this event in the language that is the appearance of a writing of power [*pouvoir*]. The theory of interpretation is going to clarify its status while suspending the risk of a fetishisation of writing.

## THE INTERPRETATION OF THE LAW: THE LETTER AND THE MEANING OF THE LAW

Hobbes approaches the problem of the interpretation of law by the examination of three questions: what is it to interpret a law? Who has the right to interpret the law? What are the laws which demand to be interpreted?

1. Let us examine the first question: what is it to interpret a law? Before even responding there, Hobbes notes that interpretation is one of the conditions that render a law obligatory; it is the final condition. Yet the necessity of an interpretation makes the question of writing redound straightaway. Indeed, considering the civil law, Hobbes declares that 'it is not the Letter, but the Intendment, or Meaning; that is to say, the authentique Interpretation of the Law (which is the sense of the Legislator,) in which the nature of the Law consisteth'.[79] The letter thus must be put into perspective: it is not necessary to fetishise the materiality of the text. Indeed, a judge who would only hold to the letter of the law will risk either pronouncing a judgement contrary to the intention of the legislator, or, when the case is not explicitly foreseen, of being put in a situation of not being able to judge. To apply the law is to interpret it. We thus understand that application demands passage from letter to meaning, that is to say, to the intention of the legislator. But under no circumstances is it a question of a re-assessment of writing's political value. Interpretation, far from reducing writing's reach, is rather aroused or rather specified by it: what specifies the interpretation of the written law and distinguishes it from the interpretation of unwritten natural law is the fundamental question of the literal meaning.

2. We can thus pass to the second question: who has the right to interpret the law? To this question Hobbes's response is clear and univocal: those whom the sovereign has instituted with the aim of fulfilling this function. In the case of natural or unwritten laws, it is a question of judges. Interpretation here coincides with judgement and rests on the exercise of the judge's natural reason alone. In pronouncing a sentence in compliance with the demands of right reason (which is the same in every man), the judge pronouncing judgement in right adapts to the sovereign's intention, which is always supposed to coincide with reason. In the case of written laws, Hobbes envisages two possibilities: interpretation can be assured either by an interpreter authorised by the sovereign but who is not himself judge, or by the judge. Consequently, neither books of morality nor jurists' quibbles can have the status of interpretation of the law. To refer to one or the other will indeed be to introduce within justice itself the controversy and dispute that it has precisely the function of deciding. It is the unity of the law's meaning

– the unity of the legislator's intention – which makes rendering justice possible. The sovereign is thus doubly the pivot of the judicial system: as ultimate meaning to which every sentence of the subordinate judge must be referred and as sole authority likely to confer onto an individual the authority to interpret the law. For Hobbes, it is a question of putting into place the questions of a univocity of the legal norm and of its application, without which there cannot be political regulation of men's conduct.

3. We thus understand that to the third question – what laws demand an interpretation? – Hobbes can respond: all the laws. Indeed, even though natural laws would be present in all men's reason, these are not only beings of reason – the political problem would not even arise at that time – but also of passions. Self-love masks the voice of reason so much that the laws of nature become most obscure. This is precisely the situation that prevails in the state of nature. In this, which concerns civil laws, interpretation is required, we have indicated, by writing: that they may be written up in a small number of words or in a great number, the multiplicity of significations that they convey renders written laws equivocal. Yet, in its very essence, the discourse of power [*pouvoir*] must banish equivocation, source of misunderstanding and disagreements. In order to surmount this difficulty, Hobbes distinguishes two modes of relation of the letter to the meaning of the law. If we understand by letter all this that we can pass on to the materiality of the text, then it is necessary to distinguish the letter from the unique meaning of the law. Considered from this point of view, the text hinders the seizure of the legislator's intention and it is legitimate to oppose the letter to the law's spirit to which it is necessary to have recourse. On the other hand, the letter of the law is found rehabilitated, if we understand by letter the literal meaning (*literall sens*),[80] which is other than what the legislator wanted to signify in the text. The notion of literal meaning thus indicates the manner in which the text of the law must be read: not according to the use or the subjectivity of private individuals, but according to the will of the sovereign. The sovereign is the institutor of a juridical code, a writing of power [*pouvoir*] that assures the unity of the letter and the meaning in the literal sense.

We thus see, at every level of the theory of civil law, that it is a question of promulgation, authentication or interpretation; writing occupies a preponderant place. This status of writing makes it possible to distinguish Hobbes's approach from Bodin and Bacon's. While Bodin[81] denied the distinction between written laws and unwritten laws and Bacon[82] would not demand, in order to fulfil his programme of overhauling laws, that these were written, Hobbes makes of writing the model for the adequate sign and for the manifest sign of the law. Better, it is the hierarchy that Hobbes himself established between speech and writing in the beginning of chapter 4 of *Leviathan* that his political theory leads one to re-examine. If speech is the most noble of inventions because, without it, the state would not exist, we can say that, once the state exists, speech no longer suffices to assure a sufficient juridico-political regulation. Writing assures the existence of norms, which makes it possible to solve in right the misunderstandings and controversies of communication between individuals that, in the state of nature, would degenerate into conflict.

It remains to be seen what the exact nature of legislative sovereignty and its relation to domination is. This is what we are going to examine now with the study of the notion of *dominium*.

*Notes*

1. [TN: in English in the original; Zarka's emphasis.]
2. Hobbes, *Leviathan*, p. 217.
3. Hobbes is not, of course, the first to define the law (both natural and civil) as command (respectively, from God and from the civil legislator). We find it already in currents of thought as opposed in principle as those of the Reformation, in particular in Luther, and the Counter-Reformation, in paricular in Suárez's *De Legibus*. This definition of the law is found again in Bodin's political and juridical thought and in the treatise on justice that Bacon develops in *De Dignitate et augmentis scientarum*. As Michel Villey has shown (*La formation de la pensée juridique moderne* (Paris: Montchrétien, 1975)), all these currents find their probable source in Ockham's political thought.
4. Hobbes, *Leviathan*, p. 217.
5. Ibid., p. 312.
6. Hobbes, *The Elements of Law*, p. 187.
7. See the definition of the eternal law in which all creatures participate in St Thomas, the natural law being for him only the specific mode by which man participates in the eternal law (*Summa Theologicae*, 1a2ae. 90 et seq.).
8. See the definition of the laws of nature in Descartes as rules according to which the movements of the body take place, *Le Monde*, ch. 7.
9. Hobbes, *Leviathan*, p. 302; see also Hobbes, *The Elements of Law*, pp. 184–5.

10. Hobbes, *Leviathan*, p. 129.
11. Ibid., p. 303; see also Hobbes, *De Cive: The English Version*, pp. 168–9; *De Cive*, pp. 312–13.
12. Thus, Hobbes distinguishes the reason why we obey, which is drawn from the will of he who commands (*a voluntate praecipientis*), from the reason why we follow a piece of advice, which is drawn from the same thing (*ab ipsa re*) which is recommended (Hobbes, *De Cive: The English Version*, pp. 168–9; *De Cive*, pp. 312–13). Before Hobbes, Suárez had established a comparable distinction between command and counsel in *De Legibus*.
13. [TN: in English in the original.]
14. Hobbes, *Leviathan*, p. 312.
15. Hobbes, *De Cive*, p. 320.
16. Hobbes, *Leviathan*, p. 396.
17. [TN: italicised English is in English in the original.]
18. [TN: Hobbes, *Leviathan*, p. 451. In English in the original.]
19. Hobbes, *Leviathan*, p. 451. [TN: in English in the original.]
20. Ibid., p. 397.
21. Ibid., p. 312. [TN: in English in the original.]
22. Hobbes, *The Elements of Law*, p. 187.
23. Cf. ibid., p. 94; Hobbes, *De Cive: The English Version*, pp. 75–6; *De Cive*, p. 198; *Leviathan*, pp. 216–17.
24. See Howard Warrender, *The Political Philosophy of Hobbes: His Theory of Obligation* (Oxford: Clarendon Press, 1957); Raymon Polin, *Politique et philosophie chez Hobbes* (Paris: Vrin, 1977); Raymon Polin, *Hobbes, Dieu et l'homme* (Paris: PUF, 1981).
25. See Chapter 9, 'On the State'.
26. Hobbes follows Suárez in this. For an in-depth study of this relationship, see Karl Schuhmann, 'La notion de loi chez Hobbes', in *Le Pouvoir et le Droit: Hobbes et les fondements de la Loi*, ed. Louis Roux and François Tricaud (Saint-Étienne: Publications de l'Université de Saint-Étienne, 1992), pp. 175–95.
27. Hobbes, *Leviathan*, p. 189.
28. See Hobbes, *De Cive: The English Version*, pp. 62–3; *De Cive*, pp. 168–70.
29. Hobbes, *The Elements of Law*, p. 75.
30. [TN: ibid.] This purely ethical definition of natural law, which temporarily isolates the latter from all theological reference and definitively extracts it from all cosmological establishment, distinguishes Hobbes's approach from that of Locke. In *Essays on the Law of Nature*, Locke, beyond the recovery of certain theses of Hobbes, inscribes the consideration of the law of nature within a cosmo-theological perspective straightaway (John Locke, *Essays on the Law of Nature*, trans. W. von Leyden (Oxford: Clarendon Press, 1954), p. 151). Natural law returns to its formal cause,

that is to say, to God, whose existence is inferred from the order of the world. Locke furthermore explicitly refers to the relation that St Thomas establishes between eternal law and natural law (cf. ibid., p. 117).
31. Hobbes, *Leviathan*, p. 189.
32. Ibid., p. 190.
33. Hobbes, *The Elements of Law*, p. 72.
34. Hobbes, *Leviathan*, p. 214.
35. Hobbes, *The Elements of Law*, p. 92.
36. Hobbes, *Leviathan*, p. 115.
37. See Zarka, *La décision métaphysique de Hobbes*, pp. 310–24.
38. Hobbes, *The Elements of Law*, p. 69.
39. See Hobbes, *Leviathan*, p. 215.
40. Hobbes takes up Psalm 14 again within the framework of his problematic: 'The fool hath said in his heart, *There is* no God' (Ps. 14:1, AV).
41. [TN: in English in the original.]
42. Hobbes, *Leviathan*, p. 203.
43. Ibid., p. 205.
44. See Chapter 4, 'Theory of Language', above.
45. Natural laws are for Hobbes known first by reason. His perspective is thus fundamentally distinguished from that of Luther for whom it is only Scripture, thus revelation, that makes it possible for us to know divine laws. There is evidently in no way a trace in Hobbes of the Lutheran decline of reason.
46. Hobbes, *The Elements of Law*, p. 95.
47. Cf., ibid., pp. 95–6; Hobbes, *De Cive: The English Version*, pp. 76–8; *De Cive*, pp. 199–200.
48. See also Hobbes, *Leviathan*, p. 396.
49. Ibid., p. 397.
50. See Hobbes, *The Elements of Law*, pp. 97–8; *De Cive: The English Version*, p. 84; *De Cive*, p. 208.
51. [TN: Hobbes, *The Elements of Law*, p. 99.]
52. Hobbes, *The Elements of Law*, p. 186. [TN: in English in the original.]
53. Hobbes, *Leviathan*, p. 318.
54. Ibid., p. 319.
55. Ibid., p. 312.
56. See Hobbes, *The Elements of Law*, p. 188.
57. Jean Bodin, *On Sovereignty: Four chapters from the* Six Books *of the* Commonwealth, ed. and trans. Julian H. Franklin (Cambridge: Cambridge University Press, 1992), p. 58; Jean Bodin, *Les six livres de la République* (Aalen: Scientia Verlag, [1583] 1977), p. 223.
58. Jean Bodin, *Exposé du droit universel = Juris universi distributio*, trans. Lucien Jerphagnon (Paris: PUF, 1985), pp. 16 and 17. [TN: my translation. To my

knowledge, this has never been translated into English. The Latin reads as follows: *'nihil aliud sit quam summae potestatis jussum sive sanctio. est enim sancire & sciscere, jubere'*. The French reads as follows: *'n'est rien d'autre, en effet, que l'ordre ou la sanction de l'autorité souveraine. Sanctionnner, c'est la même chose que decreeter, c'est-à-dire commander'*.]
59. [TN: in English in the original.]
60. See Thomas Hobbes, *Dialogue between a Philosopher and a Student of the Common Law*, ed. Joseph Cropsey (Chicago, IL: University of Chicago Press, 1971). See also Paulette Carrive, 'Hobbes et les jurists de la Common Law', in *Thomas Hobbes: de la métaphysique à la politique*, ed. Martin Berman and Michel Malherbe (Paris: Vrin, 1989), pp. 149–71, and Simone Goyard-Fabre, 'La legislation civile dans l'état-Léviathan', in *Thomas Hobbes: de la métaphysique à la politique*, pp. 173–92.
61. Francis Bacon, *De Dignitate et augmentis scientarum*, in *The Works of Francis Bacon*, ed. Basil Montagu, vol. 9 (London: William Pickering, 1828), pp. 67–83.
62. Francis Bacon, 'Proposition touching the amendment of the laws', in *The Works of Francis Bacon*, vol. 5 (London: William Pickering, 1826), pp. 337–52.
63. Francis Bacon, 'Of judicature', in *Essays or Counsels, Civil and Moral*, in *Francis Bacon*, ed. Brian Vickers (Oxford: Oxford University Press, 1996), p. 449.
64. [TN: in English in the original.]
65. Hobbes, *Leviathan*, p. 312.
66. [TN: in English in the original.]
67. Hobbes, *De Cive: The English Version*, pp. 174–5; *De Cive*, p. 320.
68. See Hobbes, *De Cive: The English Version*, pp. 174–5; *De Cive*, p. 320.
69. See Hobbes, *De Cive: The English Version*, pp. 174–5; *De Cive*, pp. 320–1.
70. Hobbes, *De Cive*, p. 322. [TN: 'Wherefore not a *writing*, but a *voice* is necessary for a *written law*' (Hobbes, *De Cive: The English Version*, p. 176).]
71. Hobbes, *De Cive: The English Version*, pp. 174–6; *De Cive*, pp. 320–2.
72. Hobbes, *Leviathan*, p. 317.
73. [TN: in English in the original.]
74. Hobbes, *Leviathan*, p. 319.
75. Ibid., pp. 319–20.
76. Ibid., p. 319.
77. Ibid., p. 321.
78. Ibid.
79. Ibid., pp. 321–2.
80. [TN: in English in the original.]
81. Bodin, *Exposé*, pp. 16 and 17.
82. Bacon, 'Proposition', pp. 345–6.

# Chapter 8

# ON PROPERTY

### PROPERTY AND POWER [*POUVOIR*]

Property does not seem, at first glance, to figure among the fundamental questions aroused so much by the doctrine of natural right as by Hobbes's theory of politics. We find in it nothing comparable with, for example, the admirable chapter 5, 'Of Property', from Locke's *Second Treatise of Government*. Certain recent studies on the history of natural right and of property in the seventeenth and eighteenth centuries give him neither a particular chapter nor even an attentive consideration.[1] This situation is not without some objective foundation: the question of property is entirely subordinated in Hobbes to the political problem. It is in fact the existence of political power [*pouvoir*] that must take account of the origin, foundation and effectiveness of property. The state does not content itself with giving positive rules to property. It more radically founds the possibility of an appropriation of things:

> Seeing therefore the Introduction of *Propriety* is an effect of Commonwealth; which can do nothing but by the Person that Represents it, it is the act onely of the Sovereign.[2]

The same passage in the Latin version of *Leviathan* states in a more suggestive manner:

> Quoniam ergo constitutio proprietatis civitatis opus est; illius opus est, qui summam in civitate habet potestatem.[3]

If property is implemented, it is not primarily the work of labour upon nature, but the work of the power that founds it through law. More precisely, the first work is conditional on the second: political power [*pouvoir*] does not give to property its material, but its juridical effectiveness. We could say in this sense that Hobbes operates a political reduction of the problem of property in subordinating the appropriation of goods to the solution of the major political problem of the constitution of a sovereign power [*pouvoir*].

However, this political reduction of the problem of property risks masking another, perhaps more fundamental, operation, namely, the resurgence of property at the very heart of political theory. Indeed, is not the loss of property's autonomy had at the cost of an underlying reinterpretation of the political in terms of property? When, in §11 of chapter 5 of *De Cive*, Hobbes designates the fundamental political attribute of the man to whom, or of the council to which individuals have subjected their particular wills, he employs the word *dominium* as equivalent of *summa potestas* and of *summa imperium*. Yet is thinking sovereignty in terms of *dominium* not implicitly, but irresistibly, to interpret the political relationship of power [*pouvoir*] in terms of property? Certainly, the concept of *dominium* has signified, from the Middle Ages, not only the possession of things or the right of possession (in a sense that it would be necessary to specify), but also other types of dominion. Better, the term *dominium* designates in Hobbes himself a certain type of interpersonal relationships as well as property in things – property even depending most often on the relation of dominion between persons. Thus, when he recapitulates the constitutive modes of a right over persons, Hobbes speaks of right of dominion, *jus dominii*.[4] For example, being king is nothing other than having dominion over a great number of persons: '*Regnem enim esse, nihil aliud est quam dominium habere in personas multas.*'[5] However, it is not sufficient to include within the term *dominium* all the political or private relationships in which an individual (sovereign or subject) has a right over one or several persons in order to discharge it of his meaning of property. So little, moreover, that in the passage from *The Elements of Law* corresponding to that from *De Cive* where the constitutive modes of a right of dominion over persons are enumerated, we find an important clarification:

> But before I enter thereunto: it is necessary to make known, upon what title one man may acquire right, that is to say *property or dominion* over the person of another.[6]

The right over other persons is thus *property or dominion over the person of another*.[7] This right of dominion can be constituted in three ways: voluntary submission, forced submission and engendering (although this last mode may be an insufficient title single-handedly). From then on, the question returns to knowing whether the application of the notion of *dominium/dominion*[8] to all forms of power [*pouvoir*][9] over others does not, at the political level, lead the Hobbesian conception of sovereignty to a seigniorial conception, where the relation of sovereignty would be based on a relationship of property over subjects and territory?

Although the model for property occupies an important place in the Hobbesian theory of political power [*pouvoir*], the principal issue for the doctrine of sovereignty, however, seems very much, on the contrary, to be extracting the political relationship from the relationship of property. Thus, on the one hand, even though Hobbes puts on the same plane the terms *dominium*, *summa potestas* and *summum imperium*, on the other hand, even though he gives the term *dominion* as equivalent of *property*, it does not follow from this that political right is reduced to the right of property.[10] This is not done without difficulties. But, in this respect, the testimony of Hobbes's contemporary who brought the concept of a seigniorial (or, rather, and more strictly, patriarchal) monarchy to the ultimate implications is unable to mislead us. Sir Robert Filmer will criticise Hobbes with precision in his *Observations Concerning the Originall of Government* (1652) for not having founded his theory of absolute sovereignty on the concept of *regnum patrimoniale*, even though he possesses this concept. We can even add that Hobbes completely modifies this concept in reinterpreting it within the framework of his own political theory.

In the path traced by Bodinien theory, Hobbes develops a theory of sovereignty, linked to a very particular concept of *auctoritas* (*authoritas* in Hobbes's written form), which emancipates sovereignty from the relation of property – that is to say, simultaneously makes it possible to recognise dependence on it [property] and liberate it [sovereignty] from it.

In order to attempt to show this, we will successively examine three points, each of which puts the relationship of two concepts into play: on the one hand, *dominium/proprietas* or the right over things; on the other hand, *dominium/potestas* or the right over persons; finally, *dominium/auctoritas* or sovereignty.

## THE RIGHT OVER THINGS: *DOMINIUM/PROPRIETAS*

In order to designate the right that a man has over things, Hobbes employs both the term *dominium* and that of *proprietas*,[11] although the second appears much more frequently than the first. This terminological equivalence engages, more profoundly, the suppression of all conceptual difference. Hobbes thus completes an operation already begun by Grotius, but deriving some of his own consequences. In order to measure the reach of this conceptual identification, it is important to go back to St Thomas Aquinas' position which, precisely, establishes a distinction between *dominium* and *proprietas*.

In the *Summa Theologica*, the two notions are defined in the course of the examination of the questions treated in two celebrated articles:[12] (1) '*is the possession of external goods natural to man?*', (2) '*is it legitimate for individual men to possess anything as their own?*' Already significant indication: the status of *dominium* is specified in the first and that of *proprietas* in the second. First of all, the notion of *dominium* is split: it is necessary to distinguish between God's *dominium* and man's. This distinction itself is based on a double consideration of things. Considered in their nature, things are in God's power [*pouvoir*] alone, which is its principle. There is thus a *dominium Dei* over all beings. However, considered in their use, certain things have been destined by divine providence to assure the satisfaction of man's corporeal needs. The hierarchical structure of the universe (the fact that less-perfect things are with a view to the more perfect) and the determinations of man as being endowed with reason and with will (the fact that he may be capable of using things) makes it possible to justify the existence of a natural *dominium* of man on the use and enjoyment of things. This *dominium* is not particular or exclusive, but common to all men. We thus see how the question of *proprietas* is going to be posed: can man appropriate what is common? St Thomas's response is positive: man can appropriate things, but only so as to manage them and have them at his disposal. Three arguments drawn from Aristotle justify property: (1) each one gives more attentive care to what belongs to him in his own right; (2) there is more order in the administration of a thing when it is entrusted to a particular person; (3) peace requires that each be satisfied with what belongs to him. The relationship between *dominium* and *proprietas* is thus sorted out in the following manner:

Community of goods is said to be part of the natural law not because it requires everything to be held in common and nothing to be appropriated to individual possession, but because the distribution of property is a matter not for natural law but, rather, human agreement, which is what positive law is about, as we saw above. The individual holding of possessions is not, therefore, contrary to the natural law; it is what rational beings conclude as an addition to the natural law.[13]

Grotius is going to rework this problem in aiming to identify *dominium* and *proprietas*,[14] even though he accepts the distinction between common right and particular right. This reworking is based, on the one hand, on the elaboration of a new concept of natural right as subjective right, that is to say, moral faculty or quality of a person, and on the substitution of a genealogy of property for St Thomas's, so to speak, structural perspective. While the latter added on to natural right, where everything is possessed in common, a property that is born from positive right, Grotius thinks that the establishment of property abolishes the originary common right. We will retain only the two principal moments of the genealogy of property traced in chapter 2 of book 2 of *De Jure belli ac pacis*. Originally, the human race had at its disposal an undivided right over the earth, considered as a common heritage. This common right is defined by five characteristics: (1) it was given by God to men just after the creation of the world; (2) it concerned the use and the consumption of things in view of the satisfaction of needs; (3) it implied that we could not take away that of which a man took possession without injustice; (4) it held place of property: 'The enjoyment of this universal right then served the purpose of private ownership';[15] (5) it was, however, not exclusive since all could freely gain access to nature's goods. This state of undivided universal right could have remained stable indefinitely if men had been able to conserve the simplicity of life and mutual friendship which condition the community of good people. Yet such was the case: the appearance of the arts, the development of the passions, the multiplication of the number of men: in sum, the search for a commodious life and the lack of love and of justice no longer allowed the maintenance of the primitive community and of undivided right. The passage to the regime of property has supposed a mutual accord, an express contract (*pactum*) – when previously common things were the object of a sharing – or tacit – when the right of property was left to the first occupant.[16]

## On Property

The right of the first occupant will remain thereafter the sole primitive mode of property's acquisition. Every other will only be derived. Thus, to the Thomist superimposition of the propriety of positive right on the common domain of natural right – in which property takes root[17] – Grotius opposes the different outline of a distinction within the space of the world between things likely to be the subject of an appropriation and of things that are not in any way likely to become it (the sea, the air, etc.).[18] Property is from then on a *real* right, as faculty of having a thing at one's disposal; *exclusive*, in opposition to the common right that we keep over the things that are not susceptible to appropriation; finally, it is an *absolute* right, even though it should distinguish between full ownership and usufruct (temporary or perpetual).[19]

Hobbes is going to bring the identification of *dominium* and *proprietas* to its most extreme by a double operation, which consists in showing the impossibility of an originary community of the good and the contradictory character of an undivided right.[20] Here the text is most significant in this regard:

> The Distribution of the Materials of this Nourishment, is the constitution of *Mine*, and *Thine*, and *His*; that is to say, in one word *Propriety* [*proprietas*]; and belongeth in all kinds of Commonwealth to the Sovereign Power [*summa potestas*]. For where there is no Common-wealth, there is (as hath already been shewn) a perpetuall warre of every man against his neighbour; And therefore every thing is his that getteth it, and keepeth it by force; which is neither *Propriety* nor *Community*; but *Uncertainty*.[21]

Five remarks on this text:

1. This passage on property finds its context in a chapter on political economy, the principal object of which is to define the production, compensation, exchange and circulation of the goods necessary to the maintenance of the life of the state. The question of property is put within the framework of the double relation of man to nature and to the state.

2. The relationship of man to the goods furnished by nature takes on, as in the authors that we have earlier considered, a theological position. Without explicitly involving the notion of a *dominium Dei* over all nature, Hobbes considers that nature's goods have been liberally given by God to the human race, in such a way that, in order to take

possession of them, men must either simply accept them or obtain them by their effort. Thus, the abundance of the things necessary to human life is conditional on God's grace or kindness (*favour*[22]/*benevolentia*) and man's effort. Hobbes could appear to reproduce here, under a somewhat bowdlerised form, the classical conception of an undivided right conferred by God to men.

3. Yet such is not the case. Just the opposite, it is going to be employed to show that the originary undivided right over things is untenable because it can take neither the form of Thomist *dominium* nor the form that Grotius gave to it. The Latin version of a sentence from the text cited below says it clearly, in emphasising the principle of the incompatibility between the idea of undivided right of all over all and that of community: 'Ubi enim civitas est, ibi omnia omnium sunt, et bellum perpetuum est.'[23] We can certainly legitimately say '*Natura dedit omnia omnibus*'[24] and conclude from it that every man has a natural right to use and enjoy things. But, on account of the dynamics of interhuman relationships, this right cannot be limited to the use of things necessary to the satisfaction of need and must necessarily extend to all things. Hobbes's anthropological presuppositions thus subtend the idea of an exclusive natural right of each over all things. This right over all things conceals a contradiction: 'that right of all men to all things, is in effect no better than if no man had right to any thing'.[25] We thus understand that, when all have a right over all, there is neither *proprietas* nor *communitas*, but *concertatio*, conflict.

4. Finding in no way a foundation in natural right, property is going to find its principle in political power [*pouvoir*]. The effectiveness of the right over all things is based on positive right: 'commonwealth, property of goods, and justice are born at the same time'.[26] There is thus neither a positive right of property that will be superimposed upon a *dominium* of natural right, as in St Thomas, nor particular appropriation of things that stand in for a non-exclusive common right, as in Grotius, but political foundation of the existence and of the rules of property starting from the internal contradiction of the idea of a natural right to distinguish *dominium* and *proprietas*. However, once established, property in Hobbes is composed of the characters that Grotius attributed to it: it is a real, an exclusive and, in a certain sense, an absolute right.

5. The property of a thing is an absolute right in the sense where the one who possesses this right can have the thing at his disposal as he sees fit, that is to say, that he can use it and make use of its products (when it

is a question of a usufruct), but also transform it, give it up, even destroy it (when it is a question of a full ownership). But property is not absolute in the sense where it would be opposable to political power [*pouvoir*]. If property implies the distinction of mine and yours, this distinction takes place only between subjects or citizens. It defines my right over a thing as exclusive of the other's right, but not as exclusive of the sovereign power [*pouvoir*]. Thus, concerning the property of the earth, Hobbes can write: 'the Propriety which a subject hath in his lands, consisteth in a right to exclude all other subjects from the use of them; and not to exclude their Soveraign, be it an Assembly, or a Monarch'.[27] How to justify this right of the political power [*pouvoir*] to recall property or transfer it from one subject to another, without the one to whom it is recalled having committed a crime?[28] Is there no contradiction in the Hobbesian idea of a political foundation for property? There is in any case a radical relativity of property in things in relation to the political power [*pouvoir*] that makes property, but also can dismantle it or remake it. But this relativity can be justified only by reference to a more fundamental absolute: 'every man by the law of nature, hath right or propriety to his own body'.[29] Now, it is essentially in order to protect this property of self that the political power [*pouvoir*] has been established. As property in things (which is from positive right) is, in principle, only a means with the aim of the conservation of the proper of self (which is from natural right), political power [*pouvoir*] has the right, when circumstances require it, to utilise the one so as to preserve the other. Thus, concerning taxes, Hobbes can write: 'Those levies therefore which are made upon men's estates, by the sovereign authority, are no more but the price of that peace and defence which the sovereignty maintaineth for them.'[30] The relativity of the right over things thus is attached to its subordination to the political guarantee of property that each has over self.

Every question is henceforth of knowing whether the Hobbesian conception of the state quite fulfils this function. Does the use of the concept of *dominium* in the field of interhuman relationships and in particular of political power [*pouvoir*] not indicate on the contrary a disappropriation of self?

## THE RIGHT OVER PERSONS: *DOMINIUM / POTESTAS*

The notion of *dominium*, brought back to that of *proprietas* when it is a question of the right over things, is going to receive a considerable extension in the field of the right over persons and actions. Power [*pouvoir*] maintains complex and criss-crossed relations with property. These relations vary according to whether we consider the simple power [*puissance*] of fact[31] or power [*pouvoir*] adorned with a right (*potestas*). However, since here it is about examining the question of the right over persons, we will limit ourselves to the relationship of the concepts of *dominium* and *potestas*.

What is especially striking in the Hobbesian doctrine of the right over persons is the generalisation of the notion of *dominium*.[32] Thus, as we have indicated, the three titles by which a right over persons is constituted – consent, submission to force and generation – belong to the category of *jus dominii*.[33] In certain cases, Hobbes sometimes even gives the term *dominion* as equivalent to that of *right*.[34] Finally, the notions of *summa potestas* and *summum imperium* are put on the same plane as that of *dominium*.[35] This generalisation is recurrent in the detail of the developments on the three modes of right over persons. We have thus been right to emphasise[36] the fact that Hobbes utilises the expressions *dominium herile* and *dominium paternum* in preference to the more classical *dominica potestas* and *patria potestas*, which are still present in Grotius.

Furthermore, Hobbes would not be able to find the principle of this generalisation in Grotius. From the definition of subjective right,[37] Grotius makes a clear distinction between power [*pouvoir*] and property. Power [*pouvoir*] (*potestas*) is specified in power [*pouvoir*] over oneself (*libertas*) and power [*pouvoir*] over others (*patria potestas* and *dominica potestas*). For its part, property (*dominium*) is specified full or imperfect ownership (usufruct, guarantee [*gage*], etc.). This distinction – which does not forbid comparing the two categories, quite the opposite – is confirmed by the chapter from *De Jure belli ac pacis* concerning the right over persons.[38] In this chapter, which, without any possible doubt, furnished the basis upon which Hobbes worked in order to write the chapters from *The Elements of Law* and *De Cive* concerning the same subject,[39] a generalisation of the notion of *dominium* is not included. Certainly, he turns to Grotius[40] to take the forms of property (*proprietas*) as a main theme of his analysis of sovereignty (*summum imperium*),[41] but there it is a question only of a comparison and not in the least of an identification under a common concept. Finally, *dominium* and *imperium* are clearly distinguished anew when Grotius writes in his chapter on the primitive acquisition of things:

Although sovereignty and ownership are generally acquired by a single act, they are nevertheless distinct. Consequently ownership passes not only to citizens but also to foreigners, while the sovereignty remains in the hands of him who previously held it.[42]

We can consequently avoid these questions: does the generalisation of *dominium* imply, in Hobbes, the effacement of the distinction between property in things and power [*pouvoir*] over persons? More particularly, is the theory of political power [*pouvoir*] not totally affected by a reinterpretation in terms of property?

In order to be in a position to respond there, two preliminary remarks should be made. First, it is necessary to take account of the distinction between the two forms of state (*civitas*) or of republic (*commonwealth*)[43] that Hobbes carries out according to the right of dominion's mode of formation. Second, it is necessary to emphasise that the right over persons is composed of two absolutely distinct aspects. It can be dominion over actions or dominion over the physical person. Yet the Hobbesian conception of natural right forbids as a matter of principle all alienation of the right that each has over his body and its limbs. There are indeed some inalienable rights of the individual that no one can transfer – save being insane, though a juridical act cannot be founded on unreason. These inalienable rights are based on the principle according to which 'every man, not onely by Right, but also by necessity of Nature, is supposed to endeavour all he can, to obtain that which is necessary for his conservation'.[44] Without it being necessary to develop the different constitutive elements of this absolutely inalienable right – that is to say, inalienable whatever the relational context within which men find themselves, whether the state of nature or the civil state – we will note that he forbids *in principle* every physical or corporeal dis-appropriation of self. On the other hand, this does not also hold true of the natural right that each has over his actions. That is perfectly alienable. The establishment of the state, for example, consists precisely in transferring the right that we have to govern our actions to the will of a man or a council. If there is thus no corporeal dis-appropriation of self – *in principle* – there can be dis-appropriation of the government of self. Following these principles, the constitutive modes of the right of dominion (despotic, paternal or instituted) thus come to concern only the private or political appropriation of the right that a man has over his actions.

These two points recalled, it is henceforth a question of knowing if, and to what extent, the three constitutive modes of the right of dominion follow the principle of this distinction between inalienable property of the physical person and alienable property of actions. Let us say straightaway that, if we stick to *The Elements of Law* and to *De Cive*, the right of dominion's first two modes (*dominium despoticum* and *dominium paternum*) go beyond the threshold of a simple property of actions in order to expand to the property of the physical person, while the third, that is to say, voluntary consent, which subtends in particular every theory of the state of the republic of institution, is insufficient to assure political property of the right over actions. In other words, the political theory of *The Elements of Law* and *De Cive* very much furnishes an interpretation of political power [*pouvoir*] in terms of property, but it also allows for detecting the difficulties – even the contradictions – that are left to it. Let us successively examine the three constitutive modes of the right of dominion over persons in these two works.

1. *Dominium despoticum* first of all supposes victory over one or several men and the fear that this victory produces in him or the vanquished. However, the pre-eminence of force would not be able to constitute a title of dominion single-handedly. In order that such a right be constituted, a promise or a pact by which the weakest commit themselves to serve the strongest is additionally necessary, which would have conceded to it beforehand not only life but also corporeal liberty. It is this pact that makes the dominion relationship between the *dominus* and the *servitus* a juridical relationship, without which there would be no right of dominion but simply *de facto* coercion.[45] In virtue of his pact, the servant owes an obedience without reservation to the master and, correlatively, the latter has a right of absolute dominion (*absolute dominion*)[46] over the former. It remains to be seen what the extent of this right of absolute dominion is. Does it stop at the government of all the servant's actions?[47] No. For the physical person and the goods of the servant are equally a property of the master.[48] Thus, can the master say of the servant, as of any other animate or inanimate thing, *hoc meum est*.[49] We can from then on itemise the consequences of the master's right of property over the servant: (a) the master can sell or bequeath his servant by will and testament; (b) whatever he may do to him, he does not commit injustice in this regard; (c) his right of property is perpetual; (d) he can, if he wishes, deliver the servant from his servitude in freeing him, in chasing him away, etc.; (e) if he himself comes to

be, voluntarily or by forced subjection, servant of another master, the property of his old servants passes to the new master. We thus see the extent of the master's right of dominion. In fact, it is distinguished from the right of full ownership of a thing only on one point alone, though a major point: if the servant is deprived of his corporeal liberty (this which can happen only if he is imprisoned, chained or, what amounts to the same thing, in danger of death), he is then liberated from all obligation to the master and can exercise the natural right to defend his life in fleeing or even in killing the master. But this reservation signifies only that the master's right of full ownership over the servant is not absolutely full. The declaration of the master, *hoc meum est*, does not totally transform the servant into a thing. In other words, the conception of servitude developed in *The Elements of Law* and *De Cive* is close to an appropriation by the master not only of the actions but also of the physical person of the slave. Without that, this appropriation is not totally realised.[50] We will better measure the conception that we are going to examine in comparing it with the analysis of the perfect voluntary servant in Grotius.[51] Perfect servitude consists in serving all his life a master in exchange for food and other things necessary to life that he must provide for the servant. Thus conceived and 'accepted within natural limits it contains no element of undue severity', says Grotius.[52] Indeed, not only does the master have the right neither to kill the servant nor to inflict physical abuse upon him, that Hobbes would accept with some reservations, but, what is more, he does not have in any way right over his children, that Hobbes would not accept: 'the children of the servant are the goods of the master in *perpetuum*'.[53]

2. *Dominium paternum* falls under the jurisdiction of a specific title of dominion. Against Grotius,[54] Hobbes refuses the two theses according to which: (a) generation alone gives a right over the child; (b) and gives it to the father, because of the superiority of the masculine sex. It is thus important to show 'by what title one man cometh to have property in a child'.[55] This title of property over the child belongs not to the one who gives life to the child, but to the one who preserves it. Yet it is the mother who first has the power [*puissance*] to preserve or destroy her progeny. It is thus she who originally has the right of property of the child. The father or any other man could obtain it only if the mother abandons the child or if she transfers to a man a right over herself. However, as a title of property must always be based on a juridical act, the child is supposed to make a pact of obedience with its mother. What is the

extent of the right of dominion over the child? It is again wider than in the servant's case. Children are indeed 'in most absolute subjection to him or her, that so bringeth them up, or preserveth them'.[56] The right enveloped within *dominium paternum* is indeed composed of the right of life and death. Let us specify, however, that this right belongs to paternal power [*pouvoir*] only in the purely theoretical hypothesis of the existence of a family in the state of nature. The fact remains that the person's full and complete ownership, which could not totally take place in the servant's case, manages, paradoxically, to become reality in the child's case. Paternal dominion indeed reduces the child to the state of thing that we can give, sell, put in the service of other persons, kill if he rebels, etc. The comparison of Hobbes's conception with that of Grotius' will here also be significant.[57] For the latter, only the father has the right to govern the child (this right covers the right to punish but only so as to coerce the child to perform its duties or so as to correct it). But this right of the father disappears as soon as the child acquires the capacity to judge necessary to the conduct of its actions and leaves its father's house. The child, thus become adult, is absolute master of its actions and totally independent of others' right. Additionally, the child has a right of property over the things that belong to it, the use of this right alone finds itself deferred. We thus see how Grotius, as opposed to Hobbes, limits paternal right to only provisional government of the child's actions.

3. Will it be otherwise in the case of the third constitutive mode of dominion over persons, namely, that which is established by institution? This third mode takes on the status of the sovereign's right in the instituted state. In order to determine the content of the sovereign's right of dominion, it is thus necessary to return to the utterance of the pact that institutes it. Now, the clause of the social pact that each makes with each other is limited to the transfer of the right of use (*jus utendi*) of each individual's power [*puissance*].[58] The sovereign's right thus must, in principle, be limited to directing the subjects' or citizens' actions enveloped and included within the will of a man or a council.[59] Having developed it at length below, we will here insist neither on this mode of possession of the right over actions in the instituted state nor on the considerable difficulties that this theory presents in the version that *The Elements of Law* and *De Cive* give of it.

We will retain only that the three constitutive modes of the right of dominion over persons are thought in terms of property. This property takes two forms politically.[60] Indeed, the right of dominion's two primary modes of acquisition give birth to the patrimonial kingdom (*patrimonial kingdom*[61]/*regnum patrimoniale*), while the third gives birth to an instituted kingdom or monarchy (*monarchia institutiva*).[62] Yet these two forms of state are only specifications of the distinction between the two great categories of state that embrace all forms of government: the *civitas acquisita* or *commonwealth by acquisition* and the *civitas institutiva* or *commonwealth by institution*.[63] These two forms of state are distinguished, as Hobbes says, by the origin or the constitutive mode of dominion, but they are also distinguished, as this results from our prior developments, by the manner in which the right of dominion is possessed by the sovereign. In going back over a distinction performed by Grotius in the chapter on sovereignty from *De Jure belli ac pacis*,[64] we were able to see that, in the same fashion that Grotius distinguishes kings who possess sovereign power [*pouvoir*] as a usufruct, Hobbes seems to confer to the sovereigns of states of acquisition a possession of power [*pouvoir*] in the form of full ownership over subjects and to the sovereigns of states of institution a possession of power [*pouvoir*] in the form of usufruct (not temporary but perpetual) over the actions of subjects.

We thus see the considerable place that property occupies in political theory. It remains to be seen if the doctrine of sovereignty is not totally dependent on it.

## SOVEREIGNTY: *DOMINIUM/AUCTORITAS*

Such does not seem to us to be the case. An argument for it constantly submitted by Hobbes is already the clue: the identity of the sovereign's rights (*sovereignty*[65]/*summa potestas*) in a state of institution as well as in a state of acquisition: 'the Rights, and Consequences of Soveraignty, are the same in both'.[66] In other words sovereignty remains the same whatever may be its origin or the constitutive mode of the right over persons. This assertion, already present in *The Elements of Law* and *De Cive*, takes on particular importance in *Leviathan* because there Hobbes additionally indicates that the practices of government must also be identical. This is indeed, on the part of the sovereign, an act

> to demand of one Nation more than of the other [this where sovereignty was established by institution], from the title of Conquest,

as being a Conquered Nation, is an act of ignorance of the Rights of Soveraignty.[67]

We said in the beginning that the Hobbesian doctrine of sovereignty emancipates the political relationship from the relationship of property. It is possible to see this by the examination of two major points. The first will consist in showing the validity in Hobbes of the distinction brought about by Grotius between the manner of possessing sovereignty and the extent of the right of sovereignty. The second, in showing that the concept of authorisation, applied in *Leviathan* to political theory, furnishes the juridical key making it possible to think the political relationship in terms other than the relationship of property. We understand from then on the considerable reorganisation that the juridico-political theory of *The Elements of Law* and *De Cive* will undergo in *Leviathan*.

1. After having defined sovereignty as the civil power [*puissance*], the acts of which are independent of a superior power [*pouvoir*] and cannot be annulled by another human will,[68] Grotius presents a certain number of remarks, the second of which we will retain. It consists in presenting a distinction between sovereignty, on the one hand, and the more or less full manner in which it is possessed, on the other hand. This distinction, established from the difference between the range of a right and the manner of possessing it in the domain of property in things, is going to have the effect of conferring an autonomy upon the concept of sovereignty in the domain of the political right of conferring. Thus, just as, regarding corporeal or incorporeal things, possession can be of full ownership, by right of usufruct or time, likewise Grotius says:

> [T]he Roman dictator held the sovereign power by a right limited in time; but most kings, both those who are the first to be chosen and those who succeed them in lawful succession, hold it as a usufruct. Some kings, however, possess the sovereign power in full right of ownership, having acquired it in lawful war, or through the submission of a people which, to avoid greater disaster, subjected itself without any reservation.[69]

But, it being a question of a sovereignty of full ownership, of a usufructary sovereignty or of a temporary sovereignty, this changes nothing in the range of the right of sovereignty which remains identical in the three cases. We in fact judge the nature of moral things by their operations, so that the rights that produce the same effects are identical and must have the same name. Thus, since, in the three cases, acts of power [*pouvoir*] are exercised in such a way that they can be annulled by any other person, there is identity of sovereignty.

It goes without saying that the distinction carried out by Grotius cannot be applied to Hobbes without some reorganisations. We know that, for Hobbes, there cannot be temporary, limited or shared sovereignty. The fact remains that the range of the right of sovereignty remains, for him, the same whatever may be sovereignty's origin (acquisition or institution) and whatever may be the manner in which it is possessed (patrimonial mode or usufructary mode). The application of Grotius' distinction thus has a double advantage in Hobbes: it allows us to understand the reason for the identity of sovereigns' rights and the autonomy of the exercise of sovereignty.

2. But Hobbes goes farther. For it is not sufficient to assure autonomy to the extent of sovereignty's right. It is additionally necessary to furnish the juridical key making it possible to think the relation between sovereign and subjects in a manner different from the relation of property. In other words, it is necessary to think the right over persons and actions some way other than the right over things, thus some way other than in terms of full ownership or usufruct. As far as the right over things is concerned, Hobbes has elaborated a theory of the transfer of right in order to take account of how a thing can be alienated.[70] It was thus necessary to form another concept likely to take account, independently of the transfer of right over things, of the constitution of a right over persons and actions. This that returns to seek the juridical key of a double operation which aims at: (1) establishing a relation between persons in such a way that one could have a right over the other without reducing this other to a thing; (2) giving a content to the idea of a right over actions that does not call into question the inalienable right that each individual has over his physical person.

Hobbes furnishes this juridical key in *Leviathan* while discovering the concept that, in the right over persons, must be substituted for the valid concept of alienation in the right over things. Yet the formulation of this substitute is played out precisely in the distinction between *dominium* and *auctoritas* or *authoritas*. The crux of the matter is contained in the following text:

Of Persons Artificiall, some have their words and actions *Owned* by those whom they represent. And then the Person is the *Actor*; and he that owneth his words and actions, is the AUTHOR: In which case the Actor acteth by Authority. For that which in speaking of goods and possessions, is called an OWNER, and in latine *Dominus*, in Greeke *xurios*; speaking of Actions, is called Author. And as the Right of possession, is called Dominion [*Dominium*]; so the Right of doing any Action, is called AUTHORITY [*Authoritas*]. So that by Authority, is always understood a Right of doing any act: and *done by Authority*, done by Commission, or License from him whose right it is.[71]

The exhaustive explanation of this text will lead too far. It will suppose indeed a complete exposition of the theory of the artificial person and of representation, to which we devote the next two chapters. We will content ourselves here to remark that the notion of *authority/authoritas* occupies, for actions, the place that the notion of *dominion/dominium* occupies for things: it defines a right over actions distinct from the right over things.[72] Correlatively, as regards actions, the *author* is substituted for *dominus*.[73] The problem of the right over persons can from then on be formulated in a manner absolutely distinct from the problem of the right over things: it puts into relation an author and an actor between whom a relationship of authorisation is established. The juridical relationships between persons must be rethought starting from this relationship where the actor's right, far from annulling the author's right, is, on the contrary, founded on it. The theory of the social contract will be a particular case of it: that by which a multitude of actors authorise all the actions of a determinate actor. Thus understood, the social contract permits constituting some rights of sovereignty which do not void but, on the contrary, suppose the permanence of subjects' rights. For the problem of the political appropriation of the person and of the subject's actions is substituted that of the constitution of a sovereign will that the subjects must recognise as theirs. In other words, in *Leviathan* a theory of sovereignty takes shape that, in the same movement by which it is emancipated from the theory of property, opens one of the fundamental problems of modern political thought: that of the formation of a sovereign will which may also be that of all the subjects.

3. We thus understand that, starting from the substitution of a theory of authority/authorisation for a theory of *dominium*, Hobbes submits, in

*Leviathan*, the whole of the conception of the right over persons from *The Elements of Law* and *De Cive* to a profound reform. One question remains unresolved, however: how is it that the notion of *dominium* keeps an important place in *Leviathan*, and precisely within the framework of the right over persons? We can sketch two responses. (1) If, in *Leviathan*, Hobbes liberates sovereignty from its dependence on the theory of property, this emancipation is fully realised, even at the level of vocabulary, only in the case of republics of institution. On the other hand, in the case of republics of acquisition, where power [*pouvoir*] is obtained by force, the notion of *dominium* is retained, and as juxtaposed to the doctrine of authorisation, which henceforth furnishes the sole model for the establishment of a right over persons.[74] (2) This juxtaposition does not leave the concept of *dominium* unchanged. It indeed signifies henceforth less a relationship of property than the exteriority of the sovereign will and of the power [*pouvoir*] of coercion that is imposed on the wills of individuals. By the convention of authorisation, each subject is indeed simply *supposed* to recognise the wills and actions of the sovereign for his own. This does not mean that he always, nor even most often, recognises himself there.

If the Hobbesian theory of sovereignty is emancipated from the theory of property, it nevertheless still lets certain aspects of the problem from which it is liberated show through.

It is henceforth important to consider for itself the profound reorganisation of the doctrine of the social pact and of the right over persons that *Leviathan* introduces, with the theory of authorisation/ representation, in relation to *The Elements of Law* and *De Cive*.

*Notes*

1. This is the case with Steven Buckle's book, *Natural Law and the Theory of Property: Grotius to Hume* (Oxford: Clarendon Press, 1991). The author passes from Grotius to Pufendorf without stopping at Hobbes. On the other hand, we will find some useful analyses, unhappily too often interrupted by biographical considerations without interest, in James Tully's work, *A Discourse on Property: John Locke and His Adveraries* (Cambridge: Cambridge University Press, 1980). A French translation of this work was published under the title of *Locke: droit naturel et propriété*, trans. Philippe Raynaud (Paris: PUF, 1992). Of overall value is Marie-France Renoux-Zagamé's excellent work, *Origines théologiques du concepts moderne de propriété* (Geneva: Droz, 1987). There we will find an impressive

documentation of Second Scholasticism and analyses of primary importance on the theology of territory. As far as Hobbes is concerned, we will recall C. B. Macpherson's work, *The Political Theory of Individualism: Hobbes to Locke* (Oxford: Oxford University Press, 1962). Finally, it is important to highlight Alexandre Matheron's two remarkable articles: 'Maîtres et serviteurs dans la philosophie politique classique', *La Pensée*, 200 (1978): 3-20, reprinted in *Anthropologie et politique au XVIIe siècle* (Paris: Vrin, 1986), pp. 171–88; and 'Spinoza et la propriété', in *Anthropologie et politique au XVIIe siècle*, pp. 155–69.

2. Hobbes, *Leviathan*, p. 296 [TN: in English in the original].
3. Hobbes, *Leviathan*, in *Opera Philosophica*, p. 186.
4. The English text of *De Cive* gives 'right of dominion'.
5. Hobbes, *De Cive*, p. 249 [TN: 'for to be a *King*, is nothing else but to have *Dominion* over many *Persons*' (Hobbes, *De Cive: The English Version*, p. 117).]
6. Hobbes, *The Elements of Law*, p. 127, my emphasis; see also Hobbes, *De Cive*, p. 249. [TN: in English in the original.]
7. [TN: in English in the original.]
8. [TN: in English in the original.]
9. Power [*pouvoir*] (*potestas*) does not come down to a simple power [*puissance*] (*potentia*) of fact, but also covers a right (*jus*).
10. [TN: italicised English in English in the original.]
11. See, for example *De Cive*, p. 251: '*proprietas* et *dominium* in res suas'. [TN: 'a *propriety*, and *Dominion* over *his own goods*' (Hobbes, *De Cive: The English Version*, p. 119).]
12. St Thomas Aquinas, *Summa Theologicae*, vol. 38, trans. Marcus Lefébure O.P. (Oxford: Blackfriars, 1975), 2a2ae. 66, 1 and 2, pp. 63 and 65.
13. Ibid., 2a2ae. 66, 2, sol. 1, p. 69.
14. *De Jure Belli ac Pacis Libri Tres*, trans. Francis W. Kelsey et al., vol. 2 (New York: Oceana Publications, 1964), ch. 2, p. 186. Chapter 2 of book 2 concerns right common to all men and chapter 3 of the same book concerns particular right. The identical terminology between *proprietas* and *dominium* is indicated from vol. 2, ch. 2, I: 'In order to understand the distinction fully, it will be necessary to know the origin of proprietorship, which jurists call the right of ownership.'
15. Ibid., vol. 2, ch. 2, II, p. 186.
16. The things that passed into property are those that were likely to be it, in opposition to those that can in no case at all become it (for example, the sea) and for which common right persists.
17. For St Thomas, the enjoyment of exterior goods remains common: 'Man's other competence is to use and manage the world's resources. Now in regard to this, no man is entitled to manage things merely for himself, he

must do so in the interests of all, so that he is ready to share them with others in case of necessity. This is why Paul writes to Timothy, "*As for the rich of this world, charge them to be liberal and generous*"' (Aquinas, *Summa Theologica*, 2a2ae. 66, 2, rep., p. 69).

18. 'Having laid down these fundamental principles, we say that the sea, viewed either as a whole or in its principal divisions, cannot become subject to private ownership. Since, however, such ownership is conceded by some in the case of individuals but not in the case of nations, we bring forward proof, first on moral grounds.'

'The cause which led to the abandonment of common ownership here ceases to be operative . . .'

'The reason is that occupation takes place only in the case of a thing which has definite limits.' (Grotius, *De Jure Belli ac Pacis*, vol. 2, ch. 2, III, pp. 190–1)

19. See the analysis given by Matheron, 'Spinoza et la propriété', pp. 155–69.
20. For detail on Hobbes's ethical and natural right [*jusnaturalistes*] positions, see our work *La décision métaphysique de Hobbes*, pp. 255–356.
21. Hobbes, *Leviathan*, pp. 295–6; *Leviathan*, in *Opera Philisophica*, pp. 185–6.
22. [TN: in English in the original.]
23. Hobbes, *Leviathan*, in *Opera Philisophica*, p. 186. [TN: 'For where there is no Common-wealth, there is (as hath been already shewn) a perpetual warre of every man against his neighbour' (Hobbes, *Leviathan*, p. 296).]
24. Hobbes, *The Elements of Law*, p. 72.
25. Ibid. [TN: in English in the original.]
26. Hobbes, *Leviathan*, in *Opera Philisophica*, p. 112. [TN: my translation. The original reads, 'civitas, proprietas bonorum, et justitia simul nata sunt'.]
27. Hobbes, *Leviathan*, p. 297.
28. See Hobbes, *The Elements of Law*, pp. 139–40.
29. Ibid., p. 131. [TN: in English in the original.]
30. Ibid., p. 140.
31. Power [*puissance*] (*potentia*) is defined in particular in chapter 10 of *Leviathan* (p. 150; Latin version, p. 68). In any event, it evidently exists before the appearance of property.
32. See Hobbes, *De Cive*, p. 257, where the notion of *dominium in personam* figures.
33. Ibid., pp. 249–50; Hobbes, *The Elements of Law*, pp. 127–8.
34. See Hobbes, *The Elements of Law*, p. 127. [TN: italicised English in English in the original.]
35. See also Hobbes, *De Cive*, p. 255, concerning paternal power [*pouvoir*].
36. François Tricaud signals this fact in his translation of *Leviathan*, p. 211n.22.

37. See Grotius, *De Jure Belli ac Pacis*, vol. 1, ch. 1, V.
38. The chapter where Grotius examines the constitutive mode of the right over persons begins thus: 'A RIGHT is acquired not only over things but also over persons. Such rights have their origin primarily in generation, consent, or crime' (Grotius, *De Jure Belli ac Pacis*, vol. 2, ch. 5, I, p. 231).
39. It is a question of *The Elements of Law*, chs 2, 3 and 4, and *De Cive*, chs 8 and 9.
40. Grotius, *De Jure Belli ac Pacis*, vol. 1, ch. 3, VII.
41. Ibid., vol. 1, ch. 3, XI.
42. Ibid., vol. 2, ch. 3, IV, p. 207.
43. [TN: in English in the original.]
44. Hobbes, *Leviathan*, pp. 209–10.
45. See Hobbes, *The Elements of Law*, pp. 128–30. The contract between the weakest and the strongest distinguishes the servant from the slave. The latter is subject only to a constraint from doing. It does not in any way make a contract with the master. The distinction between servant and slave is given in French in *De Cive*, because the Latin has only a single term for the two: *servus* (Hobbes, *De Cive*, p. 250). *The Elements of Law* (Hobbes, *The Elements of Law*, p. 128) correlatively distinguishes between *servant* and *slave* [TN: italicised English in English in the original]. The Hobbesian difference approximately corresponds to the one that Grotius effects between the perfect servant, on the one hand, and the slave who falls under the jurisdiction of the right of people, on the other (cf. *De Jure Belli ac Pacis*, III, VII, 1–7), that is to say, the prisoner of war. There is, however, this difference, that Hobbes's slave is always an imprisoned or chained slave. He does not thus have corporeal liberty at his disposal. This is why in *De Cive* he is named *ergastulus*.
46. [TN: in English in the original.]
47. With a limitation concerning what contravenes natural laws. But this reservation is of little weight.
48. 'Qui enim jure disponit de *persona* hominis, de omnibus rebus disponit de quibus disponere potuit *persona*' (Hobbes, *De Cive*, p. 251). [TN: 'for he that can by Right dispose of all those things that the *Person* of a man, may surely dispose of all those things which that *Person* could dispose of' (Hobbes, *De Cive: The English Version*, p. 119).]
49. Hobbes, *De Cive*, p. 251.
50. We cannot develop this point here, yet let it be enough for us to say that, pushed to its ultimate implications, it would attest to the contradictory character of the Hobbesian conception of a servitude founded on a pact.
51. See Grotius, *De Jure Belli ac Pacis*, vol. 2, ch. 5, XXVII.
52. [TN: Ibid., vol. 2, ch. 5, XXVII, p. 255.]
53. Hobbes, *The Elements of Law*, p. 133. [TN: in English in the original.]

## On Property

54. See Grotius, *De Jure Belli ac Pacis*, vol. 2, ch. 5, I.
55. Hobbes, *The Elements of Law*, p. 131. [TN: in English in the original.]
56. Ibid., p. 134.
57. See Grotius, *De Jure Belli ac Pacis*, vol. 2, ch. 5, I–VII.
58. '[F]or each Citizen compacting with his fellow, says thus, *I conveigh my Right on this Party, upon condition that you passe yours to the same*; by which means, that Right which every man had before to use his faculties to his own advantage, is now wholly translated on some certain man, or Councell, for the common benefit' (Hobbes, *De Cive: The English Version*, p. 105; *De Cive*, p. 234).
59. '[U]nion; which is defined . . . to be the involving or including the wills of many in the will of one man, or in the will of the greatest part of any one number of men, that is to say, in the will of one man, or of one COUNCIL' (Hobbes, *The Elements of Law*, p. 103).
60. In fact, the theory of the transfer of right in *The Elements of Law* and *De Cive* is incapable of founding simultaneously the subjects' positive obligation to act and the sovereign's right to punish. See Chapter 9, 'On the State', and Chapter 10, 'On the Right to Punish'.
61. [TN: in English in the original.]
62. See Hobbes, *The Elements of Law*, p. 135; *De Cive*, p. 260.
63. [TN: italicised English in English in the original.]
64. Grotius, *De Jure ac Pacis*, vol. 1, ch. 3, XI.
65. [TN: in English in the original.]
66. Hobbes, *Leviathan*, p. 252.
67. Ibid., p. 257.
68. See Grotius, *De Jure Belli ac Pacis*, vol. 1, ch. 3, VII.
69. Ibid., vol. 1, ch. 3, XI, p. 114.
70. See Hobbes, *The Elements of Law*, pp. 74–81; *De Cive*, pp. 168–80; *Leviathan*, pp. 128–42.
71. Hobbes, *Leviathan*, p. 218; *Leviathan*, in *Opera Philosophica*, p. 123.
72. [TN: italicised English in English in the original.]
73. [TN: italicised English in the original.]
74. See the definition of the republic of acquisition given in *Leviathan*, pp. 251–2.

*Chapter 9*

# ON THE STATE

### REPRESENTATION, CIVIL PERSON AND STATE

The theory of juridical representation – a particular case of which is the theory of political representation – formulated in chapter 16 of *Leviathan* is not only one of the absolutely new aspects of this work in relation to *The Elements of Law* and *De Cive*. It is a centrepiece starting from which Hobbes reconstructs the whole of his theory of the social contract. Indeed, the social contract puts into play the passage from a multiplicity of natural persons in conflict to a single civil person. Hobbes formulates the passage thus in *The Elements of Law*: 'a multitude of persons are united by covenants into one person civil, or body politic'.[1] *De Cive* takes up a comparable formulation again: 'By what hath been sayd, it is sufficiently shewed, in what degrees *many naturall persons*, through desire of preserving themselves, and by mutuall feare, have growne together into *a civill Person*, whom we have called a *City*.'[2] Finally, we can read in *Leviathan*: 'A Multitude of men, are made *One* Person, when they are by one man, or one Person, Represented.'[3] The fundamental difference in relation to the two preceding utterances is that henceforth the notion of representation takes account of the notion of the civil person.

Yet the versions of the social pact from *The Elements of Law* and *De Cive* do not allow for taking account of the constitution of the civil person, so that the political edifice, no sooner erected, collapses. The notion of the civil person (*persona civilis*) that appears in each of these works will never be truly operational. It is thus upon the debris of the theory of the social contract and of the state from *The Elements of Law* and *De Cive* that *Leviathan* is going to reconstruct the juridical armature of a new political edifice with political representation.[4]

## POLITICAL THEORY WITHOUT REPRESENTATION: THE INSTITUTION OF THE CIVIL PERSON IN *THE ELEMENTS OF LAW* AND *DE CIVE*

In order to examine political theory without representation, it is necessary to again take up the problem of the social pact at its starting point such as it is spelled out in chapter 19 of the first part of *The Elements of Law* and in chapter 5 of *De Cive*. We find almost the same formulation in the two works:

> In this estate of man therefore, wherein all men are equal, and every man allowed to be his own judge, the fears they have one of another are equal, and every man's hopes consist in his own sleight and strength; and consequently when any man by his natural passion, is provoked to break these laws of nature, there is no security in any other man of his own defence but anticipation. And for this cause, every man's right (howsoever he be inclined to peace) of doing whatsoever seemeth good in his own eyes, remaineth with him still, as the necessary means of his preservation. And therefore till there be security amongst men for the keeping of the law of nature one towards another, men are still in the estate of war, and nothing is unlawful to any man that tendeth to his own safety or commodity; and this safety and commodity consisteth in the mutual aid and help of one another, whereby also followeth the mutual fear of one another.
>
> It is a proverbial saying, *inter arma silent leges*.[5]

This very dense text sums up, on the threshold of the state's institution, all the elements that form the problem that the social contract will have to resolve. Let us again take up the two principal points that characterise the logic of the situation for individuals within the state of war. This is first of all a state of equality of fact between men which consists less of an equality of force than of an equality of power [*puissance*]. Since each is capable of the utmost, namely, killing the other, individual differences become negligible. This equality implies that none of them can establish his dominion over others. More, each individual being in total uncertainty of others' designs, equality of power [*puissance*] is transformed into equality of fear. So that, in the absence of all natural justice, each is to himself his own judge. There is thus a third form of equality: the equality of liberty.

Equality under these forms, far from being a factor for peace and harmony, leads to violence. Since the outcome of a fight is not played out in advance, each can hope to have advantage over the other. But, at the same time, equality impeding anyone from being able to win a decisive victory, it is thus the condition for a war which it is impossible to get out of except by death. In this condition of generalised insecurity wherein all the signs of human behaviour are suspect, the worry of defending oneself leads each individual to anticipate a real or imaginary aggression the object of which, at any instant, he can be.

Reason supports this factual situation in right through the formulation of the natural right which is nothing other than the verbal expression of the *conatus* of self-preservation. Thus, all individuals have an equal right over all. However, this right is a 'right for' ['*droit de*'] which gives no 'right to' ['*droit à*'] anything. It is a subjective right which in no way creates reciprocal obligation. Thus, natural right, far from furnishing the means to get out of war, reinforces it, and consequently 'we manifestly contradict that our intention'.[6] Let us remark in passing that, in its essence or its definition, right is not reduced to fact or to power [*puissance*]. Thus, we do not have right to do what will be contrary to our preservation since the latter is the end of right. But, within the state of nature, individuals cannot distinguish with certainty what is necessary to their preservation from what is not necessary and even from what is contrary to it. The result is that only within the state of war is right reduced to power [*puissance*]:

> Out of which may also be collected, that irresistible might in state of nature is right.[7]

Yet, precisely, this reduction of right to power [*puissance*] puts natural right into contradiction with itself. In order to prevent this contradiction, reason dictates to each the natural law that prescribes seeking peace. However, natural law is not the sole means given to it, since it obliges only *in foro interno* and not *in foro externo*. It concerns only intention or predisposition, but, without any external guarantee on others' intentions, natural law keeps quiet. The means for peace must furnish a double guarantee (*security*):[8] that of mutual support against an exterior enemy and that from a fear such that it could bring to each a certainty concerning others' designs. The social contract will thus have to bring a response to the search for this double guarantee that the simple concord (*concord*)⁹ or simple consent (*consent*)¹⁰ of several wills cannot furnish. The search for this double guarantee must thus lead to the constitution of a common power [*pouvoir*].

How can such a power [*pouvoir*] be constituted? The response is identical in *The Elements of Law* and in *De Cive*: by union (*union*,¹¹ *unio*). *The Elements of Law* defines this 'union' as 'the involving or including the wills of many in the will of one man, or in the will of the greatest part of any one number of men, that is to say, in the will of one man, or of one COUNCIL'.¹² A few lines below, we can read that this union is 'BODY POLITIC or civil society . . . which may be defined to be a multitude of men, united as one person by a common power, for their common peace, defence, and benefit.'¹³ The union thus constitutes a civil person in making us pass from a multiplicity of wills to a single will:

> Now *union* thus made is called a *City* [civitas], or *civill society* [societas civilis], and also a *civill Person* [persona civilis]; for when there is *one will* of all men, it is to be esteemed for *one Person* [una persona].¹⁴

The constitution of this civil person endowed with a single will must be carried out in such a way that it 'may use all the power and faculties of each particular person, to the maintenance of peace, and for common defence'.¹⁵ Subsequently, three questions are posed: (1) what type of contract gives existence to the civil person? (2) Does this contract make it possible to take account of the rights which are attached to it? (3) Finally, does this contract assure the transfer of power [*pouvoir*] without which the state could not have the means to assume its function?

Let us begin with the first question: what type of contract gives existence to the civil person? In order to understand it, it is necessary to remove two impasses, one of which comes from an impossibility of fact and the other from an abuse of words.

First, the social contract does not involve the subjects actually transmitting their power [*pouvoir*] or their force:

> [B]ecause it is impossible for any man really to transfer his own strength to another, or for that other to receive it; it is to be understood: that to transfer a man's power and strength, is no more but to lay by or relinquish his own right of resisting him to whom he so transferreth it.¹⁶

This impossibility concerns natural powers [*pouvoirs*], that is to say, the faculties of the body and of the mind. The impossibility of transmitting natural powers [*pouvoirs*] allows us to fundamentally distinguish the unity of the political body from the unity of a natural body, which is realised by the composition of movements and of the directions of its small parts the summation of which allows for calculating force. The institution of the civil person, no more than the functioning of the state, falls under the jurisdiction of a simple physics of force or of the composition of conatus. The birth and function of the state imply, as we have seen, a dynamics of signs and not only of force. This is why the transfer of power [*pouvoir*] comes under a juridical theory of transmission of right. The civil person, having a juridical act for an origin, will have only a juridical existence. It draws its unity from the contract that institutes it, thus it is no longer necessary to confuse it with an individual's natural unity. Thus explained why a monarch as well as a council can be considered as a single civil person. The fact remains that the whole question is of knowing whether the theory of transferring right that we find in *The Elements of Law* and *De Cive* makes it possible to take account of it. We will revisit this point soon.

The second impasse draws from the abuse of words that compose the phrase 'will will':[17]

> And though will of man, being not voluntary, but the beginning of voluntary actions, is not subject to deliberation and covenant; yet when a man covenanteth to subject his will to the command of another, he obligeth himself to this, that he resign his strength and means to him, whom he covenanteth to obey.[18]

The phrase 'voluntary will' runs afoul of the same critique as that of free will [*volonté libre*]. In these two cases we verbally transform an accident into substance when we attribute to it other accidents: 'Lastly, from the use of the word *Freewill*, no liberty can be inferred to the will, desire, or inclination, but the liberty of the man; which consisteth in this, that he finds no stop, in doing what he has the will, desire, or inclination to doe.'[19] And just as the phrase 'free will' arouses the fallacious dogma of a free will [*libre arbitre*] opposed to necessity, likewise that of voluntary will subtends the opinion of those who intend to remove every obligatory character in the sovereign's orders. In fact, the will is the last of the passions that succeed one another in deliberation. To will is thus to have ceased deliberating. We cannot understand the social pact along the lines of a voluntary will that renders the rights of the sovereign conditional. The voluntary act of the contract must thus consist of a submission (*to subject his will to the command of another*)[20] of the will. The civil person is thus produced by a pact of submission.

The modalities of this pact of submission consist of a commitment from individuals to transfer their natural right to a man to whom or to a council which, for its part, promises nothing: 'each Citizen compacting with his fellow, sayes thus, *I conveigh my Right on this Party, upon condition that you passe yours to the same*; by which means, that Right which every man had before to use his faculties to his own advantage, is now wholly translated on some certain man, or Councell, for the common benefit'.[21] From this interindividual pact must follow a double obligation: (1) a mutual obligation: the subjects are committed to each other; (2) an obligation with regard to the man or the council to which right has been transferred. The social contract must have the effect of constituting '*one Person*, whose *will*, by the compact of many men, is to be received for the *will* of them all; so as he may use all the power and faculties of each particular person, to the maintenance of peace, and for common defence'.[22] It is thus necessary to examine the content of the transfer of right in *The Elements of Law* and *De Cive* in order to attempt to respond to the second question: does the social contract permit taking account of the rights that are attached to the civil person?

In these two works, there are two manners of relinquishing a right that one possesses, without any distinction being made between the relinquishment of a right that we have over a thing and the relinquishment of the right that we have over ourselves: abandoning it or transferring it to another.

> To RELINQUISH it, is by sufficient signs to declare, that it is his will no more to do that action, which of right he might have done before. To TRANSFER right to another, is by sufficient signs to declare to that other accepting thereof, that it is his will not to resist, or hinder him, according to that right he had thereto before he transferred it.[23]

Only the second manner interests us here since the social contract consists of a transfer and not an abandonment of right. If we follow to the letter the terms by which the nature of the transfer is expressed, we must say that, strictly speaking, it transmits nothing at all. It consists simply in not standing in the way of the other's natural right. On the threshold of the state's institution, each one has a natural right over all. To transfer one's right is to leave enjoying one's own to others, without impediment on our part. It is thus a question of knowing, starting from this definition of the transfer of right, what the social contract commits us not to resist. The purpose of the institution of the state being the conservation of life, non-resistance will not be unlimited. First of all, it focuses on all the things that we possess. Indeed, as we have seen in the previous chapter, there is no property (wealth or land) so absolute that it would deprive the sovereign of the right to make use of it. The social contract makes the sovereign the source of the difference between 'mine' and 'yours'. There is thus never absolute 'yours' and 'mine'. But if we do not have absolute right over the things that we possess, this is not true for the rights that we have over ourselves. Articles 18 and 19 of chapter 2 of *De Cive* will thus show that there are some inalienable rights of the individual, like the right to resist those who attack us by force in order to take away our life, to wound us or to imprison us, a right that is extended to the right to resist punishment even when it is legitimate.[24] Likewise, a contract stipulating that we are committed to accusing ourselves is null.[25] The subjects thus preserve their natural right over their life and over all the actions that have the function of preserving it when it is in peril. This is why *The Elements of Law* introduces a reserve within non-resistance for individuals when the sovereign's power [*pouvoir*] of coercion is exercised:

> This power of coercion, as hath been said chapt. 15, sect. 3, of the former part, consisteth in the transferring of every man's right of resistance against him to whom he hath transferred the power of coercion. It followeth therefore, that no man in any commonwealth whatsoever hath right to resist him, or them, on whom they have conferred this power coercive, or (as men use to call it) the sword of justice; supposing the not-resistance possible. For (Part I, chapter 15, sect. 18) covenants bind but to the utmost of our endeavour.[26]

What thus are those of our actions the right of which we will transfer to the state or to the civil person? What is the domain of non-resistance to power [*pouvoir*]? To what obligations are subjects held? In order to take account of this, *De Cive* involves a distinction between the right of resistance in general and the right of defending oneself. Indeed, the submission of all men to the will of one man alone or one council alone occurs 'when each one of them obligeth himself by contract to every one of the rest, not to resist the *will* of that *one man*, or *counsel*, to which he hath submitted himselfe; that is, that he refuse him not the use of his wealth, and strength, against any others whatsoever (for he is supposed still to retain a Right of defending himselfe against violence) and this is called UNION.'[27] If we follow the distinction from *De Cive*, the pact of submission will imply an obligation of non-resistance when it is a question of others, but not when it is a question of self. But the difficulty is then only displaced, for the subjects' obligation of non-resistance thus restrained, will remain totally negative: to commit oneself not to resist is not to commit oneself to doing something. If not to resist really does mean not placing obstacles to the sovereign's rights, we do not see in the name of what could the obligation not to resist found a positive obligation to obey. The contract of submission thus does not confer right to oblige to act in any way. This is what makes up all the ambiguity of the text of *The Elements of Law* where Hobbes matches some obligations of non-resistance of the subjects to the sovereign's rights but where he pretends, at the same time, that the subjects are obliged to obey:

> [T]hat man or assembly, that by their own right not derived from the present right of any other, may make laws, or abrogate them, at his, or their pleasure, have the sovereignty absolute. For seeing the laws they make, are supposed to be made by right, the members of the commonwealth to whom they are made, are obliged to obey them; and consequently not to resist the execution of them; which not-resistance maketh the power absolute of him that ordaineth them.[28]

Between not resisting the application of a law and accomplishing what this law orders, there is a juridical gap that nothing allows you to fill in. Political power [*pouvoir*] seems here to exceed what the transfer of right accords to it.

This difficulty is clearly recognised by Hobbes in *De Cive* where, making power [*pouvoir*] found obligation immediately on the social contract, he mediately founds it on the aim of the state's institution.[29]

It is indeed one thing to say: *I give to you the right to command it is not important what*, and another thing to say: *I will do all what you will command*. But, from then on, is not the contract that institutes the state or the civil person null and void at that very instant when it appeared? For how could the aim of the political body found a positive obligation which would not be inscribed within the contract of submission? *Leviathan* expresses this consequence explicitly: 'For in the act of our *Submission*, consisteth both our *Obligation*, and our *Liberty*; which must therefore be inferred by arguments taken from thence; there being no obligation on any man, which ariseth not from some Act of his own; for all men equally, are by Nature Free.'[30] If *Leviathan* still appeals to the aim of the state's institution, it is not in order to found the subjects' political obligation, but only in order to calculate its extension.

The juridical theory of the transfer of right from *The Elements of Law* and *De Cive* thus proves incapable of founding the rights that Hobbes attributes to the state in these very works. The sovereign's rights infinitely exceed the pact of non-resistance to which the subjects commit themselves. The notion of the civil person endowed with a single will, which must be taken for the will of all the subjects, will never be truly operational.[31] We already see to what re-elaboration *Leviathan* will submit the whole of the profoundly tottering political edifice of *The Elements of Law* and *De Cive*.

But it is necessary to go farther, for this deficiency of the juridical theory leads to another point of view of the fact, that is to say, of political power [*pouvoir*]. Indeed, to the third question – does the social contract permit the transfer of power [*pouvoir*] without which the state would not have the means to assume its function? – the response must be negative. For, failing to create obligation, the transfer of right will not transmit to the sovereign any new power [*pouvoir*]. In other words, the sovereign's absolute power [*puissance*], characterised as the greatest that men can confer and the greatest that a man or a council can receive, is absolutely empty because it is only based on the subjects' passivity. Thus, absolute power [*pouvoir*] is based on the social contract no more than the rights of the sovereign. The concepts of civil person and of absolute power [*pouvoir*] are simply juxtaposed to a theory of the social contract which cannot take account of it.

If we would follow the theory of the transfer of right understood in the sense of non-resistance all the way, then we would end neither at the civil person nor at absolute power [*pouvoir*]. In fact, the social contract will add nothing to the natural right the holder of which will already be the sovereign as individual in the state of nature, just as it will add nothing to his natural power [*pouvoir*]. The person of the sovereign is redirected then to his natural person (individual or multiple, according to whether it would be a question of a man or a council).

Will the social pact thus conceived make it possible to get out of the state of war? It is this that we can doubt, for how could the sovereign guard his unlimited natural right when it was conditional on war? Would civil peace have for its condition that the sovereign remain in the state of war with his subjects? Thus, far from permitting the constitution of a single will which was that of all and which fixed society's unity, there was rather the constitution of a will totally foreign to the subjects and even radically archaic since it will find the foundation of legitimacy of his acts only in the natural right of the state of war.

## THE STATE AND JURIDICAL ORDER: THE THEORY OF POLITICAL REPRESENTATION IN *LEVIATHAN*

The two principal difficulties for Hobbes's first juridico-political theory come, on the one hand, from the reduction of the transfer of right over persons and actions to the transfer of right over things, and, on the other hand, from this, that the notion of the civil person remained non-elucidated. It is precisely to these two points that the theory of representation of *Leviathan* attempts to bring a new response.

First of all, the theory of representation is a juridical theory the goal of which is to define the notions of natural person and artificial person (the civil person will be a particular case of this), and to determine the constitutive mode as well as the conditions for the validity of an artificial person's acts. It is thus a question for Hobbes of establishing a juridical structure making it possible to interpret the transfer of right over persons and over actions in a way that is not reduced to the transfer of right over things. Thus, to the transfer of right by which we lose all right over the thing that we possessed before transferring it (which is held in chapter 14 of *Leviathan*) is going to be joined a theory of authorisation which has a different content.

The latter essentially aims to take account of the constitution of a subordinate right over persons and actions and to surmount the fundamental difficulty of the transfer of individuals' right to the sovereign from *The Elements of Law* and *De Cive*, which accorded simultaneously too much and too little right to the state. Too much, since to relinquish his right over himself and his actions was to lose all right over self, as we lose all right over a thing in selling or in giving it. Too little, since the transfer of right over self consisted only in non-resistance, and that this in no way implied subjects' positive obligation. The alienation contained in the social contract of submission will no longer consist of a total loss of right by which subjects would become the sovereign's, so to speak, unseizable thing, but in a creation of a right over the natural right that each has over himself.

The theory of political representation is, in a first sense, a particular case of juridical representation, that by which a simultaneously artificial and civil person is constituted. But, in a second sense, it is the foundation of all the other forms of representation and of juridical contract since it must guarantee the validity of the execution of past contracts [*contrats*] between subjects within the state. There thus must be a self-foundation of right and of fact for the social contract. It must in fact itself create the conditions of its own juridical validity and of its own effectiveness. In other words, the social contract will come to be such that it could not be contested, neither in right nor in fact. It will thus come to constitute a right of the state not subject to the judgement of particular subjects and a power [*pouvoir*] likely to enforce it. It is also to the problem of this self-foundation that the theory of political representation has to bring a solution.

Chapter 16 of *Leviathan* begins with the definition of the notion of the person:

> A PERSON, is he *whose words or actions are considered, either as his own, or as representing the words or actions of an other man, or of any other thing to whom they are attributed, whether Truly or by Fiction.*
>
> When they are considered as his owne, then is he called a *Naturall Person*: And when they are considered as representing the words and actions of an other, then is he a *Feigned* or *Artificial person*.[32]

The notion of person designates the juridical relation between an individual and actions or speeches. When speeches or actions are attributed to an individual who speaks and acts, we are dealing with a natural person. When there are two different individuals, one of whom speaks and acts in place of the other, that is to say, in his name, the first is the representative and the second the represented. The representative is then an artificial or a fictive person. The attribution is said to be true when an individual gives to another the right to represent him. It is said to be fictive when the relation between the two individuals is mediated by a thing. A thing can thus be represented by a person, for example: 'Inanimate things, as a Church, an Hospital, a Bridge, may be Personated by a Rector, Master, or Overseer.'[33] The attribution is fictive because the thing cannot authorise itself the speeches or actions of the artificial person and because the authorisation is accorded by the proprietor or the governor: 'But things Inanimate, cannot be Authors, nor therefore give Authority to their Actors: Yet the Actors may have Authority to procure their maintenance, given them by those that are Owners, or Governours of those things. And therefore, such things cannot be Personated, before there be some state of Civill Government.'[34]

This said, it will seem at first glance that the notion of representation is involved in the previous definition only regarding the artificial person. If such were the case, it is not representation that will take account of the notion of natural person, but, on the contrary, that of natural person which will explain that of representation. In fact, a few lines later, Hobbes specifies what the definition of person left in doubt:

> *To Personate*, is to *Act, or Represent* himselfe, or an other; and he that acteth another, is said to beare his Person, or act in his name (in which sence *Cicero* useth it where he saies, *Unus sustineo tres Personas, Mei, Adversarii, & Judicis*, I beare three Persons, my own, my Adversaries, and the Judges).[35]

Thus, the notion of representation is applied not only in the case of an artificial person, but also in the case of a natural person. In the first case, an individual acting in the name of another, there is thus distinction between the representative and the represented. In the second case, an individual acting in his own name, he is simultaneously the representative and the represented. It is thus necessary, in order that there may be a juridical person, that there be representation.

Of what does representation consist? As F. Tricaud signals in note 5 on page 162 of his translation, representation has a double aspect expressed by the double use of the verb *to act*,[36] which signifies simultaneously to act and to play a role. The natural person acts in his name and plays his own role. The artificial person acts in the name of another and plays the role of this other. This double signification of the verb *to act*,[37] which characterises the double function of representation, is rooted, according to Hobbes, in the Greco-Roman origin of the word 'person'. In Greek, it designates the face and, in Latin, disguise, the exterior appearance or again the mask of the actor who imitates someone on the scene. The word 'person' thus has a theatrical sense which is going to pass into juridical language: 'from the Stage, hath been translated to any Representer of speech and action, as well in Tribunalls, as Theatres'.[38] Hobbes exploits this semantic origin, since the couple representative/represented, which defines the notion of person, is identical to the couple, actor/author. The representative is the actor and the represented the author.

Yet, since political representation is a particular case of juridical representation, the sovereign who assumes the person of the republic will himself be a representative, an actor in the double sense of one who acts and one who plays the role of another – as it happens, that of the subjects. In other words, it is not only the tribunal that is going to be dramatised, but also the whole political edifice. The theory of political representation transforms the state into a gigantic real theatre, the boards of which it erects. We will soon ask ourselves how the roles are distributed in this theatre, and in particular whether it does not inaugurate, as soon as established, a reversal of the actor/author relation. For the moment, we can remark that the state of nature was already, in a certain way, a theatre, but a theatre where (each being simultaneously author and actor) each wants to play his own comedy and imposes it on others, whence, as a result, a conflict of authors, a generalised cacophony and a mutual uncertainty of roles. The state of nature, which inevitably drifts into the state of war, is the theatre of a multitude of discordant pieces. The institution of the state thus has the function of making the spectacle possible by imposing a single text.

The notion of representation takes account both of the natural person and of the artificial person. In this regard, it is important not to confuse the physical individual and the juridical person.[39] There is in Hobbes's text a polyvalence in the use of the notion of person.[40] It signifies: (1) the representative or the actor: 'then the Person is the *Actor*';[41] (2) a relationship between author and actor: 'he that acteth another, is said to beare his Person';[42] (3) the represented or the author in particular in the case of the civil person: 'A Multitude of men, are made *One* Person, when they are by one man, or one Person, Represented'.[43] In the same sense, in chapter 42 of *Leviathan* Hobbes can confirm, this time regarding the triple representation of God by Moses, Jesus Christ and the Holy Spirit, that 'a Person, (as I have shewn before, chapt. [16].) is he that is Represented, as often as hee is Represented'. A few lines later we can read that the proper meaning of the word 'person' is 'that which is Represented by another', and that it is for this reason that we can say, regarding God, that he is 'three Persons'.[44] Thus, the notion of person seems at first glance to be composed of a quasi-insurmountable ambiguity.

This ambiguity disappears, however, when we distinguish the physical individual from the juridical notion of person and we focus our attention on the relationship that the latter implies between represented and representative. We can thus formulate the general rule: (1) if the relationship between represented and representative is unique, there is only one person; (2) if the relationship between represented and representative is multiple, there is a multiplicity of persons; (3) in one case as in the other, the unique relationship or the multiple relationship does not depend on the number of individuals who compose the represented or the representative.

Let us again take up point (1) of the rule: when the relationship of representation is unique, that is to say, when a represented confers upon a representative the right to pronounce certain speeches or to carry out certain actions, we can say that they both juridically constitute a unique person to the extent that the acts that the representative carries out in virtue of the right that he has received are considered as those of the represented. From the uniqueness of the relationship, we could say as well that the representative is the person, or that the represented is the person, or yet that the representative assumes the person of the represented. Represented and representative are both juridically the same person: the first acts through the second and the second in the name of the first.

Point (2) of the rule: when the relationship is multiple – as in the case of God who maintains a triple relationship of representation with Moses, Jesus Christ and the Holy Spirit, who are his three representatives, investing each with a particular right to pronounce certain speeches or to carry out certain acts in his name – we can say that each relationship of representation constitutes a different person, the juridical relationship of God/Moses = one person, God/Jesus Christ = a second person, God/Holy Spirit = a third person.[45] From then on, it will be possible to say, as in chapter 16 of *Leviathan*, that God is represented by three persons who act in his name:

> The true God may be Personated. As he was; first, by *Moses*; who governed the Israelites, (that were not his, but God's people,) not in his own name, with *Hoc dicit Moses*; but in God's Name, with *Hoc dicit Dominus*. Secondly, by the Son of man, his own Son our Blessed Saviour *Jesus Christ*, that came to reduce the Jewes, and induce all Nations into the Kingdome of his Father; not as of himselfe, but as sent from his Father. And thirdly, by the Holy Ghost, or Comforter, speaking, and working in the Apostles: which Holy Ghost, was a Comforter that came not of himselfe; but was sent, and proceeded from them both.[46]

It will also be possible to say, as in chapter 42, that God is 'three Persons'.

Point (3) of the rule: the relationship of unique or multiple representation that gives place to a single person or a plurality of persons is in each case different in the number of individuals who compose the represented or the representative. We have seen, in the case of God, a represented who is a single individual becoming three persons because he maintained three relationships of different representation. In return, if we suppose a unique relationship of representation between a represented constituted of a multiplicity of individuals and a representative constituted of a single individual or multiple individuals, we will have one person alone. Let us first of all examine the first case: a multiplicity of individuals in relation to unique representation signifies that the actions of the representative will be recognised in the same way by each of the represented individuals. In other words, the represented confers to the representative the right to carry out actions. The actions carried out by the representative are thus in the name of each of the particular individuals. This is what happens in the case of subordinate political or private organisations the representative of which is an individual, or of independent and sovereign political organisations the representative of which is also an individual. In the latter case, it is of course a question of the monarchical state (the difference between subordinate organisations and the state is that, for the first, the representative has a limited mandate, while, for the second, the mandate – or the authorisation – is unlimited. Additionally, the first have possible existence only inside the state). If we retain the example of the monarchical state, there will be only one person since the sovereign's acts are recognised according to an identical relationship by each of the subjects. From then on, we could say as well that the sovereign is this single person, or that the multiple individuals, each of whom recognising the sovereign's acts for his own, become, by this unique relationship of representation, a single person, or, finally, that the sovereign assumes the person of the republic. Let us now examine the second case: a multitude of individuals are represented by a representative composed of several individuals, this which takes place within the subordinate organisations the representative of which is a council or within the aristocratic state. The juridical relationship of representation being here also unique – each of the subjects authorises in the same way as the others the actions of the aristocratic state's sovereign council, so that each one will recognise as his own any of these actions – there will be a single person who will be able, as previously, to designate the representative, the represented or the relationship of the one to the other. However, when the representative is composed of multiple individuals, a supplementary condition is required, namely, that the representative be able to express itself by a single majority voice:

> And if the Representative consist of many men, the voyce of the greater number, must be considered as the voyce of them all . . . the onely voyce the Representative hath.
> And a Representative of even number, especially when the number is not great, whereby the contradictory voyces are oftentimes equall, is therefore oftentimes mute, and uncapable of Action.[47]

It is from this point forward possible to explain the most important but also the most obscure passage from chapter 16: 'A Multitude of men, are made *One* Person, when they are by one man, or one Person, Represented.'[48] We stop on this first sentence in order to remark: (1) The first use of the notion of person designates the multitude of represented men. (2) This multitude becomes a single person only in the relationship of representation, an effect of which is the uniqueness of the person. (3) The second use of the notion of person designates this time the representative. When Hobbes says that the representative must be 'one man, or one Person', it is not necessary to hear that he is a single person because he is a single man. We know indeed that the representative can be a single person even when it is composed of multiple men, as in the case of a council. The notion of single person is juridical. It is thus valid that the representative physically be a single individual or a multiplicity of individuals. (4) The unity of the person of the representative is itself an effect of what Hobbes names in this text 'consent', which is the authorisation that each singular individual of the multitude accords to the representative pronouncing certain speeches or carrying out certain acts in his name. We can thus say that the text regresses from condition to condition: the effect expressed in (2) is conditional on the effect expressed in (4). The unity of the person of the representative retroactively implies that of the represented. The unity of the person of the representative, which is founded on the identity of the act by which each individual of an unorganised multitude authorises it (the authorisation can be limited or unlimited) to act and to speak in his name, founds the unity of the person of the represented in return, that is to say, shifts the unorganised multitude to organisation or to juridical unity. In other words, through the representative's acts, it is each of the singular individuals who is supposed to act. The act of the representative can from then on be considered as a collective act of the represented, individuals who thus become a single person. Now we understand the next sentence of the passage from chapter 16: 'For it is the *Unity* of the Representer, not the *Unity* of the Represented, that maketh the Person *One*.' This time the notion of person specifically designates neither the representative nor the represented, but the unity of the juridical being that they both constitute. Finally: 'it is the Representer that beareth the Person, and but one Person'. This time the person characterises the relation of the representative to the represented. Representative and represented being a single person, we can say that the representative in his actions bears or assumes the person of the represented. Hobbes concludes the passage by claiming: 'And *Unity*, cannot otherwise be understood in Multitude.' Such is indeed the objective of the theory of representation: to furnish the juridical means for thinking the passage from a multiplicity of singular individuals to the unity of a juridical person endowed with a single will which may be that of all, without presupposing that this unity may already be given in the multitude and without abolishing the multitude by the institution of the unity. We already see the fundamental interest that the juridical theory of representation could present for political theory. It is going to make it possible to conceive, from the act of institution produced by the social contract, the unity of a representative who confers in return to the multitude of individuals a unity by which this multitude becomes a political body or a civil person that the sovereign representative assumes. We also understand that the unity of the state is dissolved at the instant when its representative disappears and that individuals fall back that way into the unorganised multitude of the state of nature. The juridical unity of the artificial person coexists with the natural multitude of physical individuals. This is what it was a question of thinking: 'Unity . . . in the multitude.' At the same time, the concept of civil person reconstructed with the theory of juridical representation will be operational henceforth: the sovereign's speeches and actions will be those of the whole political body. Far from being foreign to the juridical order of the state, the sovereign will be its foundation and guarantor.

But, having pursued the analysis of the political consequences of the theory of representation, it is appropriate to study the juridical content of the contract that institutes an artificial person, a particular case of which will be the social contract that institutes the civil person.

There is, we have seen, an artificial person when there is a representative whose speeches and actions are attributed to a represented different from the representative. This attribution being juridical, it supposes a transfer of the right of the represented to the representative that it is a question now of elucidating:

> Of Persons Artificiall, some have their words and actions *Owned* by those whom they represent. And then the Person is the *Actor*; and he that owneth his words and actions, is the AUTHOR: In which case the Actor acteth by Authority. For that which in speaking of goods and possessions, is called an *Owner*, and in latine *Dominus*, in Greek *xurios*; speaking of Actions, is called Author. And as the Right of possession, is called Dominion; so the Right of doing any Action, is called AUTHORITY. So that by Authority, is always understood a Right of doing any act: and *done by Authority*, done by Commission, or License from him whose right it is.[49]

The representative, as its actions are recognised as their own by the represented, is thus the actor, and the represented is the author. What is the juridical content of this recognition that Hobbes names authorisation? The authority that the actor received from the author does not come down to a pure and simple transfer of right, such as chapter 14 of *Leviathan* defines it in terms identical to those of *The Elements of Law* and *De Cive*. For to authorise an actor's actions is not for the author to lose his right over the actions that he authorises. Quite to the contrary, the actor's actions can be recognised for his own by the author only as far as they are accomplished in virtue of a right that is again his own, thus that it always preserves. Let us again take up the parallel that the text carries out between proprietor and author: the proprietor (*dominus*) as author has a right, the one over the thing that he possesses, the other over himself and his actions. The proprietor is able to transfer his right to another (in the terms of chapter 14 of *Leviathan*). That way he loses all right over the thing that will henceforth no longer be his own. It is in these terms that *The Elements of Law* and *De Cive* had conceived the transfer of right realised by the social contract. We have seen in that case we found ourselves at an impasse: (1) individuals, in becoming the sovereign's subjects, are dispossessed of all right over themselves and their actions. Their sovereign's will was thus totally foreign; (2) this total loss of right was incompatible with the theory of inalienable rights, in particular the right of resistance. In order that the notion of civil person has a meaning, in order that the will of the sovereign be that of the subjects, and in order that the institution of the state let the inalienable rights of the subjects remain (reaffirmed in chapter 14 of *Leviathan*),[50] it is thus necessary to conceive a type of transfer of right that does not dispossess individuals of all right over themselves while constituting a right over their right. It is the solution to this problem that the theory of authorisation must furnish. The contract by which the author authorises certain (or all) of the actor's actions lets the right of the first remain while conferring to the second a right of use, thus a right subordinated to the author's right.[51] The actor will be able to accomplish actions that will be considered as emanating from the author, and the latter will act by the intermediary of the actor. To recognise for him someone else's actions is to give him the right to carry out actions which commit us. The actor acquires, so to speak, a right of use of the author's right for the category of actions that the contract that they pass among themselves stipulates. The application of this theory on the political plane makes it possible to understand that civil right does not take away the natural right that individuals had over themselves and over their actions, but, on the contrary, is founded upon it. But, at the same time, the constitution of civil right limits natural right in order to prevent it from entering into contradiction with itself because the subjects will not have the right not to obey the sovereign's commands, that is to say, the civil laws. The social contract permits the constitution of a right over the actions of others inconceivable in the state of nature.

The theory of authorisation can henceforth be understood in the transfer of right over things. Indeed, the proprietor can, as we have seen, purely and simply transfer his right over the thing that he possesses in giving it or in selling it to another, but he can also authorise this other to assure the maintenance, the management or the administration of it. In this last case, the proprietor does not lose every right. He only confers to another a right to carry out actions that, as proprietary, he could carry out himself. There is thus here constitution of a right subordinate to the right of proprietor over the thing. Since authorisation concerns actions relative to a determinate thing, the actor who received authorisation (the subordinate right) will represent not the proprietor but the thing itself. We can thus understand the passage where Hobbes claims:

> Inanimate things, as a Church, an Hospital, a Bridge, may be Personated by a Rector, Master, or Overseer. But things Inanimate, cannot be Authors, nor therefore give Authority to their Actors: Yet the Actors may have Authority to procure their maintenance, given them by those that are Owners, or Governours of those things. And therefore, such things cannot be Personated, before there be some state of Civill Government.[52]

Representation is here fictive because it is only fictively that the thing is the author of the actor's actions.

The conditions for the validity of contracts of authorisation remain to be examined. This examination will allow us to understand why all authorisation supposes the existence of the state. The contract by which the author gives to the actor the right to carry out actions or to pronounce speeches in his name is a permission (*a licence*)[53] or a mandate (*a commission*).[54] From then on, every contract concluded by the actor with a third in virtue of authorisation (permission or mandate) commits the author as if he had committed it himself. The actor's action creates an obligation for the author within the limits of the authorisation, but not beyond. Every contract concluded by the actor with a third party counter to or beyond the authority that the author has given him does not commit the latter: 'For no man is obliged by a Covenant, whereof he is not Author.'[55] From then on, two possibilities could be presented: either the contract will be null or it will commit the actor who is himself going to be made author in the contract with the third. The general rule being that, when 'the Authority is evident, the Covenant obligeth the Author, not the Actor; so when the Authority is feigned, it obligeth the Actor onely; there being no Author but himselfe'.[56]

We can consider that there are two types of mandate or permission that the theory of authorisation renders possible: (1) a mandate limited to one or several actions; (2) an unlimited mandate. In the case of limited mandates, the author is obliged by the actor's action only if the latter can render his authorisation manifest, but in the case where he exceeds the limits, he alone will be responsible for it. Thus, in a limited mandate, the actor remains held to the clauses of the mandate. But in the state of nature this type of mandate is totally impossible since there is no judge for deciding if the mandate's clauses have or have not been respected. The mandate, if it takes place, will thus remain simply verbal, the actor always being able to claim that he has acted in virtue of the authority that the author has given to him, and the latter always being able to deny it. Within the state of nature, every limited mandate is void. All contracts between particular private individuals thus supposes the existence of a supreme judge, that is to say, the state. But the state must itself be born of a contract of authorisation. The institution of the civil person thus supposes a type of mandate which itself founds its own validity. In other words, a mandate that could not be refused. Yet the unlimited mandate alone is likely to fulfil this condition. Within the social pact, individuals indeed agree between them to authorise all the sovereign's actions. Even the wording [*énoncé*] of the contract of each to each stipulates it: '*I Authorise and give up my Right of Governing my selfe, to this Man, or to this Assembly of men, on this condition, that thou give up thy Right to him, and Authorise all his Actions in like manner.* This done, the Multitude so united in one Person, is called a COMMON-WEALTH, in latine CIVITAS.'[57] By this contract indeed is it impossible for any of the authors to refuse any act whatsoever of the actor become sovereign. No dispute can be raised between them, none of the sovereign's actions will be able to be considered as invalid or unjust by the subjects. The author will thus be bound by any one of the commitments taken by the actor. Much more, the actor becomes, by the unlimited mandate, judge of the author's actions. The social contract is thus an absolutely specific contract since it institutes a supreme judge, thus conveying individuals from the state of nature to the civil state. All the sovereign's speeches or actions thus come back to the subjects under the form of obligations. The social contract itself thus founds its own validity. Beyond every possible challenge, the sovereign becomes the instituted judge of the subjects' actions, alone having the right to abandon sovereignty or to transmit it to another. The succession to the head of state falls under the jurisdiction of a juridical and not of a hereditary act.

The self-founding political representation of its own validity is going to be able to found, in turn, all the other forms of contract and of political or private representation. From the point of view of relationships between subjects, all contracts [*contrats*] (for example, commercial contracts [*contrats*]) and all private representations (for example, the representation of children by parents or tutor, or the representation of things) become possible insofar as they are not forbidden by civil laws. They are henceforth guaranteed by the existence of a supreme judge suitable for resolving disputes and for claiming the right, and, through this, of a political power [*pouvoir*] capable of enforcing the laws. From the political point of view, the institution of the sovereign introduces a reversal in the relationship author/actor, represented/representative, as well as in the notion of authority. Indeed, as soon as the civil person is constituted, we can say that the sole true political author is the sovereign, whereas the subjects become actors. Since the prince's actions and speeches return to the subjects under the form of obligations, these become the actors of the sovereign author's commands. Hobbes formulates this reversal in explicit terms in *Leviathan*, in chapter 26, dedicated to civil laws:

> There is therefore requisite, not only a Declaration of the Law, but also sufficient signes of the Author, and Authority. *The Author, or Legislator* is supposed in every Common-wealth to be evident, because he is the Soveraign, who having been Constituted by the consent of every one, is supposed by every one to be sufficiently known.[58]

The subjects for their part become actors. Thus, concerning the violation of the civil law, Hobbes writes:

in the violation of the Law, both the Author, and Actor are Criminalls. From hence it followeth that when that Man, or Assembly, that hath the Soveraign Power, commandeth a man to do that which is contrary to a former Law, the doing of it is totally excused: For he ought not to condemn it himselfe, because he is the Author.[59]

This reversal of the initial author/actor relationship also implies a reversal of the act of authorisation that can henceforth be accomplished, from the political point of view, only by the sovereign. It is the sovereign who authorises, who confers to the subjects a mandate (order or permission), and who authorises the laws: 'the Verification, is but the Testimony and Record; not *the Authority of the Law; which consisteth in the Command of the Soveraign only*'.[60] The same reversal is going to affect representation. Not only will the sovereign be able to be represented by ministers in public affairs or by governors in the administration of provinces – who will be able to act in his name – but much more: every organisation ruled subordinate, that is to say, that one where an assembly or a man is instituted as representative (in commercial or other affairs) of the actions of a group of individuals within the state, will be able to be constituted only by the mediation of the sovereign representative who determines the conditions and the limits of its validity.

We thus see how the theory of political representation, which was at first only a specific case of juridical representation, becomes the condition for the validity of all other forms of contract or of subordinate representation.

The consequences of the theory of representation on political theory are thus considerable. *Public space is a juridical space in Hobbes*; power [*puissance*] has no other goal than guaranteeing its functioning. *Leviathan* puts into place a juridical structure of the state which does not have its equivalent in *The Elements of Law* or *De Cive*. The pairs of concepts around which it is organised: author/actor, represented/representative, authorisation/authorised make of the Hobbesian state something completely different than a cold monster. The act of authorisation no longer implies only the obligation of non-resistance, but creates a positive obligation for the subjects – authors/actors – to recognise as theirs the speeches or actions (law or command) of the sovereign – actor/author. Moreover, authorisation no longer implies for individuals the loss of their natural right over themselves. It creates, on the contrary, a civil right which is founded upon it and which returns to the subjects under the form of obligations which assure an intersubjectivity and guarantee peace. The institution of the state thus confers new rights to the sovereign, rights founded directly on the social contract. The constitution of the political body thus no longer leaves the sovereign as outside of society, keeper of a natural right of the state of war. The will of the sovereign actor/author is the will of the republic's civil person, since it is that of each author/actor subject. Every right conceded by the author/subject to the actor/sovereign returns to the actor/subject under the form of laws of the author/sovereign. Conversely, the subjects are not despoiled of all right. Certainly, they do not evidently have the right not to obey the laws. But they preserve their natural right, that is to say, their liberty to act or not to act there where the civil laws do not impose any obligation or ban. The civil right which permits the distinction between mine and yours gives a content, an effectiveness and a guarantee to the subjects' right.

The initial act of institution continues to support each instant of the state's existence. The subjects are neither given nor are sold to the sovereign. This is why their obedience to the sovereign remains suspended from the guarantee that this brings to the security of their individual existence. As soon as the state is no longer in a position to assure their defence, they rediscover their natural unlimited right of the state of nature. The political body's factual existence is thus supported by the gnawing fear, always latent, of a regression into civil war. The power [*puissance*] of the sovereign is itself only the summation of the power [*puissance*] of each of the subjects; to weaken his subjects is thus for the sovereign to be weakened himself. That the sovereign may not have obligation to the subjects, that he may not himself be submitted to the civil laws, does not signify that the exercise of power [*pouvoir*] is reduced to the caprices of his good pleasure. Discernment in Hobbes echoes the prudence that characterised political virtue in Aristotle. The sovereign is at the same time the foundation and guarantor of the state's juridical functioning, that is to say, as a last resort, of the civil peace. Abuse of power [*pouvoir*], bad example given to subjects, non-respect for natural laws will be causes of degeneration and of regression into war. There are bad sovereigns, that is to say, sovereigns who do not know or do not respect the rules that govern the political artifice, who do not know, or do not want to know, that, if a law is always just, it must additionally be good, that is to say, necessary for subjects. Hobbes knows this and repeats it. But human existence is never exempt from harms and, on the whole, a bad sovereign would be better than no state at all. The good sovereign is the one who – in the image of the Platonic king not subjected to the civil laws and who directs his action from the contemplation of the intelligible world – founds his action on the knowledge of God's natural laws, the fundamental principle of which is that of equity. But the Hobbesian sovereign draws his legitimacy neither from knowledge nor from God, but from each of the individuals who compose the people. Certainly, the social contract is conceived as realised once and for all and indissoluble, but so much of it is necessary that, 'without the help of a very able Architect', men may be 'compiled, into any other than a crasie building, such as hardly lasting out their own time, must assuredly fall upon the heads of their posterity'.[61] If it is true that *Leviathan* has the function of teaching the subjects their duties and sovereigns their rights, we can also say that these rights are returned in duties,[62] and that, in another sense, *Leviathan* aims to teach sovereigns what they must do or not do so that the state be maintained.

There remains, however, a question of quite first importance for the Hobbesian theory of the state. We have encountered it on several occasions without being able to thematise it for itself: it is about the question of penal right. Hobbes claims of course that the right to punish or to inflict punishment is essentially linked to the idea of sovereignty and follows from the right to render justice. The existence of this right thus does not seem to make a problem: is it not that which must generate the fear of power [*pouvoir*] and, correlatively, the respect for the laws? Nevertheless, we are going to see, the right to punish is paradoxically the most difficult public right to think.

*Notes*

1. Hobbes, *The Elements of Law*, p. 108.
2. Hobbes, *De Cive: The English Version*, p. 90; *De Cive*, p. 215.
3. Hobbes, *Leviathan*, p. 220.
4. On the historical origin of the use that Hobbes makes of the notion of 'civil person', see Polin, *Politique et philosophie chez Hobbes*, pp. 221–50, and Simone Goyard-Fabre, 'Le concept de *Persona civilis* dans la philosophie politique de Hobbes', *Cahiers de philosophie politique de l'Université de Caen*,

3 (1983):. 49–71. We could also consult on this question our work, *La décision métaphysique de Hobbes*, pp. 325–56.
5. Hobbes, *The Elements of Law*, p. 100.
6. Ibid., p. 74.
7. Ibid. [TN: in English in the original.]
8. [TN: in English in the original.]
9. [TN: in English in the original.]
10. [TN: in English in the original.]
11. [TN: in English in the original.]
12. Hobbes, *The Elements of Law*, p. 103.
13. Ibid., p. 104.
14. Hobbes, *De Cive: The English Version*, p. 89; *De Cive*, p. 214. Cf. *De Cive*, pp. 214–15. Hobbes indicates there that the notion of civil person has a validity that is not limited to the city, for if a city is very much a civil person, every civil person is not a city. For example, companies of merchants are civil persons without actually constituting cities. In *The Elements of Law*, p. 174, Hobbes takes into consideration being the first to have extended the theory of the civil person to the *commonwealth* [TN: in English in the original]. On these points, see Polin, *Politique et philosophie chez Hobbes*, pp. 224–5.
15. Hobbes, *De Cive: The English Version*, p. 89; *De Cive*, p. 214.
16. Hobbes, *The Elements of Law*, p. 104; see also *De Cive*, p. 215.
17. [TN: Hobbes, *The Elements of Law*, p. 63.]
18. Hobbes, *The Elements of Law*, pp. 103–4.
19. Hobbes, *Leviathan*, p. 262.
20. [TN: in English in the original.]
21. Hobbes, *De Cive: The English Version*, p. 105; *De Cive*, p. 234.
22. Ibid., p. 89; p. 214.
23. Hobbes, *The Elements of Law*, pp. 75-6.
24. We will come back to this point in the next chapter.
25. It should be noted that *The Elements of Law*, p. 88, extends inalienable rights to things that are necessary to life, like the right to use fire, water, free air, a place for living.
26. Hobbes, *The Elements of Law*, p. 111.
27. Hobbes, *De Cive: The English Version*, pp. 88–9; *De Cive*, pp. 213–14.
28. Hobbes, *The Elements of Law*, p. 117.
29. See Hobbes, *De Cive*, p. 226.
30. Hobbes, *Leviathan*, p. 268.
31. Polin, *Politique et philosohie chez Hobbes*, p. 234, insists on a correlative difficulty to this that we are going to develop. It concerns a text from *De Cive*, p. 241, where, when the people has abandoned its every right to one man alone it ceases to be *persona una* and becomes *multitudo dissoluta*.

32. Hobbes, *Leviathan*, p. 217.
33. Ibid., p. 219.
34. Ibid.
35. Ibid., pp. 217–18.
36. [TN: in English in the original.]
37. [TN: in English in the original.]
38. Hobbes, *Leviathan*, p. 217.
39. See David P. Gauthier, *The Logic of Leviathan: The Moral and Political Theory of Thomas Hobbes* (Oxford: Clarendon Press, 1969), pp. 120–77.
40. See François Tricaud, n. 62, p. 168 of his translation of *Leviathan*.
41. Hobbes, *Leviathan*, p. 218.
42. Ibid., p. 217.
43. Ibid., p. 220.
44. Ibid., p. 522.
45. This is said explicitly in Hobbes's text, *An Answer to a Book Published by Dr. Bramhall, Late Bishop of Derry; Called the 'Catching of the Leviathan'*, in *The English Works of Thomas Hobbes*, vol. 4, pp. 310–11.
46. Hobbes, *Leviathan*, p. 220.
47. Ibid., p. 221.
48. Ibid., p. 220.
49. Ibid., p. 218.
50. Ibid., p. 192.
51. See Gauthier, *The Logic of Leviathan*, p. 124.
52. Hobbes, *Leviathan*, p. 219.
53. [TN: in English in the original.]
54. [TN: in English in the original.]
55. Hobbes, *Leviathan*, p. 218.
56. Ibid., p. 219.
57. Ibid., p. 227.
58. Ibid., p. 320; my emphasis.
59. Ibid., p. 346.
60. Ibid., p. 320; my emphasis.
61. Ibid., p. 363.
62. See chapter 30 of *Leviathan*, titled '*Of the* OFFICE *of the Sovereign Representative*'.

*Chapter 10*

# ON THE RIGHT TO PUNISH

> There is a question to be answered, of much importance; which is, by what door the right, or authority of punishing in any case, came in.[1]
>
> Thomas Hobbes, *Leviathan*

## THE RIGHT TO PUNISH AS A PROBLEM

The state represents a relationship in which people *rule over* other people. This relationship is based on the legitimate use of force (that is to say, force that is perceived as legitimate). If the state is to survive, those who are ruled over must always *acquiesce* in the authority that is claimed by the rulers of the day. When do they do so and why? By what internal reasons is this rule justified, and on what external supports is it based?[2]

In this text by Max Weber, the definition of the state and the questions that it raises are evidence of the repercussion of problems opened by Hobbes's political thought through sociology at the beginning of the twentieth century and, beyond that, to our own. Certainly, the perspective and the speculative context within which Weber deploys his analysis are very different from those that animate Hobbes's thought,[3] but this does not prohibit encounters or even revivals since, beyond the diversity of the circumstances of thought, there is the same definition of political order. For us, in keeping to the cited text, we can read that Weber rediscovers Hobbes on the fundamental question of the relation between state and violence. Political domination is not the only important type of domination. Political power [*pouvoir*] is distinguished from other types of power [*pouvoir*]. In homogenising the concept of power [*pouvoir*] and in dissolving it into a network of relations or connections of force that cross social devices and institutions, we lose the political concept of power [*pouvoir*], and perhaps even that of power [*pouvoir*] full stop.[4] Not that political power [*pouvoir*] would be the only kind to make use of violence as a means: in more or less evident ways, all power [*pouvoir*] supposes or engenders violence (whether it would be physical or not). What is more, we cannot define the power [*pouvoir*] of the state by the simple exercise of violence. What characterises political domination is another trait: not monopoly on violence, but monopoly on legitimate violence. A state exists only when the use of power [*pouvoir*] or of force is enveloped within a process of legitimation. A monopoly on legitimate violence signifies for Weber, who follows in this way a properly Hobbesian determination, that groups or individuals have 'the right to use physical violence only insofar as the *state* permits them to do so. The state is regarded as the sole source of the "right" to use violence.'[5]

Weber's sociology, in defining three foundations of legitimacy, so as to explain the structure of domination, and also in designating a pure typology established from a historical reality which presents only 'highly complex variations',[6] comes close to and is simultaneously distinguished from Hobbes's political thought, which constructs in a purely rational manner, that is to say, ahistorically, the pure type, the prototype of sovereignty. The difference between the two paths concerns not only method, since for Hobbes the mediation of power [*puissance*] and of right, the regulation of power [*puissance*] by right within the power [*pouvoir*] of the state appears not only in the manner in which men represent or justify it in a given moment of their history, their submission to a political domination, but falls, more profoundly, under the jurisdiction of a demand internal to the very concept of political power [*pouvoir*] the foundation of which it is possible to exhibit rationally.

We thus understand that the question of the right to punish would be a privileged field for testing the value of this foundation. The power [*puissance*] of the state, public force, is exercised as a constraint, a particular case of which is punishment. Let us clarify: we are not talking about fact. Every state pretends to possess the right to punish, that is to say, to practice a punishment upon an individual found guilty under its domestic legislation. This claim is even the necessary condition of its viability. Perhaps no one has insisted on this point more than Hobbes.

Thus, the state cannot survive 'when there is no visible Power to keep them in awe, and tye them by feare of punishment to the performance of their Covenants, and observation of those Lawes of Nature'.[7] On the other hand, we are talking about the foundation for this claim. In order to reach this foundation, it is necessary to pass from the necessity of fact to the justification of right: to exhibit the status in the name of which the state can legitimate its claim. Hobbes tackles this problem head-on in the chapter in *Leviathan* on punishment: 'there is a question to be answered, of much importance; which is, by what door the Right, of Authority of Punishing in any case, came in'.[8] Now, within Hobbes's system, it is in principle from the social contract, as the protofundamental act of the state,[9] that the sought-after status must be found, since it is from this contract that 'are derived all the *Rights*, and *Facultyes* of him, or them, on whom the Soveraigne Power is conferred by the consent of the People assembled'.[10] The problem can thus be made clear: does the social contract make it possible to give an *a priori* foundation to penal right? But the difficulty is more precisely because, in the same chapter on punishment, Hobbes maintains by way of a response: 'no man is supposed bound by Covenant, *not to resist* violence; and consequently *it cannot be intended, that he gave any right to another to lay violent hands upon his person*'.[11] It is thus the antinomy between penal right and the right of resistance, even within the Hobbesian conception of the social contract, that should be considered first. In order to then approach the different attempts by which Hobbes struggles to overcome this antinomy, and finally coming from it to the principle of a solution which substitutes an *a posteriori* foundation for the untraceable *a priori* foundation of the right to punish.

## THE ANTINOMY OF THE RIGHT TO PUNISH AND OF THE RIGHT OF RESISTANCE

In order to make the antinomy clear, it is important to define its terms. The right of resistance and penal right are not symmetrical.

The first is a natural, subjective right that every human individual possesses, whatever the relational context within which his or her existence is deployed may be. Both within the state of nature and within the civil state, the individual 'cannot lay down the right of resisting them, that assault him by force, to take away his life'.[12] This right is thus attached to man's natural person and finds itself founded on the fundamental ethical principle according to which 'every man, not onely by Right, but also by necessity of Nature, is supposed to endeavour all he can, to obtain that which is necessary for his conservation'.[13] It is obvious that abandoning our right of resistance would be to break this ethical principle. We can add three remarks to this.

First, the right of resistance consists not only in resisting what could put our life in danger directly, but also what could put it in danger indirectly, and that which, without putting it into danger directly or indirectly, could affect persons whose injuries or death would plunge us into grief.[14] And so we have the right to resist the one or those who would want to attack us by force in order to kill us, to cause us injuries or to imprison us; but also the one or those who would want to prevent us from enjoying air, water, movement, free passage from one place to another; and again the one or those who would want to make us testify against ourselves – which can only occur in the state – or against those 'by whose Condemnation a man falls into misery; as of a Father, Wife, or Benefactor'.[15]

Second, it is a question of an absolutely inalienable right of man. A contract or a man engaged in abandoning his right of resistance to another (whoever he was) is always null. The alienation of the right of resistance in effect contravenes the reason or the cause which founds every transfer of right: namely, the *consideration* of some good for oneself.[16] Alienating his right of resistance would be, for the one who alienates, putting the object of his will into contradiction with the presiding cause. The act would thus be contradictory, it could result only from an error or from a lack of knowledge. And it goes without saying that we do not know how to found a right on error or a lack of knowledge.

Third, the right of resistance, being absolutely inalienable, eluded the rights that we transfer to the sovereign in the social contract. It thus defines that part of natural right or liberty that the individual retains within the state, even though the individual abandons its right over all things. Let us recall that the right over all things is not identified with natural right, but constitutes the enlarged form of natural right in the state of war.[17] Within the state, the right of resistance constitutes the sphere of the rights of man in the name of which an individual can always legitimately resist political power [*pouvoir*]. The application of this principle to punishment is clear: punishment, 'being Force, a man is not obliged not to resist'.[18] Man, become citizen, thus retains, as man, a right of resistance that he cannot transmit to the state and that it cannot take from him. The rights of man can neither be lost nor be received.

On the other hand, penal law can exist only in the state. Better, it belongs exclusively to the state. Indeed, first, if, within the state of nature we have the right, in accordance with the relational context established there, to kill another man, there is no punishment: no authority exists capable of producing an accusation or of establishing a culpability. Second, within the political edifice, only the representative sovereign is authorised to decide on a punishment, in opposition to representatives of civic systems (*systemata civium*) – groups or associations of subjects certain of which are subordinate political bodies – which are constituted within the state.[19] The right to punish is thus very much an exclusive right – a monopoly – for the state, so constitutively tied to it that it is simultaneously an inalienable attribute of its sovereignty and the sign of its absolute power [*pouvoir*]:

> To the sovereign is committed [by virtue of the social contract, as a means of attaining the goal of political institution] the Power of Rewarding with riches, or honour; and of Punishing with corporall, or pecuniary punishment, or with ignominy every Subject according to the Law he hath formerly made; or if there be no Law made, according as he shall judge most to conduce to the encouraging of men to serve the Common-wealth, or deterring of them from doing dis-service to the same.[20]

Within the state, the coexistence of these two inalienable, essentially different, rights is a necessity. Indeed, on the one hand, the right of resistance which belongs to man inasmuch as man subsists within the citizen and, on the other hand, penal right is an attribute of the state without which laws and justice will remain dead letters. Yet is this necessary coexistence conceivable? Can we simultaneously admit the existence of a penal right for the state and of a right of resistance for man – become citizen?

> But in case a great many men together, have already resisted the Soveraign Power unjustly, or committed some Capitall crime, for which every one of them expecteth death, whether have they not the Liberty then to joyn together, and assist, and defend one

another? Certainly they have: For they but defend their lives, which the Guilty man may as well do, as the Innocent.[21]

This example, among others, seems to testify that the state's right to punish (here, the condemnation to death of one or several criminals) and the individual's right of resistance (here, the liberty of each of the criminals to give active support to the others in order to attempt to mutually defend their lives) can coexist, even if contentiously. Better, 'this is granted to be true by all men, in that they lead Criminals to Execution, and Prison, with armed men, notwithstanding that such Criminals have consented to the Law, by which they are condemned'.[22] What is decisive, within this contentious coexistence, for determining which of the two opposed rights is going to carry the day is evidently the sovereign's power [*puissance*], which is, in principle, incomparable in relation to that of one or a number of subjects: the sovereign claims the penal right of the state because he holds public power [*puissance*].

However, coexistence thus conceived presupposes that of which it is necessary to take account, namely, the existence of a right to punish: whence does the state hold this right? The right to punish appears at the same time as sovereignty, thus it is necessary to return to the social contract in order account for it. Now, paradoxically, resituated at this level, the question, far from bringing a solution, on the contrary makes the antinomy suddenly appear.[23] We know, indeed, that on account of the inalienable character of the right of resistance, 'no man is supposed bound by Covenant, not to resist violence; and consequently it cannot be intended, that he gave any right to another to lay violent hands upon his person'.[24]

The antinomy can be formulated thus: if the right of resistance is inalienable, then subjects have never conceded the right to punish them to the sovereign. The right to punish cannot therefore be conceived as an essential attribute of sovereignty emanating from the contract that institutes the state. Conversely, if the penal right is an inalienable attribute of sovereignty founded on the social contract, then the right of resistance cannot be considered as an inalienable right of man. Under this contradiction, the political edifice totters. Worse, it risks being toppled because the antinomy is internalised by affecting the relation between the state's ends and means. Its ends are to assure, through peace and security, the preservation of citizens' being and well-being. The means that it uses to achieve this is a right to punish, that is to say, to take away their being or their well-being. Does the state have the power [*pouvoir*] to assure the perpetuation of life or of commodious life in appropriating the right to interrupt it or to render it difficult?

## THE UNTRACEABLE *A PRIORI* FOUNDATION FOR THE RIGHT TO PUNISH

It is appropriate to consider the successive attempts by which Hobbes attempts to overcome the antinomy.

From *The Elements of Law*, we simultaneously encounter the ethical principle of man's inalienable right of resistance[25] and the juridico-political demand for a right to punish inseparable from the right to render justice. Thus is the right to punish conceived as the greatest power [*pouvoir*] and the infallible mark of sovereignty:

> And first it is an infallible mark of absolute sovereignty in a man, or in an assembly of men, if there be no right in any other person natural or civil to punish that man, or to dissolve that assembly . . . For a greater power is required to punish and dissolve, than theirs who are punished or dissolved; and that power cannot be called sovereign, than which there is a greater.[26]

It remains to be seen in what terms the relation between the right of resistance and the right to punish is thought. Now, what is surprising is that, within the paragraph from *The Elements of Law* that we just mentioned, the right to punish is explicitly founded on the negation of the right of resistance for subjects to political power [*pouvoir*]:

> For he that cannot of right be punished, cannot of right be resisted; and he that cannot of right be resisted, hath coercive power over all the rest, and thereby can frame and govern their actions at his pleasure; which is absolute sovereignty.[27]

Have men abandoned their right of resistance in becoming subjects or citizens of the state? This seems to be affirmed in another passage from *The Elements of Law*: 'This power of coercion . . . consisteth in the transferring of every man's right of resistance against him to whom he hath transferred the power of coercion. It followeth therefore, that no man in any commonwealth whatsoever hath right to resist him, or them, on whom they have conferred this power coercive, or (as men use to call it) the sword of justice.'[28] But if it is possible to transfer his right of resistance, it is no longer inalienable. The juridico-political demand to found the right to punish is thus accepted at the cost of the ethical principle in question.

However, the difficulty is such that we cannot suppose that Hobbes did not see it. One clue makes it possible to confirm this: the reservation that simultaneously concludes and restrains the scope of the text just cited: *'supposing the not-resistance possible'*.[29] This is very much the signal that the non-resistance of the individual to the state is not unlimited: *'For . . . covenants bind but to the utmost of our endeavour.'*[30] Yet it is precisely impossible for an individual, as much by natural necessity as by natural right, not to resist any power [*pouvoir*], being that of the state, when it attempts to coerce him. It would indeed be absurd to suppose that an individual could, between two evils, choose the worst.

We can thus legitimately conclude that the attempt to think penal right and the right of resistance together from *The Elements of Law* ended in failure. The difficulty, glimpsed for a moment, is put in brackets, as if reserved for a later revival.

This revival is performed in *De Cive*, where Hobbes thematises the difficulty and struggles to overcome it by specifying the concept of the right of resistance, but within a general framework which was already that of *The Elements of Law*. Regarding the right to punish, *De Cive*[31] indicates that its existence rests on the fact that men agree – at the moment of the social contract – not to offer security to those who must undergo punishment. And he adds that most of them observe these contracts well enough when punishment is not practiced upon themselves or upon their neighbours.

We see that *De Cive* attempts, as does *The Elements of Law*, to found penal right on the transfer of the right of resistance, but this time distinguishing, within the right of resistance in general, two rights: (1) the right to defend oneself extended to neighbours (those whose suffering or death would render our life difficult); (2) the right to defend any others (those whose suffering or death would leave us indifferent). Of these two rights composing the right of resistance in general, only the first would be inalienable, whereas the second would be alienable. The social contract that founds penal right would thus not involve the total abandonment of our right of resistance, but only one of its parts. It would be necessary in this sense to differentiate, in the citizen, an inalienable right of resistance that he keeps as man and a duty of non-resistance that he keeps as citizen.

Can we find within this distinction the means of overcoming the antinomy, that is to say, the means of furnishing an *a priori* ground (by the social contract) for the penal right, all while maintaining man's inalienable right of resistance? To this question, *Leviathan* responds in the negative:

> In the making of a Common-wealth, every man giveth away the right of defending another; but not of defending himselfe. Also he obligeth himselfe, to assist him that hath the Soveraignty, in the Punishing of another; but of himselfe not.[32]

Let us stop there for a moment in order to remark that this is the solution proposed by *De Cive*. But in the following sentence Hobbes explicitly emphasises the deficiency:

> But to covenant to assist the Soveraign, in doing hurt to another, unlesse he that so covenanteth have a right to doe it himselfe, is not to give him a Right to Punish. It is manifest therefore that the Right which the Common-wealth (that is, he, or they that represent it) hath to Punish, is not grounded on any concession, or gift of the Subjects.[33]

In other words, if the social contract, conceived in the terms of *De Cive*, makes it possible to take account of a citizen's duty to or obligation of non-resistance when the sovereign wants to punish a guilty person, better, if it also makes it possible to explain that the citizen would have an obligation to assist the sovereign in practicing punishment (with the exception that the latter does not practice it upon the citizen's neighbours), on the other hand, it does not make it possible to found the right to punish as such. For the very simple reason that individuals could not have delivered to the sovereign a right to punish that they did not formerly possess in the state of nature: to make one's own justice, in the name of one's own reason, by inflicting an evil (injuries or death) upon the other in order to react to the real or imaginary danger that the other represents for us, is not to punish. In the social contract, individuals thus could not give to the sovereign a right that they had never possessed as individuals. The impossibility of individuals conceiving a right to punish in the state of nature essentially distinguishes Hobbes from Locke. As to this last point, in the state of nature, *'every man hath a right to punish the offender, and be executioner of the law of nature'*.[34] That is, from Hobbes to Locke, the law of nature changed in meaning and status.

In hoping to resolve the difficulty of *The Elements of Law*, *De Cive* goes too far in the other direction: maintaining the inalienable character of the right of resistance (at least partly) in rendering problematic the idea of an *a priori* foundation for the right to punish. This right, as an essential attribute of sovereignty, thus remains, it seems, suspended without foundation in the void. Certainly its necessity survives, but this necessity cannot by itself alone furnish a rational justification for right. It remains to be seen if *Leviathan* contains the resources necessary for overcoming the impasses of *The Elements of Law* and of *De Cive*.

The special feature of the juridico-political doctrine of *Leviathan* resides first of all, we have seen, in the theory of authorisation. This theory makes it possible to think the social contract anew: the authorisation that individuals confer to the sovereign is fundamentally distinguished from the transfer of right which reduced the contract of submission in *The Elements of Law* and *De Cive* to an alienation.[35] Authorisation is not an alienation: in instituting the state, individuals, become citizens, do not lose every right for themselves and their actions. This theory permits a complete reorganisation of the political doctrine. It is thus important to examine the consequences for the theory of crime and that of punishment.[36]

In chapter 18 of *Leviathan*, on 'the Rights of Soveraignes by Institution', Hobbes uses, in order to show that citizens cannot change the form of government and depose the sovereign, an argument that we found in the corresponding passage of *De Cive*.[37] *De Cive* used two arguments: to depose the sovereign would be to commit (1) an injustice against the contracting parties [*co-contractants*], (2) an injustice against the sovereign to whom the contracting parties [*co-contractants*] have transferred their rights. *Leviathan* takes up these arguments again, but adds a third to them:

> Besides, if he that attempteth to depose his Soveraign, be killed, or punished by him for such attempt, he is author of his own punishment, as being by the Institution, Author of all his Sovereign shall do: And because it is injustice for a man to do any thing, for

which he may be punished by his own authority, he is also upon that title, unjust.[38]

We see the very precise link that this text establishes between the theory of authorisation and the theory of punishment. Individuals, at the moment of the social contract, authorise *all* the sovereign's actions: citizens thus become the authors of all the actions carried out by the sovereign actor. The consequence for the theory of punishment is immediate: the one who commits an injustice, in the occurrence of the injustice par excellence of attempting to depose to sovereign, is, if it fails, himself author of the punishment that the sovereign will inflict upon him. This idea of the criminal as author of his own punishment has led commentators[39] to reinterpret an important distinction:

> by allowing him [the sovereign] to *kill me*, I am not bound to kill my selfe when he commands me. 'Tis one thing to say, *Kill me, or my fellow, if you please*; another thing to say, *I will kill my selfe, or my fellow.*[40]

The first formula would be continued in the social contract of authorisation, but not the second. In authorising the sovereign to punish me (eventually by death), I am in some way the indirect author of my own punishment.

We are thus not yet at the Hegelian theory where the punishment that 'is inflicted on the criminal is not only just *in itself* (and since it is just, it is at the same time his will as it is *in itself*, an existence of his freedom, *his* right); it is also a *right for the criminal himself*, that is, a right *posited* in his *existent* will, in his action', and where 'In so far as the punishment which this entails is seen as embodying *the criminal's own right*, the criminal is *honoured* as a rational being.'[41] Hobbes not only does not and never will consider punishment as an honour rendered to the criminal as the author, but even when he considers, as in the text cited, the criminal as author – indirect – of his own punishment, it is conceived as the result of an injustice that the criminal commits with regard to himself, and in no way to his right.

What fundamentally separates Hegel from Hobbes clearly springs from the remark in §100 of the *Elements of the Philosophy of Right*. It is dedicated to a critique of Beccaria's thesis, in the treatise *Of Crimes and Punishments*, according to which the state does not hold the right to inflict the punishment of death upon an individual because we cannot presume that, at the moment of the social contract [*contrat*], men had consented to be put to death. Hegel critiques this thesis in the name of a doctrine where 'The state is by no means a contract ... and its substantial essence does not consist unconditionally in the *protection* and *safeguarding* of the lives and property of individuals as such. The state is rather that higher instance which may even itself lay claim to the lives and property of individuals and require their sacrifice.'[42] It is in rejecting the idea of contract [*contrat*] and in making the state a reality superior to individuals that Hegel claims to refute Beccaria's argument. But, more fundamentally, the critique of the theory of the contract [*contrat*] and of its implications for the right to punish makes Hegel struggle with Hobbes because the latter presents the problem in all its generality, while Beccaria retains only a particular case. The Hobbesian theory of authorisation is a theory of the contract [*contrat*] which always assigns, as the aim of the state, the preservation of the life and of the well-being of individuals. It thus cannot be regarded as the prefiguration of the Hegelian doctrine.

Let us note that Kant, in the Doctrine of Right, also criticised Beccaria's thesis, but now within the framework of a theory of the contract [*contrat*]. For Kant, the criminal is punished not because he wanted punishment, but because he willed a punishable action: 'for it is no punishment if what is done to someone is what he wills, and it is impossible *to will* to be punished. – Saying that I will to be punished if I murder someone is saying nothing more than that I subject myself together with everyone else to the laws, which will naturally also be penal laws if there are any criminals among the people.'[43] The Kantian solution rests on the distinction between the self as co-legislator and the self as subject punished according to the law.

The Hobbesian theory of authorisation would doubtlessly have been able to open the path to a distinction of perspective between man as author of the contract [*contrat*] and man as subject submitting to penal laws. However, it is clear that, far from correcting the thesis in chapter 18 in order to rethink the doctrine of the right to punish, Hobbes seems on the contrary to deliberately discard it when he explicitly reaches, in chapter 28, the fundamental problem of this right:

> It is manifest therefore that the Right which the Common-wealth (that is, he, or they that represent it) hath to Punish, is not

grounded on any concession, or gift of the Subjects. But I have also shewed formerly, that before the Institution of Common-wealth, every man had a right to every thing, and to do whatsoever he thought necessary to his own preservation; subduing, hurting, or killing any man in order thereunto. *And this is the foundation of that right of Punishing, which is exercised in every Common-wealth.* For the Subjects did not give the Soveraign that right; but onely in laying down theirs, strengthened him to use his own, as he should think fit, for the preservation of them all: so that it was not given, but left to him, and to him onely; and (excepting the limits set him by naturall Law) as entire, as in the condition of meer Nature, and of warre of every one against his neighbour.[44]

Who does not see the considerable difficulty enveloped within this text? Not only does Hobbes no longer use the concept of authorisation,[45] but he explicitly affirms that the existence of the right to punish does not result from the social contract. The foundation for the right to punish is purely and simply recalled in the *right to every thing*[46] that the sovereign possessed as an individual in the state of nature. The reservation that introduces the reference to the limits imposed by the law of nature seems without real scope, for we see evil in how that law could with more efficiency limit the right over every thing for the individual become sovereign than it did with regard to the same individual in the state of nature.

Let us examine the impasses towards which this text drives:

1. The theory of authorisation was used in chapter 18 to found the doctrine of the inalienable rights of sovereignty, a part of which is the right to punish. Yet, if this right no longer finds its foundation in the social contract of authorisation, it simultaneously loses the character that specifies the rights of sovereignty and distinguishes them from natural right expanded to the state of war.

2. Hobbes often distinguishes the natural person from the civil person of the sovereign. This distinction is all the more necessary as it is possible that a single civil person would be composed of several natural persons without the artificial unity of sovereignty being challenged, as happens in an aristocracy where a council governs. However, in giving the right over every thing that the individual-sovereign (or the individuals comprising the sovereign council) possessed before the contract as a foundation for the state's right to punish, penal right is reduced to

being only an attribute of the sovereign's natural person (or of natural persons, which leads to considerable problems) and not an essential attribute of the state.

3. If the individual-sovereign continues, alone, to have at his disposal a right over every thing, it comes out of, in the exercise of the right to punish which is supposed to follow from it, the juridical relationship which is established between a sovereign and a guilty subject or citizen, in order to enter into the essentially non-juridical relationship which is established between an individual and his enemies. But, consequently, the fundamental difference that Hobbes establishes between punishment (as evil inflicted upon an enemy of the public) and act of hostility (as evil inflicted upon an enemy of the commonwealth) no longer holds. If the guilty citizen loses, by his crime, his citizenship and becomes an enemy of the commonwealth, the very idea of punishment loses all sense.

4. The right over every thing cannot found the right to punish. Pufendorf noted this:

> Hobbes ... asserts, That the Right the Commonwealth has to punish is not grounded on any Concession, or Gift of the Subjects, but that the Foundation of that Right is built upon that other, which, before the Institution of Commonwealths, every Man has to every thing, and to do whatever he thought necessary to his own Preservation ... To this it may be answer'd, That the Right of Punishing is different from the Right of Self-preservation: and by the Exercise of it upon Subjects, we can never understand what a State of Nature allowed.[47]

In other words, the right to punish does not exist in the state of nature, nor can the right over every thing be retained in the state by the sovereign because it provides the condition for war. We are restricting the extent of the difficulties. Pufendorf will attempt to overcome them in claiming that,

> as in natural Bodies the Mixture and Temperament of several simples form a compound, in which we often perceive such Qualities as cannot be found in any of the Ingredients that compose the Mixture: So Bodies politick, which are compounded of a number of Men, may have a Right resulting from such a

Composition, which no one of the particulars was formally possess'd of; which Right, derived from the Union, is lodged in the Governors of such Bodies.[48]

Far from overcoming the impasses of the earlier works, it thus seems that *Leviathan* multiplies them. If man's inalienable right of resistance is maintained and even reinforced here, on the other hand, the right to punish seems to find only an apparent foundation in recalling an archaism (natural right expanded to the state of war) which risks affecting the state's structure in its very heart.

Should we then say that the antinomy of the right of resistance and of the penal right is insurmountable? Does Hobbes's work contain the resources necessary to found, if not directly at least indirectly, the state's right to punish? It is possible to respond positively to these questions when, for the *a priori* (to the social contract), untraceable foundation for the right to punish, we substitute the search for an *a posteriori* foundation.

## CRIME AND PUNISHMENT: THE SOVEREIGN'S ETHICS AND THE *A POSTERIORI* FOUNDATION OF THE RIGHT TO PUNISH

In order to highlight this *a posteriori* foundation, it is appropriate to examine the doctrine of crime and punishment proposed by *Leviathan*. The theory of crime is simultaneously juridical and anthropological.

Crime is first of all situated on a juridical plane, which distinguishes it from wrongdoing. This consists in a transgression of the law, whether of natural or civil law. We can thus speak of wrongdoing both in the state of nature and in the civil state. It consists in the deliberate intent to transgress the law, that intent leading to an act or not. In the state, fault keeping its moral character, deliberate intent must this time concern the transgression of civil laws (which cover the laws of nature) or contempt for the legislator (because this contempt includes a transgression of all laws at the same time). Every fault thus does not necessarily constitute a crime: if every crime is a fault, the opposite is not always true. Two elements make it possible to specify crime. First, crime implies not only deliberate intent, but also the act by which we commit what is contrary to the law. Second, there must be a human judge in order to establish the crime and blame it on someone. It is in this that crime falls under jurisdiction of the law.

The explanation of the causes and consequences of crime is situated on the anthropological plane. This explanation has two functions: to indicate why men are driven to commit acts contrary to civil laws which are meant to protect them, and to establish a scale for the gravity of crimes. The anthropology of crime is interesting in the standard where it testifies to the modification that takes place within the dynamics of interhuman relations in the state compared with those that prevail in the state of nature. Indeed, every crime results either from a lack of understanding, from an error of reasoning or, finally, from a sudden violence of the passions. If we are attached to the third point, we see that the passions (for example, glory) that maintain the desire to increase our power [*puissance*] indefinitely (in particular, instrumental powers [*puissances*]: wealth, friends, reputation) are the causes of crimes more dangerous for the state than those that result from the other passions (for example, hatred, concupiscence, greed, etc.). The difference comes from this: the first passions risk making interhuman relationships regress into a dynamic which was precisely that of the state of war, and thus bringing about a destruction of the state.

As with the theory of crime, the theory of punishment first of all aims to bestow a juridical status onto punishment. Here is the definition:

> A PUNISHMENT, *is an Evill inflicted by publique Authority, on him that hath done, or omitted that which is Judged by the same Authority to be a Transgression of the Law; to the end that the will of men may thereby the better be disposed to obedience.*[49]

Three points characterise punishment.

First, as an evil inflicted by the public authority, punishment is distinguished from vengeance. When some man is himself taking the law into his own hands as a private man, he commits an act of vengeance. Only the sovereign in his civil person is thus empowered to inflict a punishment upon the criminal.

Second, punishment supposes that an individual would be guilty of having transgressed a law. We thus understand that all circumstances that could impede a citizen from learning of a civil law (for example, the non-publication of the law), which he would then unknowingly transgress, constitute either complete excuse or attenuating circumstances which remove or reduce the crime and, consequently, the punishment. The legal assignment of transgression and the juridical status of punishment allow for distinguishing it from an act of hostility. The act of hostility finally has the character of an evil inflicted beyond civil law.

However, it is important to distinguish the two cases. On the one hand, the case where the hostile act is exercised by the sovereign against an individual who does not belong or who no longer belongs to the commonwealth. On the other hand, the case where the act of hostility is committed by the sovereign against a citizen. In the first case, the act of hostility is justified since it is exercised either against an (actual or virtual) enemy of the state, or against a rebel (one who has explicitly refused the commitment which makes a citizen). The rebel places himself beyond civil legality, he cannot thus be the object of a punishment but suffers 'as an enemy of the Common-wealth'.[50] The rebel is a citizen who becomes an enemy. On the other hand, in the second case, that is to say when the act of hostility is exercised by the sovereign against a citizen in his own right, this act, without being illegal in a civil manner, is morally illegal. It is not illegal in a civil manner because the sovereign is not himself subject to the positive laws that he prescribes. On the other hand, it is morally illegal because the sovereign is bound to respect the laws of nature which include a duty to God.

We know that on several occasions Hobbes examines the morally illegal acts that a sovereign commits when he condemns the innocent, when he inflicts an evil without public condemnation, etc. Now, it is clear from this examination that the act of hostility exercised against the citizen is not only morally condemnable, but also politically thoughtless. It can result only 'from the unskilfulnesse of the Governours, ignorant of the true rules of Politiques'.[51] There are, of course, bad, ignorant or cruel sovereigns who exercise acts of hostility against their subjects. But such leaders are politically irresponsible in view of their functions or their duties as representative of the commonwealth. First of all, because, in so doing, a sovereign places himself in the condition of a single individual who acts within his natural or private person. Next, and above all, because he sows one of the germs that weaken and eventually destroy the institution that he represents. Just as his subjects are weakened by this, the sovereign is himself weakened. Just as acts of hostility against citizens are committed by this, he places the political institution in contradiction with itself. The bad sovereign thus not only commits an injustice from God's point of view: he again puts into question, in a manner more or less serious, more or less irreversible, the existence of the state.

This is why under both the moral obligation of the laws of nature and political prudence, that is to say, of the art of governance, the first principle of which is *salus populi*, a sovereign worthy of the name must not commit acts of hostility against his subjects. Respect for the laws of nature and knowledge of the art of governance define what we can call an ethics of the sovereign, which consists in a full exercise of sovereignty in all its laws but also in its duties.[52] Freely resurrecting one of Weber's concepts, we could characterise this ethics of the sovereign as an ethics of responsibility. In Hobbes's work, this entails a moral dimension and a political dimension because it covers the consideration of the effects or consequences of an act. Thus, to instruct the people as to the foundation for civil obligation, making good laws (that is to say, laws necessary for the well-being of the people), not to commit acts of hostility against subjects are, among others, the essential characteristics of the ethics of the sovereign as an ethics of responsibility.

Third, the political dimension of this ethics is inscribed within the purpose of punishment: disposing the will of men to obedience. Thus, when the sovereign inflicts a more severe punishment than that which is fixed and prescribed by the law itself, 'the excesse is not Punishment, but an act of Hostility'.[53] The excess of the evil inflicted does not intend to dispose men to obedience. Even when the evil inflicted is less than the satisfaction gained by the crime, this evil is less a punishment than the price or the cost of the crime: far from disposing to obedience, it incites the transgression of laws.

What thus defines punishment is not only the fact that it proceeds from public authority, but also respect for procedures that must control the exercise. Now if, as we have seen, the *a priori* foundation for the right to punish remains untraceable, the ethics of the sovereign can doubtlessly furnish a substitute for it. In other words, the right to punish, which cannot be founded on the social contract, finds the justification for its existence in the modalities of its exercise. For the first, impossible foundation in the contract is substituted a second foundation in the art of governance. If the sovereign is the height of sovereignty, that is to say, if he exercises violence only having established the guilt of a subject, using a publicly declared law and conforming to the penalty provided, we can say that this violence is a justification of right in the conscience of the subjects.

More profoundly perhaps than any other political thinker, Hobbes, in refusing to make the inherent difficulties disappear in searching for a foundation for the right to punish within the framework of a theory of the contract [*contrat*], opens the path for a solution that is without doubt still our own. Do we have the means today to found the penal right by means other than on the modalities of its exercise?

### Notes

1. [TN: in English in the original.]
2. Max Weber, 'Politics as a vocation', in *The Vocation Lectures: 'Science as a Vocation' and 'Politics as a Vocation'*, trans. Rodney Livingstone, ed. David Owen and Tracy B. Strong (Indianapolis, IN: Hackett, 2004), p. 34.
3. We will keep ourselves in this chapter to the question of the foundation for the right to punish. This is why we will limit our examination to Hobbes's three great ethico-political works. A complete examination of this question would need to include the *Dialogue between a Philosopher and a Student of the Common Laws of England*.
4. The loss of the properly political concept of power [*pouvoir*] is shown in Foucault's work: 'It is in the sphere of force relations that we must try to analyse the mechanisms of power [*pouvoir*]. In this way we will escape from the system of Law-and-Sovereign which has captivated political thought for such a long time. And if it is true that Machiavelli was among the few – and this no doubt was the scandal of his "cynicism" – who conceived the power [*pouvoir*] of the Prince in terms of force relationships, perhaps we need to go one step further, do without the persona of the Prince, and decipher power [*pouvoir*] mechanisms on the foundation of a strategy that is immanent in force relationships' (Michel Foucault, *The History of Sexuality, vol. 1: An Introduction*, trans. Robert Hurley (New York: Random House, 1978), p. 97). Better, it is the concept of power [*pouvoir*] full stop that seems to be dissolved under the appearance of its obscure omnipresence: 'The omnipresence of power [*pouvoir*]: not because it has the privilege of consolidating everything under its invincible unity, but because it is produced from one moment to the next, at every point, or rather in every relation from one point to another. Power [*pouvoir*] is everywhere; not because it embraces everything, but because it comes from everywhere' (ibid., p. 93). Note that Foucault indicates one of the aspects of Hobbes's thought on the central question for our study of the right to punish (ibid., pp. 135–6).
5. Weber, 'Politics as a vocation', p. 33.
6. Ibid., p. 34.
7. Hobbes, *Leviathan*, p. 223.
8. Ibid., p. 353.
9. On the social contract as the protofundamental act, see my *La décision métaphysique de Hobbes*, pp. 241–54 and 325–56.

10. Hobbes, *Leviathan*, p. 229.
11. Ibid., p. 353; my emphasis.
12. Ibid., p. 192; see also Hobbes, *The Elements of Law*, p. 88; *De Cive*, p. 177.
13. Hobbes, *Leviathan*, pp. 209–10.
14. Cf. ibid., p. 202.
15. Ibid., p. 199.
16. Cf. ibid., p. 192.
17. On the *jus in omnia* as enlarged form of *jus naturale*, see *La décision métaphysique de Hobbes*, pp. 312–17.
18. Hobbes, *Leviathan*, p. 199; cf. *De Cive*, p. 177.
19. Cf. ibid., pp. 283–4.
20. Ibid., p. 235; see also *The Elements of Law*, p. 117.
21. Hobbes, *Leviathan*, p. 270.
22. Ibid., p. 199.
23. See the interesting analyses in Francesco Viola, *Behemoth o Leviathan? Diritto e obbligo nel pensiero di Hobbes* (Milan: Giuffré, 1979), pp. 243–7.
24. Hobbes, *Leviathan*, p. 353.
25. 'As it was necessary that a man should not retain his right to every thing, so also was it, that he should retain his right to some things: to his own body (for example) the right of defending, whereof he could not transfer; to the use of fire, water, free air, and place to live in, and to all things necessary for life' (Hobbes, *The Elements of Law*, p. 88). Note that Hobbes clearly suggests here the distinction that we have established elsewhere between natural right and the right over every other. The part of natural right that each retains in the civil state defined the sphere of legitimate resistance to political power [*pouvoir*].
26. Ibid., p. 117.
27. Ibid.
28. Ibid., p. 111.
29. Ibid.; my emphasis.
30. Ibid.; my emphasis.
31. See Hobbes, *De Cive*, p. 220.
32. Hobbes, *Leviathan*, p. 353.
33. Ibid., pp. 353–4.
34. John Locke, *Two Treatises of Government*, ed. Peter Laslett (Cambridge: Cambridge University Press, 1988), p. 272.
35. See Chapter 9, 'On the State', above.
36. See Hobbes, *Leviathan*, chs 27 and 28.
37. See Hobbes, *De Cive*, pp. 232–4.
38. Hobbes, *Leviathan*, p. 229.
39. See Gauthier, *The Logic of the Leviathan*, p. 147. Viola, *Behemoth o*

*Leviathan?*, pp. 243–7, criticises, very pertinently to our mind, Gauthier's interpretation.
40. Hobbes, *Leviathan*, p. 269.
41. G. W. F. Hegel, *Elements of the Philosophy of Right*, trans. H. B. Nisbet, ed. Allen W. Wood (Cambridge: Cambridge University Press, 1991), p. 126.
42. Ibid.
43. Immanuel Kant, *The Metaphysics of Morals*, trans. and ed. Mary Gregor (Cambridge: Cambridge University Press, 1996), p. 108.
44. Hobbes, *Leviathan*, p. 354; my emphasis.
45. Contrary to what Gauthier maintains (p. 148), we cannot see here a simple complication of the theory of authorisation, but a veritable negation of the capacity of contract of authorisation to directly or indirectly found the right to punish, even though it directly founds all the other inalienable rights of sovereignty.
46. [TN: in English in the original.]
47. Samuel von Pufendorf, *Of the Law of Nature and of Nations*, trans. Basil Kennett (1729), pp. 762–3.
48. Ibid., p. 762.
49. Hobbes, *Leviathan*, p. 353.
50. Ibid., p. 356.
51. Ibid., p. 251.
52. Cf. ibid., ch. 30.
53. Ibid., p. 355.

# *PART IV*

# HOBBES ACCORDING TO TWO CONTEMPORARIES

Two major lessons appear from the reworking of some of the fundamental concepts of politics by Hobbes. First, Hobbes extracts the concept of sovereignty from that of property in discovering one of modern political philosophy's central problems: that of knowing how a multiplicity of particular wills are able to give birth to a single political public will. Second, Hobbes elaborates a juridical model for resolving the problem of the origin and the structure of the state.

We are going to see that these two points find themselves critiqued in the work of two of his contemporaries: Filmer and Pascal. On one hand, Filmer explicitly opposes to Hobbes's theory of institution a return to a patrimonial theory of political power [*pouvoir*]. On the other hand, Pascal implicitly opposes to the juridical model of the social contract a conception of the institutionalisation of force in right: for the Hobbesian belief in the political effects of reason is substituted an analysis of the reason of the effects that lead to a demystifying critique of the political.

*Chapter 11*

# HOBBES AND FILMER: *REGNUM PATRIMONIALE* AND *REGNUM INSTITUTIVUM*

### FILMER'S JUDGEMENT

> With no small content I read Mr Hobbes' book *De Cive*, and his *Leviathan*, about the rights of sovereignty, which no man, that I know, hath so amply and judiciously handled. I consent with him about the rights of exercising government, but I cannot agree to his means of acquiring it. It may seem strange I should praise his building and yet mislike his foundation, but so it is.[1]

Everything is somehow already said in this assessment from Filmer. In order to take account of his reading of Hobbes's politics, it is thus necessary to elucidate this paradox that makes him approve the edifice while condemning the foundation, that is to say, retain the doctrine of the rights of sovereignty while rejecting the theory of institution that subtends it. Can the Hobbesian concept of sovereignty preserve the same content when we separate it from the concepts of natural right and social contract in order to replace it within a doctrine that makes of the 'right of fatherhood'[2] the foundation for 'royal authority'?[3] Thus formulated, the question calls for a negative response: the concept of sovereignty is evidently bound to the doctrinal framework within which it is constructed. Sovereignty according to Bodin is not identical to sovereignty according to Filmer, and the latter is not identical to sovereignty according to Hobbes. Certainly, there are numerous and real convergences between Filmer and Hobbes, to which we will return, but there are also some fundamental divergences which affect the content of the concept of sovereignty and explain the incommensurate posterity of their works. This double relation between Filmer and Hobbes can be truly understood only if we perceive the existence of an important differentiation in the work of the second: there are not one but, in a sense, two theories of sovereignty's foundation in Hobbes. Yet these two theories are supposed to agree with an identical definition of sovereignty's rights. It is a question of the distinction between the concepts of *regnum patrimoniale* and *regnum institutivum*.[4] The Filmerian critique of Hobbes is going to consist in privileging the first against the second, that is to say, in opposing Hobbes to himself. What is the value of this critique? Is the double foundation of sovereignty in Hobbes internalised in a splitting of the concept of sovereignty? How to understand from then on that the political rights that are attached to it may be recognised as identical? Can we say that Filmer, by a path evidently independent of Hobbes,[5] had supported throughout a doctrine of the foundation of sovereignty that Hobbes had also envisaged but that in the final analysis he had gone beyond by the institutional doctrine of sovereign will and public rights.

In order to respond to these questions, I will examine three points: (1) Filmer and Hobbes's convergences on sovereignty; (2) the concepts of *regnum patrimoniale* and *regnum institutivum*; (3) private sovereign will or public sovereign will.

## CONVERGENCES ON SOVEREIGNTY

Filmer and Hobbes's convergences on sovereignty are numerous. For our two thinkers, political theory does not have the function of scrutinising the secrets of the art of governing, the *arcana imperii*, but defining the content of the rights of sovereignty and, correlatively, the extent of subjects' obedience. Yet if we bracket the fundamental opposition on the origin and theoretical justification of sovereignty for the moment, we can say that Filmer and Hobbes agree on the absolute character of sovereignty. This means for them: (a) that the sovereign is not responsible before any other human authority, but only before God; (b) that no other terrestrial power [*pouvoir*] can be compared with his own; (c) that sovereignty resides entirely within the will of the one who possesses it; (d) that the people, as such (Hobbes maintains, we have seen, an inalienable right of resistance of the *individual*, we will return there) does not have at its disposal any right of resistance and that it cannot thus change the form of government or the keeper of power [*pouvoir*].

*Filmer*: I see not then how the children of Adam, or of any man else, can be free from subjection to their parents. And this subjection of children is the only fountain of all regal authority, by the ordination of God himself. It follows that civil power not only in general is by divine institution, but even the assignment of it specifically to the eldest parent, which quite takes away that new and common distinction which refers only power universal as absolute to God, but power respective in regard of the special form of government to the choice of the people. Nor leaves it any place for such imaginary pactions between kings and their people as many dream of.[6]

*Hobbes*: And whosoever thinking sovereign power too great, will seek to make it less; must subject himself, to the power, that can limit it; that is to say, to a greater.

The greatest objection is, that of the practise; when men ask, where, and when, such power has by subjects been acknowledged. But one may ask them again, when, or where has there been a kingdom long free from sedition and civil war. In those Nations, whose Common-wealths have been long-lived, and not been destroyed, but by foreign war, the subjects never did dispute of the sovereign power.[7]

Thus, putting aside the patriarchalist or contractualist [*contractualiste*] justification of sovereignty, Filmer and Hobbes agree on the constitutive elements of its nature. This convergence persists in this doctrine of the sovereign's rights. We know that Hobbes furnishes a rigorous deduction and a classification of these rights starting from the institution and the goal of the republic.[8] On the other hand, Filmer is much more brief; he emphasises that three rights are necessarily attached to sovereignty: the rights of life and death, of declaring war, and of concluding peace.[9] These rights are also of the marks of sovereignty because they are inseparable from it and express its ultimate and irresistible character.

From these positions on sovereignty, we understand that Filmer and Hobbes can converge on the status of civil law. This is defined identically by them as the command of a superior:

*Filmer*: We all know that a law in general is the command of a superior power.[10]

> *Hobbes*: Law, properly is the word of him, that by right hath command over others.[11]

This definition concerns both divine law and civil law, the first being a command of God and the second a command of the sovereign. Civil sovereignty is thus conceived as the power [*pouvoir*] to give and to break the law. The sovereign legislator transcends the laws that he sets down, which are, according to Filmer, only his instruments.[12] The revival by Filmer of a principle from Ulpian, *Princeps legibus solutus est*,[13] orders the whole of the third chapter of *Patriarcha*:

> There can be no laws without supreme power to command to make them. In all aristocracies the nobles are above the laws, and in all democracies the people. By the like reason, in a monarchy the king must of necessity be above the laws. There can be no sovereign majesty in him that is under them. That which giveth the very being to a king is the power to give laws; without this power he is but an equivocal king.[14]

In these theses are echoed those of Hobbes:

1. The Legislator in all Common-wealths, is only the Soveraign, be he one man, as in a Monarchy, or one Assembly of men, as in a Democracy, or Aristocracy . . .
2. The Soveraign of a Common-wealth, be it an Assembly, or one Man, is not Subject to the Civill Laws. For having power to make and repeal Laws, he may when he pleaseth, free himself from that subjection, by repealing those laws that trouble him, and making of new, and consequently he was free before.[15]

The convergence of these two thinkers' conceptions on civil law, *Statute Law*,[16] presents itself as an almost identical position on the *Common Law*,[17] common right or common custom of the kingdom. A custom, itself so ancient, does not know how to bestow the authority of a law upon a use. Neither time passed, nor experience acquired, nor the jurisprudence of subordinate judges can bestow this dignity upon it. If the *Common Law*[18] can assume the status of a legislation, this is only insofar as it possesses, at least indirectly, the status of the sovereign's command. Thus, for Filmer,[19] far from customs having come to be from laws because of their age, they on the contrary originally had this character of law that was kept despite the progressive effacement of the recollection of their source: the sovereign will. What we perceive as customs were thus at first from the unwritten commands of kings. Hobbes's explanation, while being inspired by the same principle, is somewhat different: custom was not originally a law but becomes so because it finds itself indirectly authorised by the sovereign. The latter can indeed signify his will in different ways: silence is one, because it is the indication of a consent. If the sovereign lets a custom take hold, we can legitimately think that he consents and that, by the same token, he wants it.

However, the central principle according to which the prince is not bound by civil laws is integrated into the concept of sovereignty in a noticeably different manner in Filmer and in Hobbes. For the latter, the fact that the prince may not be submitted to the laws is an essential attribute of sovereignty: it is the current will of the sovereign that makes the law. If this will is contrary to a previous will, this simply signifies that a new law replaces the old. This principle is responsible for assuring the logic of juridical institution in removing the possibility of a contradiction between laws. The Hobbesian doctrine thus excludes all theory of special exemption from common right. On the other hand, in Filmer, the sovereign's transcendence in relation to laws takes the form of a theory of prerogative, or of the power [*pouvoir*] to depart from common right. Indeed, if common right is in general just and good, one needs, if necessary, to correct it in making appeal to some extraordinary means, that is to say, to the absolute and indefinite authority of the prince.[20] Royal prerogative is thus defined in its territory, its means and its aim, that is to say, respectively, the state of urgency, the use of absolute power [*pouvoir*] beyond common right, the safety of the people. Far from the king's prerogative to put subjects in a servile and onerous condition, it makes it possible to, among other functions, correct or mollify this, that a too-severe application of right could be tyrannical. Filmer again takes up his principle account: *Summum jus, summa injuria*.[21]

We thus see how, without being in all points identical, Filmer and Hobbes's theories of sovereignty converge in some major points. How to subsequently take account of their radical divergence on the foundation of sovereignty? How to explain that the one maintains that the right of paternity and subordination of children are the true foundation of sovereignty, while the second posits, on the contrary, that all men's natural liberty – to which natural equality is joined – and the social contract furnish its true principles? Does this complete divergence on the foundations not affect the concept of sovereignty itself?

## REGNUM PATRIMONIALE AND REGNUM INSTITUTIVUM

In his *Observations Concerning the Originall of Government*, Filmer expresses a perplexity: why has Hobbes founded his theory of sovereignty on the right of nature and the social contract when he has at his disposal the concept of *regnum patromniale*, by which he had himself defined a totally different and more coherent path in order to found it?

Filmer's question is perfectly justified. There are indeed in Hobbes not a single but two conceptions of the foundation of sovereignty. This distinction is initiated from the end of the chapter concerning the causes of the political body's constitution from *The Elements of Law*[22] and *De Cive*.[23] Men are indeed brought to submit to another man for two reasons: either because they fear him or because they think him capable of protecting them. The first attitude is that of the conquered who, in a war, submit to the enemy in order to save their life, the second is the attitude of those who have not yet been conquered but who fear being so. The political translation of this distinction is the following: when men submit in the first way, 'there ariseth thence a body politic, as it were naturally'.[24] *De Cive* takes account of this 'naturally' by the fact that the *civitas* finds here its origin in natural power [*puissance*].[25] On the other hand, when men submit in the second way, that is to say, in virtue of the agreement and consent of several, the political body is then a republic, a *commonwealth*.[26] In response to *The Elements of Law* which distinguishes *commonwealths* (in the narrow sense) from *bodies politic patrimonial and despotical*, *De Cive* concludes: 'Hinc est quod duo sint genera civitatum, alterum *naturale*, quale est *paternum* et *despoticum*; alterum *institutivum*, quod et *politicum* dici potest.'[27] Thus, there are two kinds of city: the one is natural, paternal and despotic, the master taking hold of the citizens there at his whim; the other is from institution and political, the citizens willingly establishing a master – a man or an assembly – with absolute power [*pouvoir*]. Whether it is quite a question there, despite Hobbes's hesitations of vocabulary,[28] of two forms of state and not only of the opposition between a natural, paternal or despotic non-political domination, on the one hand, and the city (*civitas*) or the Republic (*commonwealth*)²⁹ properly and politically instituted, on the other hand, this is what testifies to two absolutely parallel texts from *The Elements of Law* and *De Cive*.

> The same family if it grow by multiplication of children, either by generation or adoption; or of servants, either by generation, conquest, or voluntary submission, to be so great and numerous, as in probability it may protect itself, then is that family called a *Patrimonial kingdom*, or monarchy by acquisition; wherein the sovereignty is in one man, as it is in a monarch made by political institution. So whatsoever rights be in the one, the same also be in the other. And therefore I shall no more speak of them, as distinct, but as of monarchy in general.³⁰

Thus, the patrimonial kingdom (*patrimonial kingdom*³¹/*regnum patrimoniale*) is a monarchy of acquisition with the same properties and the same rights as monarchies of institution. We thus understand that Filmer can ponder the reason for which Hobbes introduces his right of nature and his *regnum institutivum*, which are adapted neither to experience, nor reason, nor Scripture. This especially as Hobbes confesses, according to Filmer, first of all, that the father was originally, that is to say, before the existence of the state, an absolute sovereign having right of life and death over the members of his family, and then that a great family is, considering the rights of sovereignty, a small monarchy.³²

From there, the Filmerian reading of Hobbesian doctrines concerning natural right, natural law, and the instituting social contract is going to consist of a critique aiming to underline implausible, impractical, even contradictory implications.

Thus, according to Filmer, natural right presents at least four major difficulties: (1) its definition as liberty that each has to use his power [*puissance*] in order to protect his life³³ is incompatible with the equally Hobbesian idea of a pre-political sovereignty of the father.³⁴ (2) This right of nature supposes that we will consider men as if they suddenly came out of earth – like mushrooms – without obligations towards each other,³⁵ which is contrary to experience and to Scripture. (3) Moreover, natural right leads to a theory of the state of nature which obliges to conceive that God has created men in a worse condition than any beast, as if he had not established an end for them other than a mutual destruction. In fact, to suppose that there was not any natural power [*pouvoir*] likely to hold men in respect by fear, the Hobbesian conception of the state of war would not be any more credible: in order to take account of it, it would be necessary to suppose what would be contrary to the truth, that God had been miserly in his creation and that there had not been enough goods and places in the world. (4) Finally, to the very extent that natural right and natural law take root in the same desire to protect its own life, their content is identical, contrary to what Hobbes claims in making them consist the one in liberty and the other in obligation.

As far as the social contract is concerned, Filmer also emphasises three major difficulties that remove him not only from all reality but even all rationality. The social contract refers to conditions impossible to meet: (1) it supposes a universal pact which could not take place even in the smallest kingdom; (2) the terms in which it is formulated are contradictory because to renounce his natural right is to renounce the right to protect his life; (3) if, as Hobbes also maintains, no man is held by the terms of his submission to carry out a command of the sovereign, under the pretext that it would be dangerous or dishonourable, this leads to a destruction of the very foundation of obedience.

We can henceforth again take up a question that we set down from the introduction of this study: can we say that Filmer, by a path independent of Hobbes, has supported throughout the conception of the foundation of sovereignty envisaged by Hobbes under the name of *regnum patrimoniale*? To this question we can now respond simultaneously yes and no. Yes, because in Hobbes already the *dominium paternum*,[36] by which children are 'in most absolute subjection to him or her, that so bringeth them up, or preserveth them',[37] confers to this paternal domination titles identical to those of political sovereignty. Next, no, because consistently Hobbes indeed reaffirms that:

> The title to dominion over a child, proceedeth not from the generation, but from the preservation of it; and therefore in the estate of nature, the mother in whose power it is to save or destroy it, hath right thereto by that power.[38]

In this text from *The Elements of Law*, and those that respond to it in *De Cive* and *Leviathan*, Hobbes opposes Filmer on two fundamental points: (1) the natural act of fathering does not constitute in any fashion a title of domination, consequently, we do not know how to found on it the subjection of children, and even less royal authority; (2) it is not the father but the mother who, within the state of nature, is the first holder of the right of domination over the child, because she is the first to assume the function of protecting it. Filmer's patriarchalism thus finds itself doubly challenged in its roots. But there is more: if nature no longer suffices to found domination over the child, this is because all title of domination depends on a contract as a last resort. What contract can a child make with its mother? This contract evidently is not necessarily explicit. It suffices that the child *be supposed* to permit its obedience in exchange for the protection of its life.[39] We understand that Filmer identifies and rejects this thesis, destructive of his whole system, according to which paternal domination and, more generally, all domination depends on a contract [*contrat*]. But does not the Hobbesian concept of *regnum patrimoniale* thereby lose the patriarchal and naturalist content that Filmer sought there?

## PRIVATE SOVEREIGN WILL OR PUBLIC SOVEREIGN WILL

The doctrinal relations between Filmer and Hobbes on sovereignty are thus complex. The convergences on its absolute character and on the rights that are attached to it are, paradoxically, supported by an essential divergence on the natural or contractual [*contractuel*] foundation of sovereignty. The question that henceforth arises is of knowing whether the political signification of the concept of sovereignty is not composed, as a last resort, of a different content in each of the two thinkers. This divergence is, we are going to see, simultaneously real and serious. Let us say that what before could partially mask it are the elements of a definition of sovereignty in terms of property that we find in *The Elements of Law* and *De Cive*, in relation to which *Leviathan* is almost completely emancipated. We have shown, in preceding pages,[40] political power [*pouvoir*] is conceived, in the first two works, as a *dominium* held by the sovereign either under the form of a full and complete ownership, in the case of *regnum patrimoniale*, or under a usufuctory form, in the case of *regnum institutivum*. Yet it is equally and fundamentally in terms of property that Filmer thinks sovereignty. Thus, starting from the right of paternity (*right of fatherhood*),[41] he founds royal authority (*royal authority*)[42] either immediately, as in the case of Adam, or mediately by a theory of the heritage of supreme jurisdiction. Filmer thus defines the traits of a seigniorial monarchy where the king is conceived as proprietor of power [*pouvoir*] over the subjects:

> It is true, all kings be not the natural parents of their subjects, yet they all either are, or are to be reputed as the next heirs to those progenitors who were at first the natural parents of the whole people, and in their right succeed to the exercise of supreme jurisdiction. And such heirs are not only lords of their own children, but also of their brethren, and all others that were subject to their fathers.[43]

The most direct consequences of this definition of sovereignty in terms of property according to Filmer, and according to the author of *The Elements of Law* and *De Cive*, is the reduction of the sovereign will to a particular and private will. For Filmer, the problem of the relation between this will and the wills of the individuals who compose the state does not come up. In Hobbes's case, on the other hand, the question comes up but is not resolved: the sovereign will remains, in his first two works, exterior and foreign to that of the subjects, because particular and private.

The fundamental divergence between Filmer and Hobbes on the concept of sovereignty clearly appears with the emergence, in *Leviathan*, of a new conception of the sovereign will as no longer private, but public will. Yet Filmer, in his *Observations*, evidently does not understand the new signification that Hobbes confers upon sovereignty in redefining the public person with the help of the concepts of representation and authorisation.[44] Two points make it possible to show it: they concern the right of resistance and the notion of the single person of the republic.

First of all, Filmer considers that there is a complete contradiction between the idea of an absolutely inalienable right of resistance and the existence of the state. Again textually taking up certain claims from *Leviathan* like '"a man cannot lay down the right of resisting them that assault him by force to take away his life; the same *may* be said of wounds, chains and imprisonment"; "A covenant *[not]* to defend myself from force by force is void"; right of defending life and means of living can never be abandoned',[45] Filmer claims that to support such a right in the state is to open the door to the use of violence against the sovereign. Better, it is even to refrain from conceiving an escape from the state of war. Thereby, Filmer completely misses the fact that, in setting down the existence of the individual's inalienable rights, Hobbes is precisely giving the means to define the social contract in terms other than those of alienation.

Next, Filmer overlooks the meaning of the notion of a unique person of the republic in bringing back this uniqueness to the unity of an individual and in concluding that Hobbes does not conceive of the possibility of a government other than monarchy.

> It seems Mr Hobbes is of the mind that there is but one kind of government, and that is monarchy. For he defines a commonwealth to be one person; and an assembly of men, or 'real unity of them all in one and the same person', the multitude so united he calls a commonwealth. This his mondling of a multitude into one person is the generation of his great *Leviathan*, the king of the children of pride. Thus he concludes the person of a commonwealth to be a monarch.[46]

What is missed in this text is Hobbes's effort to think, with the notion of the sovereign as representative and actor, the transformation of a multiplicity of individual wills into a single sovereign will. This transformation is realised by the substitution of a theory of authorisation to the theory of the transfer or the alienation of right. Authorisation in fact makes it possible to conceive the existence of a public sovereign will provided with political rights which do not annul but, on the contrary, suppose the existence and the permanence of rights for subjects. We recognise here one of the central problems of modern political philosophy, that through which is begun the definition of a sovereignty thought in terms other than those of property and domination: a sovereign will that is no longer solely private but truly public.

## CONCLUSION

Filmer and Hobbes's considerations give us a suggestive indication on the divergence of the two thinkers' political doctrines. This indication concerns the use of the term of common-wealth by Hobbes.[47]

> I wish the title of the book had not been of a common-wealth, but of a weal public, or common weal, which is the true word carefully

observed by our translator of Bodin *De Republica* into English. Many ignorant men arte apt by the name of commonwealth to understand a popular government, wherein wealth and all things shall be common, tending to the leveling community in the state of pure nature.[48]

In regretting that the complete title of *Leviathan* includes the term *common-wealth*, republic, in place of that of *common-weal*, wealth or common good, Filmer overlooks a fundamental dimension of Hobbes's *common-wealth* which, without opening the door to the idea of a popular government, is *common-weal* only insofar as it is *common-will* (common political will).[49]

## Notes

1. Sir Robert Filmer, *Observations Concerning the Originall of Government*, in *Patriarcha and Other Writings*, ed. Johann P. Sommerville (Cambridge: Cambridge University Press, 1991), pp. 184–5. [TN: in English in the original.]
2. Sir Robert Filmer, *Patriarcha*, in *Patriarcha and Other Writings*, p. 6. [TN: in English in the original.]
3. Ibid. [TN: in English in the original.]
4. Filmer, *Observations*, p. 185. See the corresponding passages in Hobbes's works, *De Cive*, p. 260; *The Elements of Law*, p. 135. In *De Cive*, Hobbes opposes *regnum patrimoniale* and *monarchia institutiva*, just as in *The Elements of Law* the opposition plays out between *patrimonial kingdom* or *monarchy by acquisition*, on the one hand, and *monarchy by institution*, on the other hand. [TN: italicised English in English in the original.]
5. As we know, Filmer wrote his *Patriarcha* in successive phases, but in any case before Hobbes produced the first version of his political doctrine in 1640. However, *Patriarcha* knew only a posthumous publication in 1680, twenty years after the death of its author.
6. Filmer, *Patriarcha*, p. 7. [TN: in English in the original.]
7. Hobbes, *Leviathan*, pp. 260–1. [TN: in English in the original.]
8. Ibid., pp. 228 et seq.
9. These three rights are again of course found in the Hobbesian deduction of the three rights of sovereignty.
10. Filmer, *Patriarcha*, p. 45. [TN: in English in the original.]
11. Hobbes, *Leviathan*, p. 217. [TN: in English in the original.]
12. Filmer, *Patriarcha*, p. 39.
13. Ibid., p. 45.

14. Ibid., p. 44. [TN: in English in the original.] The same passage continues thus: 'It skills not which way kings come by their power, whether by election, donation, succession or by any other means, for it is still the manner of the government by supreme power that makes them properly kings, and not the means of obtaining their crowns' (ibid. [TN: in English in the original.]). This thesis, according to which it is not so much the manner by which a king achieved power [*pouvoir*] as the exercise of supreme power [*pouvoir*] which properly makes him a king, seems in one sense to limit the impact of patriarchalism in the elaboration of the concept of sovereignty.
15. Hobbes, *Leviathan*, pp. 312–13. [TN: in English in the original.]
16. [TN: in English in the original.]
17. [TN: in English in the original.]
18. [TN: in English in the original.]
19. Filmer, *Patriarcha*, p. 45.
20. Ibid., p. 49.
21. Ibid., p. 44.
22. Hobbes, *The Elements of Law*, p. 105.
23. Hobbes, *De Cive*, pp. 215–16.
24. Hobbes, *The Elements of Law*, p. 105: 'And when many men subject themselves the former way, there ariseth thence a body politic, as it were naturally.' [TN: in English in the original.]
25. Hobbes, *De Cive*, p. 215.
26. [TN: in English in the original.] Even though, in *The Elements of Law*, the term *commonwealth* [TN: in English in the original] can also be worthy as a general denomination for the two kinds of political body (Hobbes, *The Elements of Law*, p. 105).
27. [TN: italicised English in English in the original.] Hobbes, *De Cive*, pp. 215–16. [TN: 'Hence it is, that there are two kinds of *Cities*, the one *naturall*, such as is the *paternall*, and *despoticall*; the other *institutive*, which may be also called *politicall*' (Hobbes, *De Cive: The English Version*, p. 90).]
28. In particular, as we have emphasised above, on the term of *commonwealth* [TN: in English in the original] in *The Elements of Law*.
29. [TN: in English in the original.]
30. Hobbes, *The Elements of Law*, p. 135. [TN: in English in the original.] The parallel text to this in *De Cive* is the following: '*Paterfamilias, liberi servique ejus, virtute imperii paterni, in unam personam civilem coaliti,* FAMILIA *dicitur. Eadem, si multiplicatione prolis et servorum acquisitione numerosa fiat, ita ut sine belli incerta alea subjugari non posit, appelabitur* REGNUM PATRIMONIALE. *Quod quamquam vi acquisitum differat a monarchia institutiva origine et modo constituendi, constitutum tamen omnes easdem habet proprietas, et idem est utrobique imperii jus, ut non sit opus quidlibet de iis seorsim dicere*' (Hobbes, *De Cive*, p. 260). [TN: 'A *Father*, with

his *sonnes* and *servants* growne into a civill Person by vertue of his paternall jurisdiction, is called a FAMILY. This *family*, if through multiplying of *children*, and acquisition of *servants*, it becomes numerous, insomuch as without casting the uncertain dye of warre, it cannot be subdued, will be termed an Hereditary Kingdome; which though it differ from an *institutive Monarchy*, being acquired by force in the original, & manner of its constitution; yet being constituted, it hath al the same properties, and the Right of authority is every where the same, insomuch as it is not needfull to speak any thing of them apart' (Hobbes, *De Cive: The English Version*, p. 126).]
31. [TN: in English in the original.]
32. Filmer, *Observations*, p. 185. The theses indicated of Hobbes are found for the first (the father as absolute sovereign) in Hobbes, *Leviathan*, p. 382, and for the second (the great family considered as a small monarchy) in *Leviathan*, p. 257.
33. See Hobbes, *Leviathan*, p. 189.
34. It is true that Hobbes writes in *Leviathan*, p. 382, 'originally the Father of every man was also his Soveraign Lord', or again in *The Elements of Law*, p. 134, 'Children therefore, whether they be brought up and preserved by the father, or by the mother or by whomsoever, are in most absolute subjection to him or her, that so bringeth them up, or preserveth them.' [TN: in English in the original.]
35. See Filmer, *Observations*, pp. 187–8. The corresponding passages of Hobbes are found in *De Cive*, p. 249, and *The Elements of Law*, p. 127.
36. See Hobbes, *The Elements of Law*, chs 2 and 4 in totality; *De Cive*, ch. 9 in totality; *Leviathan*, ch. 20 in totality.
37. Hobbes, *The Elements of Law*, p. 134.
38. Ibid., p. 132. [TN: in English in the original.] See also Hobbes, *De Cive*, pp. 255–6; *Leviathan*, pp. 253–4.
39. See Hobbes, *The Elements of Law*, pp. 132–3; *Leviathan*, pp. 253–4.
40. See Chapter 8, 'On Property', above.
41. [TN: in English in the original.]
42. [TN: in English in the original.]
43. Filmer, *Patriarcha*, p. 10. [TN: in English in the original.] See the definition given by Jean Bodin of seigniorial monarchy in Bodin, *Six Books of the Commonwealth*, abridged and trans. M. J. Tooley (Oxford: Blackwell, 1967), pp. 56–9.
44. See Chapter 9, 'On the State', above.
45. Filmer, *Observations*, p. 195. In the cited text, Filmer is literally referring to three passages of *Leviathan*, which are successively the following: Hobbes, *Leviathan*, pp. 192, 199, 196.
46. Filmer, *Observations*, p. 193. [TN: in English in the original.]

47. [TN: 'Common-wealth' in English in the original.]
48. Filmer, *Observations*, p. 186. [TN: in English in the original.]
49. [TN: italicised English in English in the original.]

*Chapter 12*

# HOBBES AND PASCAL: TWO MODELS OF THE THEORY OF POWER [*POUVOIR*]

### BEYOND THE CONVERGENCES

The convergences of Hobbes and Pascal's anthropological and political conception have often been emphasised.[1] These convergences concern points as important as the theory of the expansion of the human self, the universalisation of the desire for domination, the doctrine of interhuman relationships, the necessity of the existence of a political authority that has the broadsword and justice,[2] etc. at its disposal. We can thus think, without great fear of being mistaken, that Pascal read or at least heard talk of Hobbes, in particular of his *De Cive*. Certain Pascalian claims on the collective conduct of men or on the necessity of power [*pouvoir*] often seem, if not simple repetitions, at least copies of Hobbes's positions. Most often, Pascal seems to recognise in it an at least partial truth that he tries hard to restore to a level of determined reading. We do not intend to recapture and re-examine these Pascalian repetitions and displacements. This, not only because much has been done on this plane, but also and above all because it seems to us that, despite their real convergences indicated, Pascal and Hobbes's politics remain very differently minded, above all when we consider the question of the nature and the functioning of political power [*pouvoir*]. Hobbes and Pascal very much seem to furnish two distinct models of the theory of power [*pouvoir*]. In order to attempt to show this, we will thus examine three points, making it possible to determine the sites of divergence of the two analyses of the political: (1) institution or institutionalisation; (2) adequation or inadequation; (3) effects of reason or reason of effects. At each of these levels, Hobbes's theses and arguments will be developed less for themselves than in view of putting the specificity of Pascalian positions into perspective.

## INSTITUTION OR INSTITUTIONALISATION

Hobbes's political doctrine is, in its central point of flexion, a theory of the contractual [*contractuelle*] institution of the state. The distinction between the republic of institution and the republic of acquisition does not affect the central character of the notion of institution itself. In opposition to this doctrine of explicit or implicit juridical institution of power [*pouvoir*], Pascal formulates a theory of the institutionalisation of force in right that has a different meaning.

In order to understand this, it is sufficient to examine the critique to which Pascal submits Hobbesian concepts which subtend the theory of institution: human nature, natural right, natural law and contract [*contrat*].

### *Human Nature*

The Pascalian critique of the notion of human nature is not political first of all, but theological. To the description of the deployment of personal individual and interhuman life starting from a univocal definition of human nature, Pascal opposes that there are not one but two natures of man. Thus echoing the *Writings on Grace*, which take up again the Augustinian distinction of two states of human nature, fragment 131 of *Pensées* declares '(*Is it not thus clear as day that man's condition is double?*) For in fact, if man had never been corrupt, he would enjoy in his innocence both truth and happiness with assurance; and if man had always been corrupt, he would have no idea of truth or bliss . . . (*Let us thus conceive that man's condition is double.*)'[3]

We could, however, object to ourselves here that the Hobbesian concept of human nature is suited to the second state of human nature according to Pascal. Things are not so simple: the consonance is only superficial. For precisely the passage from a first nature to a second nature of man seems to render problematic the concept of human nature itself. Indeed, why does man have only two natures? Why does he not have more of them? In fragment 129, we can in fact read: 'How many natures exist in man? How many vocations?' It is the very concept of human nature that thus seems to be shaky: 'Custom is a second nature which destroys the former. But what is nature? For is custom not natural? I am much afraid that nature is itself only a first custom, as custom is a second nature.'[4] In fragment 419, Pascal claims it directly: 'Custom is our nature.' In other words, the idea of a fixed and attributable nature of man seems to fade. We do not know exactly what in man falls under the jurisdiction of nature and what falls under the jurisdiction of custom and habit. This deconstruction of the univocal concept of human nature also extends to the notions of natural right and natural law.

### Natural Right

The concept of natural right is subject to a critical examination in the *Three Discourses on the Station of Noblemen*: there is no natural right which could naturally found a domination over persons or things. There is very much a natural equality of men, but this equality, far from finding expression in the idea of a natural right, on the contrary, functions as a critique of the illusion of such a right.[5] What we call right is only the fruit of luck or of the will of legislators. In other words, it is only from positive right, upon which all possession or all mastery finds itself definitively founded.

### Natural Law

There is very much a natural law or a natural justice, but it is no longer accessible to human reason. The natural law to which the fourteenth Provincial Letter[6] made reference is, in *Pensées*, if not lost, at least obscured by the loss of man's first nature. Thus, Pascal can write:

> Men admit that justice does not consist in these customs, but that it resides in natural laws, common to every country. They would certainly maintain it obstinately, if reckless chance which has distributed human laws had encountered even one which was universal; but the farce is that the caprice of men has so many vagaries that there is no such law.
> ... Doubtless there are natural laws; but good reason once corrupted has corrupted all.[7]

As the natural law is no longer either directly or positively accessible to human reason, we understand that 'Justice and truth are two such subtle point that our tools are too blunt to touch them accurately.'[8]

## Social Contract [Contrat]

The uselessness and invalidity of the notion of the social pact, in the double status of event and juridical structure that Hobbes conferred to it in order to take account of the state's existence, follows from this analysis of the notions of natural right and natural law. What in Pascal takes the place of the Hobbesian conception of the contract [*contrat*]? Two things essentially: first, a dialectic of force and of justice elucidated in particular in fragments 81, 85 and 103 from *Pensées*.[9] This dialectic, which always seems to turn to the profit of force, also covers the demand for an immanent justification in the establishment of this force. This type of relation between force and justice is not Hobbesian. Both in *The Elements of Law* and in *De Cive* or *Leviathan*, it is rather the powerlessness [*impuissance*] of force to assure an absolute domination that opens up the juridical problematic of the contract [*contrat*]. Right is not founded on force in Hobbes. Second, a theory of the formulation of political power [*pouvoir*] developed in fragment 828: 'Let us, then, imagine we see society in the process of formation.' Yet this text is constituted of five moments which define the Pascalian conception of institutionalisation: (1) universal desire for domination; (2) the war that results from it is not of all against all, but of one party to another; (3) taking of power [*pouvoir*] by a certain party; (4) substitution of positive rules of right for the exercise of force in order to assure the longevity of domination; (5) indication of the mode by which this substitution takes place which is in truth an institutionalisation of force in right:

> And this is the point where imagination begins to play its part. Till now power makes fact; now power is sustained by imagination in a certain party, in France in the nobility, in Switzerland in the burgesses, etc.[10]

In Pascal, the principle of the institutionalisation of force in a political establishment governed by laws, that is to say, in positive right, is done according to a double movement: on the one hand, the initial takeover continues in giving itself the appearance of right; on the other hand, with the establishment of laws, force is henceforth regulated and, so to speak, tamed.

Within this double route – explained by the Pascalian formula from fragment 81 'they have justified might' – by which we simultaneously have given to force the appearance of justice and have caught force within the rules of justice thus established, imagination and opinion have a constitutive function. Thus, the essential aspect of the Pascalian theory of power [*pouvoir*] is going to consist in demonstrating the resilience of the formation and reproduction of individual and collective opinion which is at the foundation of the process of institutionalisation. Fragment 665 gives the general principle for the mechanism of political institutionalisation:

> The government founded on opinion and imagination reigns for some time, and this government is pleasant and voluntary; that founded on might lasts for ever. Thus opinion is queen of the world, but might is its tyrant.

It is indeed by the imagination that opinion is formed: 'The imagination disposes of everything; it makes beauty, justice, and happiness, which is everything in the world.'[11] Thus, magistrates, doctors, scholars, lawyers owe their self-importance only to the process by which they are capable of duping the world by 'so original an appearance'.[12] The very duality of those who establish themselves by force and those who establish themselves with a grimace [*par la grimace*], that is to say, signs and imagination, is superficial. The establishment is also made with a grimace of men-at-arms and kings:

> The habit of seeing kings accompanied by guards, drums, officers, and all the paraphernalia which mechanically inspire respect and awe, makes their countenance, when sometimes seen alone without these accompaniments, impress respect and awe on their subjects; because we cannot separate in thought their persons from the surroundings with which we see them usually joined. And the world, which knows not that this effect is the result of habit, believes that it arises by a natural force.[13]

This function of opinion in the institutionalisation of force in custom and in positive right leads to the second pair of concepts which define the difference of Hobbes and Pascal's theories of power [*pouvoir*].

## ADEQUATION OR INADEQUATION

The state's juridical institution in Hobbes and the takeover's institutionalisation into customs and laws in Pascal engage different positions on the question of the truth of the political. Thus, once established, the Hobbesian state can persist only on the condition that it function on the mode of adequation. Adequation is inscribed as much within the theory of civil laws, which, in order to be obligatory, must be adequately signified; and within the doctrine of the official education of subjects' duties and of the rights of sovereigns who aim to balance the subjects' present actions with the terms of the originary social contract; and as within the conception of social communication inside the civil state (the reduction of uncertainty that characterised the state of nature). Unlike the Hobbesian state, the Pascalian state functions on the unsurpassable mode of inadequation. We could show it by analysis of fragment 93, which consists of the application of a continual reversal of the pros and cons in the people's opinions. In this fragment, Pascal shows: (1) that the people's opinions are shallow; (2) then, that 'the people are not so foolish as is said'; (3) finally, 'that it remains always true that the people are foolish, though their opinions are sound because they do not perceive the truth where it is, and, as they place it where it is not, their opinions are always very false and very unsound'. We could also show it in fragment 90, on the gradation of the people's points of view in the half-skilled, the skilled, the sanctimonious and in perfect Christians. Only these last adequately possessing the truth, but because they are situated beyond the political order. However, here I would like to show that inadequation is the mode of functioning for political power [*pouvoir*] in Pascal because the very existence of this power [*pouvoir*] is based on a hidden truth, the process of institutionalisation examined just now having the function of hiding or masking this, as it were, inexpressible truth of the political.

The idea that there is a hidden, and necessarily hidden, truth of the political is found in numerous texts of Pascal. The first, in the *Three Discourses on the Station of Noblemen*, is even entirely structured by the distinction between hidden thought and public thought:

> [H]e [the despised king or the king of substitution] had two ways of looking at things; the one according to which he acted as king, the other by which he recognized his real state, and that it was mere chance that had put him in the place where he was. He hid this latter thought and brought the other to light. By the former he dealt with his people, and on the basis of the latter he dealt with himself.[14]

The thought that the despised king hid was thus a true thought, in opposition to the one, illusory, through which he dealt with the people. We thus understand how Pascal, speaking to Noblemen, claims:

> What follows from this? It follows that, like the man of whom we were speaking, you must have two ways of looking at things; that if you deal outwardly with men in accordance with your rank you must recognize by a *more hidden* but *more rightful* way of thinking that you are not by nature above them. If public opinion raises you above the common run of men, let the other humble you and keep you in perfect equality with all men, for that is your natural station.[15]

The hidden and true thought is also that which debases, but this is another secret which will say why the glories of establishing are nonetheless legitimate.[16] The first of the *Three Discourses*, which has the function of bringing 'into genuine understanding' the condition of Noblemen, thus makes us pass from the public to the hidden which must remain such.

In *Pensées*, the idea of a hidden truth of the political is found. This time, it is not a question of the secret that presides over the formation of the glory of establishment, but of a truth hidden in and by order of laws and customs: 'We [the people] must not see the fact of usurpation; law was once introduced without reason, and has become reasonable. We must make it regarded as authoritative, eternal, and conceal its origin, if we do not wish that it should soon come to an end.'[17] Two questions thus arise: what is this hidden truth? Why must it remain thus?

The response to the first question takes on the foundation: that of the authority of the laws as well as of the entire political order. The foundation of the political order is implied in the beginning, that is to say, in the act by which domination was established: in the beginning of power [*pouvoir*] there is usurpation, be it due to chance and to illusion, as in the *Three Discourses*, or to takeover, as in fragment 828 of *Pensées*. Yet such a beginning affects the whole structure of the political edifice and the process of its institutionalisation. The latter is going, in fact, to have the function of masking luck or takeover in transforming fact into right or force into justice.[18] Takeover or fruit of luck, the beginning of power [*pouvoir*] must be hidden, otherwise everything drifts away from it: the dominant party, the laws, in sum, everything produced by human establishment will be likely to be overwhelmed. The laws' foundation must remain equally hidden: 'Custom creates the whole of equity, for the simple reason that it is accepted. It is the mystical foundation of its authority; whoever carries it back to its first principles destroys it.'[19] If the mystical foundation of the laws' authority must remain hidden, it is because this foundation does not consist in justice but in age, and because the people yet obey them only because it believes them just: 'He who obeys them because they are just obeys a justice which is imaginary and not the essence of law; it is quite self-contained, it is law and nothing more.'[20]

If fragment 66 maintains that we can say to the people 'that they must obey them [the laws] because they are laws, just as they must obey superiors, not because they are just, but because they are superiors. In this way all sedition is prevented, if this can be made intelligible and it be understood what is the proper definition of justice,' on the other hand, fragment 525 clearly indicates that 'people cannot accept this doctrine; and, as they believe that truth can be found, and that it exists in law and custom, they believe them and take their antiquity as a proof of their truth, and not simply of their authority apart from truth'. Obedience to the laws is bound to the formation of opinion and belief.

As to the second question: why must the truth remain hidden? The previous examination has already partially responded. It is in obedience. The people obey the laws only because it believes them just. There is thus very much a hidden truth constitutive of the political in Pascal. In order to bring out its special features, it is sufficient to remark that, just the opposite, Hobbes puts at the origin of political power [*pouvoir*] a social contract that makes explicit its principle under the form of a clear statement and commonly re-assumable [*réassumable*] self. Likewise, the fact that the laws' authority resides in the sovereign's will alone, far from having the status of a hidden truth, must, on the contrary according to Hobbes, be the object of a recognition of all the subjects.

The regime of inadequation (hidden truth), on which the theory of political power [*pouvoir*] functions in Pascal, is thus reflected in the theory of public discourse of the holder of power [*pouvoir*], in the status of the laws and customs, as well as through the doctrine the formation of the people's belief linked to its incapacity to recognise the truth in the place where it is found. Fragment 91 explains this inadequation well enough: 'We must keep our thought secret, and judge everything by it, while talking like the people.'

In the gradation of discourses and attitudes, only the true Christian is, according to Pascal, in a position to adequately grasp the truth of the political because, finding himself beyond the political, he can arrange the complete series of opinions from the pro to the con succeeding each other.

## EFFECTS OF REASON AND REASON OF EFFECTS

The third aspect of the difference in Hobbes and Pascal's politics is established between the theory of the effects of reason from the first and that of the reason of effects from the second.

Effects of reason in Hobbes means that the political institution can remain stable only by a double effect of reason. The effect of reason in the subjects who must understand why the state, with its apparatus of laws and the use of public force, is necessary to the maintenance of their being and their well-being. The effect of reason in the sovereign who must conform to the rules that govern the political artifice, that is to say, have in view the people's good. Yet these two effects of reason refer to a single calculating rationality in which the sovereign and subjects participate. There is in Hobbes no doctrine of the *ratio Status* by which the *ratio civitatis* would transcend common reason.[21]

The Pascalian concept of reason of effects has another meaning and other implications on the political plane. Reason of effects signifies not only a cause of effects, but also puts into sequence a gradation of discourse that contrasts pros and cons and the decryption of a rationality there where there seems to be only the irrational or disorder.

> The reasons of effects indicate the greatness of man, in having extracted so fair an order from lust.[22]
> 
> All men naturally hate one another. They employ lust as far as possible in the service of the public weal.[23]
> 
> In having distinguished men by external marks, as birth or wealth. The world again exults in showing how unreasonable this is; but it is very reasonable.[24]
> 
> The greatness of man even in his lust, to have known how to extract from it a wonderful code, and to have drawn from it a picture of benevolence.[25]

To pass from effects to the reason of effects is to leave from the sequence of the effects in order to examine them from a superior point of view or to pass from one discourse to another likely to render reason from the first. In rising in gradation from discourse to the most elevated level, that of the perfect Christian, we discover the rationality of the inferior degrees in the particular point of view which is theirs. Thus, in the *Three Discourses*, the concupiscent king who is 'master of several things after which men lust', disposing of the power [*pouvoir*] to 'satisfy the needs and the desires of some men', appears as figure of the charitable king: 'God is surrounded by people full of benevolence who ask of him the blessings of benevolence within his power.'[26]

The reason of effects thus consists of a critique of the political which decrypts its hidden truth by placing it back within its order: that of bodies. Thus resituated, political power [*pouvoir*] must not pretend to reign by paths other than those that constitute it, otherwise it would become tyrannical:

> It is not your strength and your natural power which make all these people subject to you. Therefore do not claim to dominate them by force, nor treat them with severity. Satisfy their desires, relieve their wants, derive your pleasure from doing good, raise them as much as you can, and you will be acting like a true king of covetousness.[27]

But resituated within its order, and thereby justified, the political order will impede no one from getting lost. In order to attain salvation, it is necessary to take another path.

## CONCLUSION

Pascal was party to a political problem rather close to that of Hobbes and that fragment 94 of *Pensées* summarises well enough:

> Civil wars are the greatest of evils. They are inevitable, if we wish to reward desert; for all will say they are deserving. The evil we have to fear from a fool who succeeds by right of birth, is neither so great nor so sure.

But he succeeds less in a political doctrine than in a critique of the political, the principal motivation of which is irony:[28]

> We can only think of Plato and Aristotle in great academic robes. They were honest men, like others, laughing with their friends, and, when they diverted themselves with writing their *Laws* and the *Politics*, they did it as an amusement. That part of their life was the least philosophic and the least serious; the most philosophic was to live simply and quietly.

If they wrote on politics, it was as in order to regulate an asylum.

> [A]nd if they presented the appearance of speaking of a great matter, it was because they knew that the madmen, to whom they spoke, thought they were kings and emperors. They entered into their principles in order to make their madness as little harmful as possible.[29]

This critical irony of Pascal on politics contrasts sharply with the doctrinal seriousness of Hobbes's politics.

## Notes

1. For Pascal's texts, we are referring to the edition of the *Œuvres complètes* by Louis Lafuma (Paris: Seuil, 1963) (indication of the page and of column A or B, when it does not concern *Pensées*). We could obviously refer with much benefit to the edition of the *Œuvres complètes* in development by Jean Mesnard (Desclée de Brouwer) (four volumes appeared). [TN: Lafuma's fragment numeration is followed by the Mesnard numbers used by Trotter in notes.]
2. On these points, see Pierre Magnard, *Nature et histoire dans l'apologétique de Pascal* (Paris: Les Belles Lettres, 1975), pp. 229–70; François Tricaud, 'Pascal disciple de Hobbes?', *Revue européenne des sciences sociales*, 20(61) (1982): 121–34; Gérard Ferreyrolles, *Pascal et la raison du politique* (Paris: PUF, 1984); Zarka, *La décision métaphysique de Hobbes*, pp. 293–309; Christian Lazzeri, *Force et justice dans la politique de Pascal* (Paris: PUF, 1993).
3. [TN: because Trotter does not translate them, the italicised sentences are my translations.]
4. Pascal, *Pensées*, fr. 126; fr. 93.

5. Pascal, *Three Discourses*, p. 213; p. 366B: 'What follows from this? It follows that, like the man of whom you were speaking, you must have two ways of looking at things; that if you deal outwardly with men in accordance with your rank you must recognize by a more hidden but more rightful way of thinking that you are not by nature above them. If public opinion raises you above the common run of men, let the other humble you and keep you in perfect equality with all men, for that is your natural station.'
6. Pascal, *The Provincial Letters*, p. 209; p. 436A: 'These, Fathers, are the principles of public peace and safety, accepted at all times and in all places, on which all the legislators of the world, sacred or profance, have based their laws. Even pagans have introduced no exception to this rule, except when there is no other way of averting loss of virtue or life.'
7. Pascal, *Pensées*, fr. 294; fr. 60.
8. Ibid., fr. 82; fr. 44.
9. '[B]eing unable to cause might to obey justice, men have made it just to obey might. Unable to strengthen justice, they have justified might; so that the just and the strong unite, and there should be peace, which is the sovereign good' (fr. 299; fr. 81). 'Hence comes the right of the sword, for the sword gives a true right' (fr. 878; fr. 85). 'And thus, being unable to make what is just strong, we have made what is strong just' (fr. 298; fr. 103).
10. Ibid., fr. 304; fr. 828.
11. Ibid., fr. 82; fr. 44.
12. Ibid.
13. Ibid., fr. 308; fr. 25.
14. Pascal, *Three Discourses*, p. 212; p. 366A.
15. Ibid., p. 213; p. 366B (my emphasis).
16. Pascal, *Three Discourses*, p. 214; p. 367A: 'Established greatness depends on the will of men who have thought it reasonable to owe honour to certain estates and to attach a certain respect to them. Power and nobility are of this kind. In one country people honour nobles, in another commoners; in this one they honour the first-born, in that other the younger. Why this? Because it is men's pleasure to do so. The matter was one of indifference before it was established; *after its establishment it became just, because it is unjust to disturb it*' (my emphasis).
17. Pascal, *Pensées*, fr. 294; fr. 60; my emphasis.
18. Cf. ibid., frr. 299, 878, 298; frr. 81, 85, 103.
19. Ibid., fr. 294; fr. 60.
20. Ibid.
21. See on this point, Yves Charles Zarka's introduction to the volume *Raison et déraison d'état: théoriciens et theories de la raison d'état aux XVIe et XVIIe siècles* (Paris: PUF, 1994), pp. 5–6.
22. Pascal, *Pensées*, fr. 403; fr. 106.

23. Ibid., fr. 451; fr. 210.
24. Ibid., fr. 324; fr. 101.
25. Ibid., fr. 402; fr. 118.
26. Pascal, *Three Discourses*, p. 215; p. 367B.
27. Ibid., p. 215; p. 368A–B.
28. See Jean Mesnard, *Les Pensées de Pascal* (Paris: Sedes, 1976), pp. 277–99.
29. Pascal, *Pensées*, fr. 331; fr. 533.

# CONCLUSION

## HOBBES'S CONTRIBUTIONS

At the end of this journey which sought to recapture Hobbesian conceptual work in the field of political thought, we can retain four essential contributions of Hobbes to the definition of the modern concept of the political. Let us clarify, first of all, that the modern concept of the political does not consist of a single and homogeneous theoretical orientation: it is crossed by fractures and antinomies. To determine Hobbes's contributions does not in any way imply the idea that these contributions must be generally shared or taken up again by subsequent thinkers: it is a question only of freeing someone from the decisive modifications or innovations introduced by Hobbes within the construction of the intellectual categories of modern political thought through his fractures and his antinomies. Let us clarify, next, that the determination of the four contributions is not intended to be exhaustive. There are indeed whole sections of Hobbes's political thought that we have not approached, in particular the relationship between politics and religion where the three non-superimposable relations between state and Church, temporal and spiritual, reason and revelation is redistributed.

Hobbes's first contribution concerns the theory of the universal individual. Certainly, the relationship between the concept of the individual and the modern theory of the state is a classical place for commentary. We have however wanted to take account of his range by way of a new angle: that by which the universalisable concept of the individual again puts into question the vision of the world and of politics linked to the definition of the heroic singularity described by Gracián. Hobbes's individual is universal in the same way as his essential ethico-political attribute: natural right. Negatively, we can say that the concept of the individual dissolves every natural social hierarchy and every organic conception of the people. The correlate of the individual is the multitude from which must be thought an institution of the people, indissociable from the institution of the state. Positively, we can say that Hobbes elaborates his ethical concept of the individual in re-elaborating the doctrine of the constitution and of the deployment of man's cognitive and affective life. It is around this ethics that the theories of right and of contract [*contrat*] are organised and reinterpreted.

The second contribution resides in the theory of the sign. Politics is a place of fundamental ambivalences: enmity/friendship, discord/agreement, submission/liberty, injustice/justice, etc. Yet it is impossible to take account of these ambivalences if we interpret power [*pouvoir*] in terms exclusive of the relation of forces, coercion or the exercise of violence. The political power [*pouvoir*] definition – but also that of the power [*puissance*] of the human individual – integrates as an irreducible component the dimension of the sign, the major, but not exclusive, form of which is language. This is why, facing the calculation of the body's force which falls entirely under the jurisdiction of a physics of movement, Hobbes elaborates an ethico-political semiology of power [*pouvoir*]. While the physical world owes its order to the composition of movements, the human world owes its own to the self-regulation of the political artifice which consists of the existence of a political right and a non-equivocal regime of communication which is assured by signs instituted from power [*pouvoir*], public force having in principle the function only of enforcing legality. Thus, Hobbes reworks the concept of power [*pouvoir*] in such a way as to integrate there, besides the force of coercing, the dimensions of signification, value and right.

The third decisive contribution consists in the construction of the notion of a public political will. Hobbes's central political problem, the one that the social contract must resolve, concerns the transformation of a multiplicity of individual wills into a unique political will: that of the civil person. But, we have seen, this problem splits. It does not in fact suffice for taking account of the institution of a single political will. It is additionally necessary that this will be public and, consequently, not be reduced to the private will of a particular man, he being sovereign. Yet the idea of such a public political will is validly thought only in *Leviathan*, with the introduction of representation, which permits the passage from one doctrine of the social contract of alienation to a doctrine of the social contract of authorisation. In other words, Hobbes discovers that the public political will can be thought only as the will of all. Yet, in constituting the concept of such a will, Hobbes accomplishes another decisive gesture: he liberates the concept of political power [*pouvoir*] and that of sovereignty from the terms of a theory of property within which they were thought. Paradoxically, even though Hobbes extends the concept of *dominium* from the right of property over things to the different forms of acquisition of a power [*pouvoir*] over men, he finds the means to escape from this same logic and gives himself theoretical instruments in order to think the constitution of a political right over men's actions which does not fall within the jurisdiction of the right of property. Modern public right finds by that way one of the paths of its emancipation with regard to private right.

The fourth contribution consists in the juridical theory of political institution. This theory concerns not only the function of the state, but also its internal functioning and the succession to sovereign power [*pouvoir*]. Yet the idea of an institutional theory of the state designates a figure of the political which can impose itself only in being theoretically opposed to other figures, in particular, but not only, in the return of a modernised version of the seigniorial conception of power [*pouvoir*], on the one hand, and in the properly modern idea of the political as institutionalisation of force, on the other hand. The first is represented by Filmer's patriarchalism which founds *royal authority*[1] on the *right of fatherhood*[2] and interprets political power [*pouvoir*] in terms of property. If Filmer's patriarchal conception constitutes a modernised version of the seigniorial conception of power [*pouvoir*], it is that, paradoxically, while tending to naturalise the political order by the superimposition of royal and paternal figures, it develops a conception of absolute sovereignty very close to that of Hobbes. The second figure of the political that refuses the problematic of the juridical institution of the political is represented by the political conceptions elaborated by Pascal. The latter indeed develops a critique of politics that aims at demystifying the whole of the beliefs and values on which political order rests. Yet, thus demystified, politics with its glory of establishment, its customs and its laws, is revealed as the order of inadequation within which force is concealed and is overtaken in becoming institutionalised. The political question is from then on less that of the constitution of a public political will as that of the formation and control of opinion.

Thus, the concepts of the universal individual, semiology of power [*pouvoir*], public political will and juridical institution of the state constitute certain of the principal results of the Hobbesian conceptual work in the constitution of the principal categories of modern political thought.

*Notes*

1. [TN: in English in the original.]
2. [TN: in English in the original.]

# BIBLIOGRAPHY

Adler, Mortimer J. (ed.), *Great Books of the Western World*, vol. 30 (Chicago, IL: Encyclopaedia Britannica, 1990).
Aquinas, St Thomas, *Summa Theologicae*, vol. 38, trans. Marcus Lefébure O.P. (Oxford: Blackfriars, 1975).
Bacon, Francis, *The Works of Francis Bacon*, ed. Basil Montagu, 16 vols (London: William Pickering, 1825–37).
Bacon, Francis, *Francis Bacon*, ed. Brian Vickers (Oxford: Oxford University Press, 1996).
Batllori, Miguel and Ceferino Peralta, *Baltasar Gracián en su vida y en su obras* (Zaragoza: Institución 'Fernando el Católico', 1969).
Bénichou, Paul, *Morales du Grand Siècle* (Paris: Gallimard, 1948).
Bodin, Jean, *Six Books of the Commonwealth*, abridged and trans. M. J. Tooley (Oxford: Blackwell, 1967).
Bodin, Jean, *Les six livres de la République* (Aalen: Scientia Verlag, [1583] 1977).
Bodin, Jean, *Exposé du droit universel = Juris universi distributio*, trans. Lucien Jerphagnon (Paris: PUF, 1985).
Bodin, Jean, *On Sovereignty: Four Chapters from the* Six Books of the Commonwealth, ed. and trans. Julian H. Franklin (Cambridge: Cambridge University Press, 1992).
Buckle, Steven, *Natural Law and the Theory of Property: Grotius to Hume* (Oxford: Clarendon Press, 1991).
Carrive, Paulette, 'Hobbes et les jurists de la Common Law', in *Thomas Hobbes: de la métaphysique à la politique*, ed. Martin Berman and Michel Malherbe (Paris: Vrin, 1989).
Cordemoy, Gerauld de, *Œuvres philosophiques, avec une étude bio-bibliographique*, ed. Pierre Clair and François Girbal (Paris: PUF, 1968).
Descartes, René, *Œuvres de Descartes*, vol. 11, ed. Charles Adams and Paul Tannery (Paris: Lépold Cerf, 1909).
Descartes, René, *Treatise of Man*, trans. Thomas Steele Hall (Amherst, NY: Prometheus Books, 2003).

Ferreyrolles, Gérard, *Pascal et la raison du politique* (Paris: PUF, 1984).
Filmer, Sir Robert, *Patriarcha and Other Writings*, ed. Johann P. Sommerville (Cambridge: Cambridge University Press, 1991).
Foucault, Michel, *The History of Sexuality, vol. 1: An Introduction*, trans. Robert Hurley (New York: Random House, 1978).
Gauthier, David P., *The Logic of Leviathan: The Moral and Political Theory of Thomas Hobbes* (Oxford: Clarendon Press, 1969).
Goyard-Fabre, Simone, 'Le concept de *Persona civilis* dans la philosophie politique de Hobbes', *Cahiers de philosophie politique de l'Université de Caen*, 3 (1983): 49–71.
Goyard-Fabre, Simone, 'La legislation civile dans l'état-Léviathan', in *Thomas Hobbes: de la métaphysique à la politique*, ed. Martin Berman and Michel Malherbe (Paris: Vrin, 1989).
Gracián, Baltasar, *Obras Completas*, ed. Arturo del Hoyo (Madrid: Aguilar, 1960).
Gracián, Baltasar, *La pointe ou l'art du génie*, trans. Michèle Gendreau-Massaloux and Pierre Laurens (Paris: L'Age d'homme, 1983), pp. 17–33.
Gracián, Baltasar, *A Pocket Mirror for Heroes*, ed. and trans. Christopher Maurer (New York: Currency Doubleday, 1996).
Grotius, Hugo, *De Jure Belli ac Pacis Libri Tres*, trans. Francis W. Kelsey et al., vol. 2 (New York: Oceana Publications, 1964).
Hegel, G. W. F., *Elements of the Philosophy of Right*, trans. H. B. Nisbet, ed. Allen W. Wood (Cambridge: Cambridge University Press, 1991).
Hobbes, Thomas, *English Works*, 11 vols, ed. Sir William Molesworth (London: Routledge/Thoemmes Press, 1839–45).
Hobbes, Thomas, *Opera Philosophica*, ed. Sir William Molesworth, 5 vols (London: John Bohn, 1839–45).
Hobbes, Thomas, *The Elements of Law, Natural and Politic*, ed. Ferdinand Tönnies (London: Simpin, Mardshall, 1889).
Hobbes, Thomas, *A Dialogue between a Philosopher and a Student of the Common Laws of England*, ed. Joseph Cropsey (Chicago, IL: University of Chicago Press, 1971).
Hobbes, Thomas, *Thomas White's* De mundo *examined*, trans. H. W. Jones (Bradford: Bradford University Press, 1976).
Hobbes, Thomas, *Leviathan*, ed. C. B. Macpherson (New York: Penguin, 1986).
Hobbes, Thomas, *De Principiis*, trans. Luc Borot, *Philosophie*, 23 (1989), pp. 5–21.
Hobbes, Thomas, *Behemoth, or the Long Parliament*, ed. Ferdinand Tönnies (Chicago, IL: University of Chicago Press, 1990).
Hobbes, Thomas, *Man*, trans. Charles T. Wood, T. S. K. Scott-Craig and Bernard Gert (Indianapolis, IN: Hackett, 1998).

Hobbes, Thomas, *De Cive: The English Edition*, ed. Howard Warrender (Oxford: Clarendon Press, 2002).
Hobbes, Thomas, *Léviathan*, trans. François Tricaud and Martine Pécharman, in *Œuvres complètes*, vol. 6/2 (Paris: Vrin, 2004).
Kant, Immanuel, *The Metaphysics of Morals*, trans. and ed. Mary Gregor (Cambridge: Cambridge University Press, 1996).
La Rochefoucauld, François de, *Maxims*, trans. Leonard Tancock (New York: Penguin Books, 1959).
La Rochefoucauld, François de, *Maximes suivies des réflexions diverses, du portrait de La Rochefoucauld par lui-même et des remarques de Christine de Suède sue les Maximes*, ed. Jacques Truchet (Paris: Éditions Garnier Frères, 1967).
La Rochefoucauld, François de, *Réflexions diverses/Miscellaneous Reflections*, in *Collected Maxims and Other Reflections*, trans. E. H. Blackmore, A. M. Blackmore and Francine Giguère (Oxford: Oxford University Press, 2007).
Lazzeri, Christian, *Force et justice dans la politique de Pascal* (Paris: PUF, 1993).
Locke, John, *Essays on the Law of Nature*, trans. W. von Leyden (Oxford: Clarendon Press, 1954).
Locke, John, *Two Treatises of Government*, ed. Peter Laslett (Cambridge: Cambridge University Press, 1988).
Machiavelli, Niccolò, *Il Principe* (1513).
Macpherson, C. B., *The Political Theory of Individualism: Hobbes to Locke* (Oxford: Oxford University Press, 1962).
Magnard, Pierre, *Nature et histoire dans l'apologétique de Pascal* (Paris: Les Belles Lettres, 1975).
Malherbe, Michel, *Hobbes, ou l'œuvre de la raison* (Paris: Vrin, 1984).
Matheron, Alexandre, 'Maîtres et serviteurs dans la philosophie politique classique', *La Pensée*, 200 (1978): 3–20; reprinted in *Anthropologie et politique au XVIIe siècle* (Paris: Vrin, 1986), pp. 171–88.
Matheron, Alexandre, 'Spinoza et la propriété', in *Anthropologie et politique au XVIIe siècle* (Paris: Vrin, 1986), pp. 155–69.
Méchoulan, Henry, *Individu et société dans la pensée baroque espagnole*, in *Studia Leibnitiana*, Sonderheft 10 (Stuttgart: Franz Steiner, 1981).
Mesnard, Jean, *Les Pensées de Pascal* (Paris: Sedes, 1976).
Pascal, Blaise, *Great Shorter Works of Pascal*, trans. Emile Cailliet and John C. Blankenagel (Philadelphia, PA: Westminster Press, 1948).
Pascal, Blaise, *Œuvres complètes*, ed. Louis Lafuma (Paris: Seuil, 1963).
Pascal, Blaise, *Œuvres complètes*, ed. Jean Mesnard, 4 vols (Paris: Desclée de Brouwer, 1964–92).
Pelegrín, Benito, *Ethique et esthétique du Baroque: l'espace jésuitique de Baltasar Gracián* (Arles: Actes Sud, 1985).
Polin, Raymon, *Politique et philosophie chez Hobbes* (Paris: Vrin, 1977).
Polin, Raymon, *Hobbes, Dieu et l'homme* (Paris: PUF, 1981).

Pufendorf, Samuel von, *Of the Law of Nature and of Nations*, trans. Basil Kennett (1729).
Redondo, Augustin, 'Monde à l'envers et conscience de crise dans le *Criticón* de Baltasar Gracián', in *L'image du monde renversé et ses representations littérarires et para-littéraires de la fin du XVIe siècle au milieu du XVIIe*, ed. Jean Lafond and Augustin Redondo (Paris: Vrin, 1979), pp. 83–97.
Renoux-Zagamé, Marie-France, *Origines théologiques du concepts moderne de propriété* (Geneva: Droz, 1987).
Rousseau, Jean-Jacques, *Œuvres complètes de Jean-Jacques Rousseau*, vol. 3, ed. Bernard Gagnebin and Marcel Raymond (Paris: Éditions Gallimard, 1964).
Rousseau, Jean-Jacques, *The Collected Writings of Rousseau*, vol. 2, trans. Christopher Kelly and Judith Bush, ed. Christopher Kelly (Hanover, NH: Dartmouth University Press, 2005).
Schuhmann, Karl, 'La notion de loi chez Hobbes', in *Le Pouvoir et le Droit: Hobbes et les fondements de la Loi*, ed. Louis Roux and François Tricaud (Saint-Étienne: Publications de l'Université de Saint-Étienne, 1992), pp. 175–95.
Skinner, Quentin, 'Meaning and understanding in the history of ideas', *History and Theory*, 8(1) (1969): 3–53.
Skinner, Quentin, 'Conventions and the understanding of speech acts', *Philosophical Quarterly*, 20(79) (1970): 118–38.
Skinner, Quentin, *The Foundations of Modern Political Thought*, 2 vols (Cambridge: Cambridge University Press, 1978–9).
Skinner, Quentin, *Reason and Rhetoric in the Philosophy of Hobbes* (Cambridge: Cambridge University Press, 1997).
Skinner, Quentin, *Liberty before Liberalism* (Cambridge: Cambridge University Press, 1998).
Skinner, Quentin and Yves Charles Zarka, *Hobbes: The Amsterdam Debate*, ed. Hans Blom (New York: Georg Olms Verlag, 2001).
Spitz, Jean-Fabien, 'Comment lire les textes politiques du passé?', *Droits*, 10 (1989): 133–45.
Strauss, Leo, *Natural Right and History* (Chicago, IL: University of Chicago Press, 1953).
Strauss, Leo, *The Political Philosophy of Hobbes: Its Basis and Genesis*, trans. Elsa M. Sinclair (Chicago, IL: University of Chicago Press, 1963).
Strauss, Leo, *'What is Political Philosophy?' and Other Studies* (Glencoe, IL: Free Press, 1959; reprinted Chicago, IL: University of Chicago Press, 1988).
Strauss, Leo, *The Rebirth of Classical Political Rationalism: An Introduction to the Thought of Leo Strauss*, selected and introduced Thomas L. Pangel (Chicago, IL: University of Chicago Press, 1989).

Strauss, Leo and Joseph Cropsey (eds), *History of Political Philosophy*, 3rd edn (Chicago, IL: University of Chicago Press, 1987).
Suárez, Francisco, *De Legibus*.
Tricaud, François, 'Pascal disciple de Hobbes?', *Revue européenne des sciences sociales*, 20(61) (1982): 121–34.
Tully, James, *A Discourse on Property: John Locke and His Adveraries* (Cambridge: Cambridge University Press, 1980).
Tully, James, *Locke: droit naturel et propriété*, trans. Philippe Raynaud (Paris: PUF, 1992).
Villey, Michel, *La formation de la pensée juridique moderne* (Paris: Montchrétien, 1975).
Viola, Francesco, *Behemoth o Leviathan? Diritto e obbligo nel pensiero di Hobbes* (Milan: Giuffré, 1979).
Warrender, Howard, *The Political Philosophy of Hobbes: His Theory of Obligation* (Oxford: Clarendon Press, 1957).
Weber, Max, *The Vocation Lectures: 'Science as a Vocation' and 'Politics as a Vocation'*, trans. Rodney Livingstone, ed. David Owen and Tracy B. Strong (Indianapolis, IN: Hackett, 2004).
Zarka, Yves Charles, *La décision métaphysique de Hobbes: Conditions de la politique* (Paris: Vrin, 1987).
Zarka, Yves Charles (ed.), *Raison et déraison d'état: théoriciens et theories de la raison d'état aux XVIe et XVIIe siècles* (Paris: PUF, 1994).
Zarka, Yves Charles, 'First philosophy and the foundation of knowledge', trans. Tom Sorell, in *The Cambridge Companion to Hobbes*, ed. Tom Sorell (Cambridge: Cambridge University Press, 1995), pp. 62–85.

# INDEX

Aristotle, 26, 51, 63, 149, 191, 244
   Aristotelian, 42, 60
Augustine, St, 25, 31n17, 235

Bacon, Sir Francis, 54–55, 134, 141–2, 142n3
Beccaria, Cesare, 205–6
Bénichou, Paul, 31n17
Bodin, Jean, 134, 141–2, 142n3, 148, 219, 229–30
Bonesana-Beccaria, Cesare *see* Beccaria, Cesare
Buckle, Steven, 163–4n1

Coke, Edward, 134
Cordemoy, Gerauld de, 78
Corneille, Pierre, 31n17

Descartes, René, 34, 60, 78, 142n8

Filmer, Sir Robert, 10, 217
   *Observations Concerning the Originall of Government*, 148, 219, 220, 224–7, 228–30
   *Patriarcha*, 219, 220, 221, 222–4, 227–8
Foucault, Michel, 213n4

Gauthier, David P., 215n45
Gracián, Baltasar, 13, 15–16, 22–4, 28, 247
   *Agudeza y arte de ingenio*, 17–20
   *Criticón, El*, 16
   *Héroe, El*, 16–17
   *Politico, El*, 20–2
Grotius, Hugo, 113, 149–52, 154–5, 159–61

Hegel, G. W. F., 3, 205–6

James I, king of England, 134
Jansen, Cornelius, 31n17

Kant, Immanuel, 206

La Rochefoucauld, François de, 15, 22–5, 28
Locke, John, 143–4n30, 146, 204

Luther, Martin, 142n3, 144n45

Machiavelli, Niccolò, 20, 21–2, 213n4

Ockham, William of, 142n3

Pascal, Blaise, 10, 15, 28, 217, 234, 249
   'Letter from Monsieur Pascal to Monsieur and Madame Perier', 25–6
   *Pensées*, 26–7, 117, 235–8, 238–42, 242–3, 243–4
   *Provincial Letters, The*, 236
   *Three Discourses by Pascal on the Station of Noblemen*, 27–8, 236, 239–40, 243
   *Writings on Grace*, 25, 235
Plato, 26–7, 35, 51, 192, 244
Polin, Raymond, 193n31
Pufendorf, Samuel von, 208–9

Renoux-Zagamé, Marie-France, 163–4n1
Rousseau, Jean-Jacques, 43, 107–8, 108–9, 133

Skinner, Quentin, vii–viii, ix, 3, 5–6
Spinoza, Baruch, 77, 86
Spitz, Jean-Fabien, 5
Strauss, Leo, viii–ix, 3, 4–5, 6–8
Suárez, Francisco, 142n3, 143n12, 143n26

Thomas Aquinas, St, 149–50, 151, 152
Tricaud, François, 179–80
Tully, James, 163–4n1

Ulpian, 222

Villey, Michel, 142n3
Viola, Francesco, 214–15n39

Weber, Max, 195–6, 212
William of Ockham *see* Ockham, William of

Zarka, Yves Charles, vii–x

EU representative:
Easy Access System Europe
Mustamäe tee 50, 10621 Tallinn, Estonia
Gpsr.requests@easproject.com

www.ingramcontent.com/pod-product-compliance
Lightning Source LLC
Chambersburg PA
CBHW061709300426
44115CB00014B/2616